Indigenous Youth in Brazilian Amazonia

Indigenous Youth in Brazilian Amazonia

Changing Lived Worlds

Pirjo Kristiina Virtanen

palgrave
macmillan

First published in 2012 by PALGRAVE MACMILLAN® in the United States—a division of St. Martin's Press LLC, 175 Fifth Avenue, New York, NY 10010.

Where this book is distributed in the UK, Europe and the rest of the world, this is by Palgrave Macmillan, a division of Macmillan Publishers Limited, registered in England, company number 785998, of Houndmills, Basingstoke, Hampshire RG21 6XS.

Palgrave Macmillan is the global academic imprint of the above companies and has companies and representatives throughout the world.

Palgrave® and Macmillan® are registered trademarks in the United States, the United Kingdom, Europe and other countries.

ISBN: 978-1-137-26534-0

Library of Congress Cataloging-in-Publication Data

Virtanen, Pirjo Kristiina.
   Indigenous youth in Brazilian Amazonia : changing lived worlds / by Pirjo Kristiina Virtanen.
      p. cm.
   ISBN 978-1-137-26534-0 (alk. paper)
   1. Indian youth—Brazil—Amazonas—Social conditions. 2. Indian youth—Brazil—Amazonas—Rites and ceremonies. 3. Indian youth—Brazil—Amazonas—Social life and customs. 4. Indigenous youth—Brazil—Amazonas—Social conditions. 5. Indigenous youth—Brazil—Amazonas—Rites and ceremonies. 6. Indigenous youth—Brazil—Amazonas—Social life and customs. I. Title.

F2519.1.A6V56 2012
305.898081'13—dc23   2012015362

A catalogue record of the book is available from the British Library.

Design by Scribe Inc.

First edition: November 2012

10 9 8 7 6 5 4 3 2 1

Transferred to Digital Printing in 2013

For the Manchineri of the Yaco River, Oskar, and Urho

Contents

Figures

x • Figures

Abbreviations

AAFi	*Agente agroflorestal indígena* (Agroforestry agent)
CAPOIB	*Conselho de Articulação dos Povos e Organizações Indígenas do Brasil* (Council for the Articulation of Indigenous Peoples and Organizations of Brazil)
CASAI	*Casa de Saúde Indígena* (Indigenous health center)
CIMI	*Conselho Indigenista Missionário* (Indigenous Missionary Council)
COIAB	*Coordenação das Organizações Indígenas da Amazônia Brasileira* (Coordination of Indigenous Organizations of the Brazilian Amazonia)
COICA	*Coordenadora das Organizações Indígenas da Bacia Amazônica* (Coordinator of the Indigenous Organizations of the Amazon Basin)
CPI-Acre	*Comissão Pró-Índio do Acre* (Pro-Indian Commission of Acre)
FUNAI	*Fundação Nacional do Índio* (National Indian Foundation)
FUNASA	*Fundação Nacional de Saúde* (National Health Foundation)
GMI-UNI	*Grupo de Mulheres Indígenas de União das Nações Indígenas do Acre e Sul do Amazonas* (Group of Indigenous Women of the Union of Indigenous Nations of Acre and Southern Amazonas)
IBGE	*Instituto Brasileiro de Geografia e Estatística* (Brazilian Institute of Geography and Statistic)

IPDP
Programa Demonstrativo dos Povos Indígenas
(Indigenous Peoples Demonstration Project)

IT
Terra indígena
(Indigenous territory)

MAPKAHA
Manxinerune Ptohi Kajpaha Hajene
(Organization of All the Manchineri of the River Yaco)

MEIACSAM
Movimento dos Estudantes Indígenas do Acre e Sul do Amazonas
(Movement of Indigenous Students of Acre and South Amazonas)

NGO
Nongovernmental organization

OPIN
Organização dos Povos Indígenas do Acre, Sul do Amazonas e Nordeste de Rondônia
(Organization of Indigenous Peoples of Acre, Southern Amazonas, and Northwestern Rondônia)

SPI
(*Serviço de Proteção ao Índio*)
(Protections Service of Indians)

UNI
União das Nações Indígenas do Acre e Sul do Amazonas
(Union of Indigenous Nations of Acre and Southern Amazonas)

Preface

In 2000 during demonstrations held in the run-up to the quincentenary of the discovery of Brazil, indigenous adolescents could be seen walking proudly side by side with elders from their communities. Many of these young people were wearing clothes derived from urban marginal cultures such as hip-hop, but they were also wearing headdresses, other indigenous ornaments, and body paintings with indigenous designs. I was at a demonstration being held by indigenous, black, and popular movements in Recife. Northeastern Brazil had become one of the regions where indigenous identities were more visible, while the number of officially recognized indigenous groups had more than doubled. The mixture of cultures, new trends, and indigenous traditions caught my attention and aroused my curiosity.

I resolved to carry out research on young indigenous people in Amazonia where the majority of Brazil's indigenous populations live in specially demarcated territories (*terras indígenas*). However, this region was also undergoing rapid cultural change from urbanization and increased social contacts. My first discussions with young Amazonians took place in an indigenous art and handicraft shop in Rio Branco, the state capital of Acre. This was my first period of fieldwork in Amazonia, and my aim was to learn about young indigenous people's lives in the Amazon lowland. I talked to a group of these young Cashinahua and Manchineri, who would hang around in the tiny square where the shop was situated. They seemed proud of telling nonnatives about the life, style of housing, types of food, and festivities typical to their indigenous territories, located a week's journey from the state capital. Undoubtedly these colorful stories also helped them sell the artifacts. The shop was frequently visited by students who came to ask questions for their studies, tourists, or people who were just interested in indigenous communities. There I was introduced to two Manchineri girls by a Cashinahua boy with whom I had already talked a few times. I am still in contact with these young women today, including now through a virtual connection over the Internet.

When I also discovered that the Manchineri were the third-largest indigenous people living in Rio Branco but that there was very little data on them in general, I decided to concentrate on this group. I also mapped out the suburbs and districts of Rio Branco, familiarizing myself with the lives of youths from all these three groups.

Before I was granted the research permit from FUNAI (the National Indian Foundation) in 2006 to study in the Manchineri reserve, Mamoadate—the first one of its kind given for work with this community—I obtained an insight into rural and urban interactions and power relations through contacts with indigenous families living in Rio Branco, indigenous teachers and environmental agents staying in the city for training courses, and other people and leaders from reserves in Rio Branco. The contacts with visitors from the Manchineri villages also helped me acquire the trust of the Manchineri people in the reserve, meaning I was frequently invited to ceremonies, and numerous stories and other topics concerning their past and present were explained to me.

Like their elders, many young people proved surprisingly good storytellers, and I am thankful to them for sharing various experiences and narratives with me. Part of my research material is highly confidential or deals with things that are sacred to the Manchineri. Selecting the information to be used was thus a challenging process. One of my working principles was to leave the private issues private if this is what the youth in question seemed to wish. However, I have still touched on various controversial issues and I shall try to show the main problems faced by the community and its younger members. At the same time, my study is also about what the youths wanted to tell me. For some adolescents explaining their thoughts was rather difficult, as is typically found to be the case when studying young people, often unused to expressing their ideas and recounting their experiences. It was the first time in their lives that they had been formally asked questions and recorded, and moreover by a non-Brazilian. My fieldwork methods therefore involved drawings and video recordings, too.

I gained a different understanding of the Manchineri community and power relations in Amazonia through my engagement with their attempts to interact in the dominant society. From the very beginning, I intended my research to benefit the Manchineri, as well as other indigenous peoples and indigenous agents, by highlighting the situations faced by their younger generations. I was also able to help the recently founded Organization of all the Manchineri of the River Yaco (MAPKAHA) by suggesting ideas for obtaining funding for its initial projects and revising their project applications. Soon I was not seen as a biopirata or a spy for the loggers and drug traffickers in those villages where few outsiders had stayed. This kind of activity also enabled me to broaden my horizontal awareness of their contemporary social relations and the networks existing between the urban and forest areas.

The final form of this work owes much to the generosity, knowledge and kindness of many people. For their inspiring ideas and invaluable practical advice during different stages of my research, my sincere thanks go to Marcelo Piedrafita Iglesias, Cecilia McCallum, Philippe Erikson, João Pacheco de Oliveira, Martti Pärssinen, Bonnie and Jean-Pierre Chaumeil, Nathalie Pétesch, Valentina Vapnarski, Peter Gow, Celia Collet, Dominique Gallois, Sidney Facundes, Minna Opas, Matti Kamppinen, and all the colleagues at the Department of World Cultures, Helsinki University, and in the Centre EREA, Université Paris Ouest-Nanterre La Défense. In Acre, especially, I am hugely grateful to Dande, Malú Ochoa, Dedê Maia, Vera Olinda, Renato Gavazzi, Gleyson, Adriano, Terri, Macêdo, Tashka Yawanawa, Alceu Ranzi, Jaco Piccoli, Mirna, Mariana, Silvana, Valeria, Magaly, Andrea and Ivana, as well as João Fontura in Brasília, all of whom accompanied and helped me in so many ways while I was in living in Acre. I also thank the reviewers, Samantha Hasey, Robyn Curtis, Desiree Browne, Erin Ivy at Palgrave Macmillan and Brittney Todd for making the publication of the manuscript into a smooth process as well as a valuable learning experience.

I am grateful to the Brazilian public authorities, CNPq and FUNAI, who processed my research requests. For supporting this work financially, I am indebted to the Academy of Finland, the Finnish National Cultural Foundation, the Finnish Konkordia Fund, the Sasakawa Young Leaders Fellowship Foundation, the Sariola Foundation, the Kone Foundation, and Bourse Lelong (CNRS). I am thankful to Antti Korpisaari for codesigning the maps of the book. For revision of the text, my thanks to David Rodgers.

I wish to express my sincere appreciation to all the people involved in my research, who dedicated their time to our discussions and shared their lives with me. I should especially like to thank the following Manchineri: the family of Ana Paula and Lazaro (I frequently wonder how their families are doing back in Extrema village), Lucas and Mariana, Alessandra, Soleane, the families of Sabá, Toya, Jaime, José Barrão Sebastião, Luis Brasil, Dona Creusa, and Chico Alves. I also wish to thank Fabiano, José and Bané Cashinahua, and Genivaldo and Wallace Apurinã. I have had the honor of being able to accompany the lives of many of my interviewees up to the present. I wish to remember two of my youngest interviewees, Heimila Cashinahua and Tânia Manchineri, whose families later told me the sad news that, despite their young age, they had departed this life in tragic circumstances. I hope this book can help keep alive their memory.

Finally I am grateful most of all to my beloved husband, our two stars, and our family, relatives, and friends for their love and kindheartedness during my absence and busy years.

Introduction

When a child is born, grows up, and reaches a certain age, the mother never comes and says, "Well, we are Indians and this is our culture." Nobody told us that . . . We never abandoned our foods, but things like music, *ayahuasca* [shamanic beverage], our stories.

Young Manchineri man, Laranjeira village

The rapid and profound intergenerational changes taking place among Amazonia's indigenous peoples, and the generational differences provoked, are present in people's attitudes toward how an indigenous community is formed. The power relations constituted by ethnic recognition, new social contacts, cooperation with different institutions, rural-urban interaction, and increased access to education have shaped the lives of today's indigenous youths in Amazonia. All these dimensions are interrelated and must be seen within the networks of actors and elements affecting young indigenous people. By documenting their values, actions, and identity in different social environments, this book presents an ethnography of indigenous youths' experiences of the transition to adulthood, shamanism, their social responsibilities, mobility between urban and forest areas, negotiations in cultural and social phenomena related to the construction of agency, and, finally, how they live their sense of indigenousness. The core of this study is an exploration of the contemporary multiple subjectivities with which indigenous youths interact.

The Amazon region is likely to face an even more extensive and interrelated series of transformations in the near future as the result of a robust wave of technological, environmental, and political changes, including the advance of hydroelectric power and mining, all of which will inevitably result in further sociocultural changes. Amazonian indigenous young people live in areas where the influx of new social agents—including nonnative migrants, governmental agencies, different indigenous groups, corporations, missionaries, environmentalists, spiritual seekers, researchers, nongovernmental organizations (NGOs), and social movements—have far more divergent interests than in earlier periods of Amazonia's history. This has changed the way in which indigenous people interact with the world, as well as their view of themselves and others. Some indigenous groups create connections with the new social agents, while others find different solutions. The non-Indians are linked to land invasions and the exploitative use of forest resources but also to new technologies and forms of knowledge that afford new ways of doing things. Both voluntary and involuntary interaction with urban areas has increased.

The study focuses on the Manchineri community in the state of Acre, in Western Brazil. The Arawak-speaking Manchineri live close to the trinational Brazilian, Peruvian, and Bolivian border. Today their reserve, the Mamoadate Indigenous Territory, is the largest indigenous territory in Acre. It is located by the Yaco River, one of the upper affluents of the Purus River (the Purus is one of the upper courses of the Amazon). The farther upriver one travels in the Mamoadate reserve, the wilder the forest becomes. The Manchineri in the reserve hunt, gather, and practice agriculture. The population numbers some eight hundred people living in the rural area and another two hundred people in urban areas. The majority of people in the reserve speak the Manchineri language, but those in the city mostly only know how to speak Portuguese.

I examine young Manchineri people, between 14 and 24 years old, who lived in the reserve, Mamoadate, or the urban area of Rio Branco, the capital of Acre, where the state's biggest urban indigenous population resides.[1] The rapid

Figure I.1 Geographical Location in Brazil

growth in the indigenous population of urban centers of Lowland South America means that ethnological studies of native peoples can no longer be limited to remote areas. As Borja and Castells suggest (1997), transitions between rural and urban areas must be seen as part of the changes posed by the emergence of urban-regional territories. The study of current beliefs, habits, and traditions in the reserve and those in the city is ever more relevant given that youth, ethnicity, and identity are usually conceived in new ways in urban centers.

Complementary research material was also gathered on Apurinã and Cashinahua[2] youths in Rio Branco, since the number of Manchineri informants in the city was far lower. The Manchineri, Apurinã, and Cashinahua are the three largest indigenous groups in the state capital, and they interact closely in native politics, rituals, and many other activities in the urban areas. The Arawak-speaking Apurinã have lands demarcated mainly in the state of Amazonas by the Purus River. Most of those who have migrated to the Rio Branco area used to live in areas close to the municipality of Boca do Acre in Amazonas State, where they have maintained relations with non-Indians over a longer period. Overall, the Apurinã number some 7,700 people, and they live divided among various indigenous lands. The Panoan-speaking Cashinahua differ from Arawak peoples through their kinship system and ontological principles and have been the focus of much more academic study. The Cashinahua population is approximately 7,300,[3] and their lands are situated on the Jurua and Upper Purus Rivers in Brazil and Peru. Cashinahua youths in Rio Branco mostly originate from the Tarauacá and Feijó areas. Although the two groups' traditions differ from the Manchineri, they experienced rubber slavery in the past and have seen demarcation of their lands and the establishment of the indigenous movement in the region. I shall examine the differences from a gender perspective, looking at how female and male youths occupy their own place in the contemporary social spaces.

According to indigenous young people in the region, their biggest problems are education, health care, and safety of their lands, even though the national constitution entitles indigenous populations to receive these services in differentiated forms. The main contemporary threats for Amazonian indigenous peoples are deforestation; cattle ranching; soya cultivation; illegal and legal logging; trafficking in drugs, animals, and plants; mining, oil exploration, and uncontrolled hunting and fishing. The difficulties and fears of indigenous youths are very concrete and linked to the immediate spaces in which they live, in contrast to many youths who are afraid of wars while living in countries with relatively stable politics. Brazil's indigenous communities still have to fight for full citizenship (Ramos 2003). At the same time indigenousness is becoming increasingly politicized. Amazonian indigenous people have come to realize that accessing resources directed toward native peoples and safeguarding their rights means having to be Indians. However, indigenousness has been defined by others. Although indigenous communities have been historically oppressed by the dominant society and attempts at assimilation have typically been drastic, their traditions are still expected to continue in a frozen fashion and to be markedly different. Indigenous lifestyles, lifeways, and sociality have not been recognized as essential elements in the making of communities (cf. Overing and Passes 2000). The situation is depicted clearly in this excerpt from a conversation recorded with a young Manchineri man: "It's like in the past when our parents were enslaved by the rubber bosses, Peruvians, Bolivians: they didn't allow anybody—our parents—to speak to us about our culture. And they were used to that, because people do become used to it, don't they? They stopped talking to us [about our culture]. We are not part of white people's culture, but neither are we part of our own. It's like that, you know."

Young indigenous Amazonian people create their social worlds differently from their grandparents and parents, who lived under other historical, political, cultural, and economic conditions, and the passage to adulthood has changed. Over recent years, the transition of native adolescents into adulthood has incorporated many new influences, some of the biggest changes being new social contacts with various actors at governmental and nongovernmental levels, the new education system, the use of technological equipment and telecommunications, a rise in economic wealth and consumer culture, and the impact of the mass media. Young indigenous people have their own voices, and more attention needs to be paid to them in our attempts to understand the present and predict the future of indigenous peoples in Latin America. Previous studies have largely overlooked Amazonian and Brazilian indigenous youths. Some academic works on young Latin Americans have already focused on the urban context (see, for instance, Mier Terán and Rabell 2005; Ruiz 2008; Velho and Duarte 2010), but not on Amazonia. Urbanization is a global question for today's young indigenous population. There is, therefore, a need for in-depth studies of indigenous lived worlds, adding an Amazonian, Brazilian, and urban dimension to the existing literature on native youths. Their voice has seldom been heard, and not even indigenous adolescents have been studied as a specific group of students in indigenous education systems or indigenous schools. More recently, though, there has been a growing interest in indigenous children as social actors (Nunes 1999; Lopes da Silva, Nunes, and Lopes da Silva Macedo 2002; Cohn 2005). As for studies of native childhood, the key point here is what being young means in cultural terms.

The concepts of *youth* and *adolescence* have been employed as sociological categories, referring to people who are physically and psychologically nearly adult, becoming independent of parents, developing their own value systems and worldviews, and on the verge of acquiring an independent position within their family (Valentine, Skelton, and Chambers 1998, 5–6). The characteristics possessed by youths and the transformations in their habitats vary according to societies, cultures, ethnicities, social classes, and gender. Recently the area of youth studies has shown a growing interest in researching young people as active agents capable of producing their own cultures within a modern multicultural context (Wulff 1995; Massey and Jess 1995; Esteinou 2005). As I shall present in this book, indigenous youths previously entered adulthood much sooner as a result of marrying at a young age.

In many of the earlier Amazonian ethnographies, adolescence is mentioned in the age-set systems and life cycles as a liminal period, preparing the person for adulthood or preadulthood. In general, ethnographers and other scholars working in remote geographical locations have shown that bodily changes at puberty (for females, almost without exception, in relation to their first menses) led to marriage and the establishment of a household unit. Hence this process meant a shift from childhood to adulthood. In the ethnology of native Lowland South America, youth as a key social construct has been addressed little, but youths have been looked at especially in studies of initiation rituals at puberty, a central aspect of almost all indigenous sociocosmologies, even though these rituals may vary considerably in content from one community to another. Rites of passage at puberty have involved some of the most beautiful and elaborate visual, musical, and verbal arts, including body paintings, chants, ritual speech, weaving, and basketry. A young person's body and closely related subjectivity have both been shown to be fabricated by other people's agencies and their actions. After a baby is born, the adults ensure the child's growth through the application of different medicinal plants, baths, body paintings, and piercing, as well as food and other social processes that help the person socially mature. Ethnographies have explored the temporary differences of the so-called liminal period involved in these rites of passage in Amazonia. Initiation rituals have usually been approached as a sequence of rigorous discipline, training, and regulations through which native youths acquire full membership in generational lines and through which gender is constructed (see, for instance, Hugh-Jones 1979; Basso 1973; Gregor 1977; Fabian 1992; Gow 2001; McCallum 2001; Lagrou 2007). Seclusion and even pain have also preceded their corporeal transformations and new identity. However these studies have tended to overlook young people's own experiences and interpretations of such rituals.

The adolescent years of indigenous Brazilians have also been studied from the viewpoint of developmental psychology, including in early studies that presented different stages in the life cycle of indigenous communities and mentioned the pubertal phase. The examination of age-set categories revealed how young people aged from 15 to 25 years learned to perform new activities, with young boys learning to make arrows, hunt, and fish, and young girls assuming certain domestic tasks (see, for instance, Florestan [1948] 1988; Goldman 1963). In recent years Brazil's native youths have more often been portrayed in the media for negative reasons, including the suicides of young Guarani, Karajá, and indigenous youths in São Gabriel da Cachoeira. Nonetheless indigenous young people are making their own claims to cultural and political autonomy. For instance, regional meetings of indigenous young people in Brazil, promoted by local governments, have given them a new visibility with which to make the histories of their peoples more widely known and their cultural differences more clearly defined. In the context of the ethnopolitical movement in particular, indigenousness functions as a form of symbolic capital and can convert and accumulate other resources: gaining educational and health care assistance as indigenous peoples or obtaining posts in indigenous organizations, as discussed in this book. Furthermore the new definitions of indigeneity found among young urban native Amazonians is reminiscent of Argentinean Mapuche punks resisting the univocal image of Mapuche Indians created by the indigenous political movement itself, which ignored the diversity found among the Mapuche people (Briones 2007).

Native youths occupy a cultural borderland in the terms set out by Renato Rosaldo in his call for studies into areas involving creative cultural production: "Such previously excluded topics prominently include studies that seek out heterogeneity, rapid change, and intercultural borrowing and lending" (1989, 208). Moreover the Manchineri living in the reserve had few contacts with non-Indians until the 2000s, but by the time I was starting my fieldwork, they had become interested in the idea of someone undertaking a cooperation project with them. If the indigenous group and the social subgroup—adolescents— was a borderland for many scholars, so, in the eyes of many Brazilians, was my fieldwork location, where I intended to carry out my research.

Acre and the Upper Purus especially is a geographical and cultural border area between the Andes and Amazonia, whose numerous indigenous population left monumental ceremonial sites that are now being more closely studied (Pärssinen, Schaan, and Ranzi 2009). The region has been a multicultural meeting point, though it was "discovered" later than other areas in the Amazon. It has also been a relatively independent area, and before belonging to Brazil formed part of Bolivia. At the end of the nineteenth century, the Purus became the destination of colonizers looking for natural wealth.

The historical literature documents Manchineri occupation of the area, and records that they were good hunters and canoe builders who knew about iron tools and made beautiful cotton clothes, which they used for trading even as far as the Jurua River. The Manchineri are also known by the names Manxineru, Maniteneri, Manitineri, and Maneteneri. The texts report the existence of "Maneteneri" at the mouth of the Aracá (or Chandless), Caspaha, and Yaco Rivers (Chandless 1866; Labre 1872; Métraux 1948; Castelo Branco 1950). The Manchineri are members of the pre-Andean Arawak group composed of the Peruvian Yine (Piro), Apurinã, Ashaninka, Mantsiguenga, and Yanesha, a classification based on their shared linguistic affiliations, which differ from other Arawak groups. The Manchineri and the Yine (Piro) living in Peru are closely related and possess many cultural similarities.[4] In fact, these two peoples are called by a generic name—*Yine*, meaning "humans"—and originate from the same ancestral groups, *nerus (nerune)*. The ancestral groups were, among others, the *Koshitshineru* (Little Bird People), *Hahamluneru* (Low River People), *Jiwutaneru* (Mouth of the River People), *Himnuneru* (Snake People), *Natshineru* (Hungry People), *Getuneru* (Frog People), *Poleroneru* (Macaw People) and *Manxineru* (People of the *Inharé* Tree) (see Matteson 1965, 153; Gow 1991, 63; and Virtanen 2011a). These groups began to intermarry when the rubber bosses arrived in the region. Today a few Manchineri also live in the Peruvian Amazon along the Urubamba, Ucayali, and Madre de Dios Rivers, as well as in the northernmost state of Bolivia. *Manchineri* is the name commonly used for both language and native group, though sometimes the group is also called *Yine* in Brazil. In Peru, *Yine* is the only official name used. The Manchineri often use the name *Piro* for the Yine in Peru. Their languages differ little in two countries, and they are mutually intelligible.

Each indigenous people has its own history of encountering dominant powers (Whitehead 2003). The relations with various actors create hierarchies and fields of power that continually reshape cultures (Gupta and Ferguson [1997] 2001). These power fields are also observable in the way people understand their lives or how they want to be seen (Rosaldo 1989). In this book, the dynamism of power relations is crucial and thus historical elements form a vital part of the analysis, insofar as social structures have their own history and develop and transform out of previous structures. Power can be wielded over others through controlling, demarcating, naming, and organizing different domains, and it refers to people's access to various kinds of resources, such as knowledge, wealth, and violence, though these are changeable (Foucault 1980; Toffler 1990; Giddens 1984). Power can also be localized and personified.

The relations between indigenous and nonindigenous actors in the region covered by this book were largely formed during the colonization of Western Amazonia. Rich in rubber (*Hevea brasiliensis*) and caucho (*Castilloa Ellastica*), exploration of these resources led to massacres of the region's indigenous peoples or their forced induction into the rubber industry's workforce. The colonizers and rubber patrons hunted the Indians, destroying their settlements and killing or enslaving their inhabitants. In the 1910s the Brazilian state's office for Indian issues, SPI (*Serviço de Proteção ao Índio*), also operated "enticement" programs to attract the region's Indians by supplying them with a range of different objects and building new settlements close to their original areas. The native peoples of the region call this period the time of flight (*tempo das correrias*). While some fled deeper into the forest, those who were captured, or who decided to cooperate with the rubber bosses, worked as guides, canoeists, or rubber tappers (*seringueiros*). These processes clearly had a traumatic effect on the region's indigenous peoples, who still carry these harsh experiences of the past with them (Piedrafita Iglesias 2010; Weinstein 1983; Taussig 1987; Castelo Branco 1947, 1950; Ôchoa and Araújo Teixeira [1997] 2002).

From the end of the nineteenth century, the Manchineri were forced to work in rubber tapping and many families lived on lands that had become the property of farmers and rubber bosses. Besides rubber extraction, work undertaken included cultivating swidden crops, clearing jungle paths, and transporting rubber by foot or river. While working on rubber production or in plantations, some Indians in the area learned Portuguese and non-Indian lifestyles. The indigenous population was also introduced to a host of contagious diseases brought to the area by the settlers. Many Indians, however, resisted the arrival of non-Indians, and some of the ensuing conflicts even led to the closure of various government "attraction posts." Castelo Branco (1947) states that in 1898 extraction of rubber was made difficult in the Guanabara area of the Yaco River following resistance from the Catiana, Canamari, Inhamaré, Capixi, and Mannchineri All these groups, except for the Manchineri, are now extinct.

For the Indians, the period from the end of the first rubber boom in the 1910s until the 1970s, when they were forced to work for the bosses, represents the time of captivity (*tempo de cativeiro*). They became indebted by the *aviamento* system. They were, in essence, obliged to hand over the rubber they produced to their bosses, who gave them the commodities and produce they needed to survive in what was effectively enslavement: since the price of these items was so high, they remained perpetually indebted. Similarly to the rubber tappers coming from other parts of Brazil, the state of Acre and its people remained dependent on the rubber economy, and all the region's principal rivers were involved in its production. Even though the price of rubber fell dramatically from 1910 onward following the introduction of rubber tree plantations in East Asia, people continued tapping rubber due to a lack of alternatives. The same occurred after the second rubber boom, which peaked in the 1940s during the Second World War.

During the periods of "flight" and "captivity" indigenous populations were dispersed and became permanently dependent on the tools and products of the national population. Additionally, indigenous rubber tappers were cheated over the price of rubber and the value of their labor and were frequently paid in sugar cane rum, *cachaça*, turning many people into alcoholics. Various indigenous peoples were unable to continue their agricultural activities, even though they had to pay exorbitant prices for the items they bought, making them dependent on their bosses (Ribeiro 2000; Piedrafita Iglesias 2010; Weinstein 1983; Hemming 1991).

In 1976, the first official identifications of Indian lands were submitted following initial surveys of indigenous peoples in the Acre state, and a FUNAI (National Indian Foundation) regional office was established in Rio Branco. FUNAI reported the Manchineri and Yaminahua working as *seringueiros* and clearing the forest for their bosses on the Guanabara and Petrópolis plantations. The report noted that these Indians had been cheated over the price and remuneration of their work. Their only economic activity had been working for the rubber farms, as well as hunting, fishing, and planting swiddens for their own sustenance when it was possible. In 1977, FUNAI opened its first indigenous post (*posto indígena*) in Acre by the Yaco River in Extrema village, to which the Manchineri and Yaminahua of the area were transferred.

It was a big change to return to the original lands, as many things had altered since contact with the non-Indians. Moreover the Manchineri now faced the new forms of domination represented by a different power structure: the military government of Brazil. According to the official reports and my own interviews, this FUNAI post differed little from others in the country during the military regime. One officer (and his wife) ran the post, with the main tasks being to control relations between the Manchineri and Yaminahua, rather than empower the Indians to pursue their own activities. As a way of compensating for the loss of the rubber-tapping revenue, FUNAI also provided the population in the Extrema village with domestic animals and introduced the cultivation of rice and beans, as well as implementing the "Coffee Project" to grow and sell coffee in Sena Madureira, an urban area downriver. The projects continued the economic system inaugurated by the rubber plantations exchanging production for commodities, and only very recently have the Manchineri assumed control over their own production in their own ways.

At this time the indigenous population was still mostly considered in negative terms as lazy, distrustful, irresponsible, and childish. In the region, they were generically called *caboclos*, whereas the local non-Indians, such as rubber tappers who had arrived from the Northeast, were referred to as *cariús* (non-Indian immigrants dwelling in forest environment) (Aquino 1977). The colonizers and owners of rubber estates (*seringais*) and the rubber bosses (*seringalistas*) were all known *Paulistas*, because they mostly came from Brazil's southern states. In the 1970s, *Paulistas* also comprised loggers and ranchers, who, backed by government policies, invested in land in the Amazon rainforest. The new landowners forced indigenous groups and independent agroextractivists, such as rubber tappers and Brazil-nut collectors, off their lands and frequently hired professional killers to murder the people who remained in their way. The history of Acre is steeped in not only devastation and violence against Indians, rubber tappers, and rural workers but also their empowerment. At the beginning of the 1980s, these peoples combined forces to claim their land rights, forming an alliance called *Povos da Floresta*. Indian leaders traveled to Rio Branco to demand the demarcation of their lands and met with new pro-Indian NGO staff in the cities, including representatives of the CPI-Acre (the Pro-Indian Commission of Acre, *Comissão Pró-Índio do Acre*) and CIMI (the Indigenous Missionary Council, *Conselho Indigenista Missionário*) (Revkin 1991; Piedrafita Iglesias and Aquino 2005). The CPI-Acre developed a pioneering program to introduce indigenous education in which trained indigenous teachers would take a lead in preparing the school curriculum and textbooks.

For Acre's indigenous movement, a milestone was reached with the establishment of UNI (the Union of Indigenous Nations of Acre and Southern Amazonas, *União das Nações Indígenas do Acre e Sul do Amazonas*). Manchineri leaders were closely involved in this project. Founded in 1979, UNI was Brazil's first pan-Indian organization working in defense of indigenous rights and also later played an influential role in the drafting of new legislation on indigenous peoples. Indigenous people's rights were established by statute and later specified in Articles 231 and 232 of the 1988 Federal Constitution.[5] Today's young adults are the first generation in Brazil have access to both individual and collective indigenous rights, a result of the fact that many of their parents had been involved in the founding of indigenous movements and indigenous politics.

The Manchineri land was officially demarcated as the Mamoadate reserve in 1986 and homologated in 1991 with 313,647 hectares. The FUNAI post in Extrema was closed in 1990. Following conflicts between the Manchineri and Yaminahua, new villages were opened, and the Yaminahua started relocating to the lower Yaco. Extrema remains the largest Manchineri village with 242 inhabitants, while Jatobá is the second largest with a population of 133 people. The others contain fewer than 100 individuals (*Fundação Nacional de Saúde* 2010). In Acre better monitoring of indigenous areas by the state and local governments is still an important issue for native populations. The recent modernization and development projects introduced by the local government, with national (and international) backing, have included the construction of highways and bridges at international borders that will change the life of the traditional populations living in the region as a result of their huge environmental, social, and cultural impacts.

The consequences of the intrusion of outside economic interests in Amazonian jungles have been social, ecological, and environmental in kind, with profound impacts on local lifestyles and livelihoods. These wide-scale changes have also spurred the emergence of indigenous voices (Ramos 1988, 1998;

Gomes 2000). In the 1990s and the early 2000s, the geopolitical interest in frontier expansion in the Amazon region resulted in large-scale deforestation.[6] The *Avança Brasil* (Forward Brazil) program, launched during the presidency of Fernando Henrique Cardoso, continued the development of Amazonia based on economic models derived from the 1960s. Indigenous activism has become stronger over the last decade. The year 2000 was also remarkable for Brazilian Indians since it was a year of massive demonstrations by the indigenous population against the large-scale celebrations planned by the state for April 22 to commemorate the quincentenary of the discovery of Brazil by the Portuguese. The slogan of the native meetings in 2000 was "Reduced yes, beaten never" (*Reducidos sim, vencidos nunca*). In the UN's Rio Earth Summit 2012, indigenous people impressively manifested for alternative development and protested, for instance, against the Belo Monte dam project and the Forest Code.

Today there are a large number of indigenous organizations and associations, in which young indigenous people have active roles. In general they have become visible subjects in ethnic and interethnic encounters. Young people often said that they "have to be connected," looking for new contacts and forums to deliver their message and point of view.

The local history of Acre's young indigenous population shows huge changes over a relatively short period of time. In 2010, the native people in the state living on indigenous lands numbered approximately 16,000, representing 15 different ethnic groups distributed across 3 linguistic families: Pano, Arawak, and Arawá. This represents 4 percent of the state's total population (IBGE 2010). The largest indigenous group is the Panoan-speaking Cashinahua. Near the borders of Peru and Bolivia, in the remotest areas, there are also settlements of "uncontacted" indigenous people (*isolados*) living in voluntary isolation from national society, and the uncontacted Mashco-Piro, nomads who pass through Brazilian territory, including Manchineri lands. In Acre, today 36 indigenous territories cover 2,390,112 hectares (14 percent) of the state's total surface area.

The state government of Acre in particular has taken "sustainable development" as its central political program. Since 2000 it has organized cultural meetings of indigenous groups, the *Encontro de Culturas Indígenas do Acre e Sul do Amazonas*. The Acre government also created the Special Advisory Service to Indigenous Peoples (*Assessoria Especial dos Povos Indígenas*), which evinces a new political recognition of indigenous issues, as well as the recently founded sectors of various state offices responsible for the indigenous population. Moreover, in April 2003 a museum, *Casa dos Povos da Floresta*, was opened to show the rural populations' way of life in the forest, their beliefs, and their traditional practices to a wider public. These and similar actions form part of the state government's set of policies developed under the slogan "Government of the Forest" (*Governo da floresta*). In the official speeches for the inauguration of the *Casa dos*

Povos da Floresta, the governor, along with other speakers, proclaimed that Acre was leaving behind an era of ignoring traditional cultures and beginning a new phase of recognizing and celebrating the richness and beauty that Indians and riverside dwellers have to offer Acre. The indigenous peoples of Acre, in contrast to their ancestors, have begun to shift away from being the objects of historical writings to become the social agents of the present. For instance, indigenous candidates have been elected to local government seats in Acre. Today most of Acre's indigenous groups have founded their own associations in order to build dialogue and defend their rights to receive educational, health care, sanitary, and economic services, as well as develop cooperative partnerships with the state and other actors.

As in various other Amazonian regions, the urbanization process in the state of Acre has been extremely fast. In 2010, according to estimates from IBGE (Brazilian Institute of Geography and Statistics), the total population of Acre was 707,125 people, approximately 70 percent of whom lived in the urban centers. This is very similar to the average for the Amazon region as a whole, where only 30 percent of inhabitants live in rural areas. The state capital, Rio Branco, is home to 335,796 people, almost half the state's population. The population of Rio Branco has increased rapidly since 2000, when it numbered 252,800. In the municipalities closest to the Manchineri reserve, the Mamoadate Indigenous Territory, urbanization over the same ten-year period was also significant: in Sena Madureira the rise was from 29,420 to 37,993 inhabitants, while the population of Assis Brasil has almost doubled—from 3,493 to 6,075. Temporary and permanent residence of indigenous people in the urban centers of Acre is still rising. The indigenous population of Acre includes 3,700 people residing in urban centers, 2,500 of them in the Rio Branco area.

In the Brazilian media, indigenous populations in urban areas have become a big issue, especially from 2005 onward with the publication of new demographic data by IBGE. The national census conducted in 2000 by the institute indicated that 350,829 Indians live in reserves and 383,298 in urban areas, the latter thus being equal to more than half the total indigenous population (52.2 percent) (IBGE 2005). This census did not count rural indigenous people outside the demarcated indigenous territories. In the 2010 IBGE census, the indigenous population was 817,963, representing 0.42 percent of the overall Brazilian population. Indians living outside indigenous lands in rural areas are now included in the census, resulting in a total of 502,783 people living in these areas, while 315,180 identified themselves as indigenous people in cities (IBGE 2010).

A remarkable number of indigenous people from the Amazon region have taken the decision to search for better living conditions, work, education, health care, or even new lifestyles in the cities. Although the situation is similar elsewhere in Latin America, one fundamental change in the Amazon region is that indigenous communities have become more permanently settled in the cities. According to IBGE (2005), the biggest age group among the indigenous population living in urban Brazil is from 15 to 19 years old, followed by the group from 20 to 24. This data also shows the need for a study of these age groups—which is precisely what this book seeks to provide.

Today the young generation not only engages with different regional, national, and global forces from those faced by their parents, but their localized bodies of cultural knowledge have also changed. The aim in this book is to show how young people's agency is constructed in relation with new types of Others and how the young generation takes a more active part in their own transition to adulthood. As Fausto and Heckenberger argue (2007, 13–14), agency in Amazonian social philosophies involves creative transformative action related to myths and the interaction with beings that can also be nonhuman. In general, structure and agency are not opposed but in a dialectical relation, implicated in the person's range of choices where agency can also vary in degree.

We need to consider the transition to adulthood through the native constitution of personhood. For Amerindians, *persons* are those social actors who have formed their personhood in legitimate processes of social interaction and relatedness within their communities (Conklin and Morgan 1996; McCallum 1996; Vilaça 2002, 2005; Overing 2003). Producing relatedness is crucial in indigenous Amazonian societies since they are usually based on convivial relations—the values of caring, generosity, and sharing but also the attempts to control anger and jealousy (Overing and Passes 2000; Overing 1988; McCallum 2001). Intimate relationships make babies who are nurtured to become members of the community, making conviviality the archetypical Amazonian form of sociality. In their convivial interactions, people live well and morally in ways that are not separate from their bodily actions. Corporeality is invested with a crucial meaning in Amazonian communities, since the human body forms the locus of sociality, connecting a person to other members of the community through eating, working, joking, and speaking together. Personhood is manifested in body paintings and adornments, as well as in the bodily behaviors manifested in ceremonies, which enable the expression of a person's status, gender, age, and so forth (Seeger, DaMatta, and Castro 1987; Turner 1991, 1995). In Amazonian indigenous communities, being in the world is about becomings, transformations, and transitions—a dimension shown in their symbolic systems—and about objectifications of human bodies that "make" bodies and thus persons (Viveiros de Castro 1992; Vilaça 2002, 2005; McCallum 1996). Here what make human beings especially human are their close relationships with kin, considered to be *real humans*.

As many scholars have argued, for the Amerindians humanity is the essential attribute shared by all cosmological agents: animals and spirits see and think of themselves and things in the same way as humans would (living in houses, eating foods, and drinking liquids that are ontologically equivalent to ours—blood for predators being equal to manioc beer, and so forth), but they see the world from a different point of view owing to the differences in their animal and spirit bodies. Thus they also communicate, eat, live, and act differently from human beings. This idea, described as *perspectivism*, highlights the similarities existing among human beings, spirits, and animals in Amerindian cosmologies. In Amerindian cosmologies animals and different spirits are equally human: their difference resides in the fact they have different bodies. Everything is seen from a perspective taken to be just one among others. The different points of view of animals and spirits can cause danger to real humans by causing the latter to start acting like animals (Viveiros de Castro 1996; Århem 1993; Stolze Lima [1996] 1999; Vilaça 2002, 2005; Londoño Sulkin 2005). Perspectivism is an important element in understanding the discussion of bodies, relatedness, and convivial living. Animal and spirit subjects see the world from different points of view owing to the differences in their bodies; thus, they also communicate, eat, live, and act in different ways from those of human beings. This concept can also be called *multinaturalism*, since beings experience different things in a similar way, and thus they have different natures where others are related in specific ways. This contrasts with multiculturalism, in which people live in a unified nature of which they have different representations (Viveiros de Castro 1996).

Amazonian ethnology has also explored how bodies and subjectivities are unstable since they depend on other subjectivities' image of the self (Taylor 1996; Vilaça 2005). The oppositions reproduce beings. The adoption of so-called nonindigenous ways of acting and being is not about turning into non-Indians but about mastering knowledge of the other and thus having two bodies. Indeed relations between Amazonian Indians and non-Indians have already been discussed in the anthropological literature in terms of the transformation of Indians into non-Indians. Aparecida Vilaça ([1999] 2007) has shown that the Wari' have two bodies simultaneously, Wari' and white, while Cristiane Lasmar (2005) argues that indigenous women in the upper Rio Negro are continually becoming either more white or more Indian. In order to maintain one's perspective as a real person, therefore, the appropriation of the other's knowledge is involved. This may occur in relations with trade partners, missionaries, enemies, health personnel, and others who are considered potential affines as they may be a source of power, knowledge, and objects (Viveiros de Castro 1992, 2001; Gow 2001; Vilaça 2002; Kelly 2011). Although they may never become real affines or kin, they play a vital part in constructing kinship. These continuous embodied transformations are also understood to result from people's production of images of themselves for others (Gow [2003] 2007). Alterity is a crucial element of identity in Amerindian sociocosmology, explaining its dynamism and its transformative aspects.

Amazonian conceptualizations of the social world and notions such as personhood, humanity, and sociality have already been used to explain interethnic contact, as well as indigenous movements and politics in Lowland South America (Turner 1991; Jackson 1995; Conklin and Graham 1995; Rosengren 2003; Lauer 2006). Here the focus has been on the transformation in indigenous social consciousness and on the strategies and resources deployed in ethnopolitics. This has provided a different view to the early studies on the integration of Amazonian Indians into Brazil's urban class society (Cardoso de Oliveira 1968, 1972; Schaden 1969).

The recent studies on the movement of indigenous populations toward urban areas have been comprehended from the perspective of native cosmology as an appropriation of the knowledge and power of white peoples (Lasmar 2005; Andrello 2006 on Northern Amazonia). These studies work from the premise that Amazonian kin relations are dependent on affinity, others, and the exterior. Some subjects within these relational structures can be called potential affines insofar as people attempt to establish an exchange relationship with them in the areas of politics, trade, rituals, and so forth, where affinity is contextually produced (Viveiros de Castro 2001). This kind of ontological approach to the experiences of indigenous people in urban areas contrasts with the image appearing in the mainstream media, where only their social problems are reported. There are also studies focusing on the relationships between migratory movements, urban indigenous politics, economic organization, labor movements, and quality of life (Ferri 1990; Brown 1993; McSweeney and Jokisch 2007; Peluso and Alexiades 2005).

My interest here resides in young people's ways of reproducing their subjectivity in multiple social spaces as they relate to native ideas of Amazonian ways of making personhood and creating relatedness, humanity, body, and perspective. These concepts form the theoretical approach of this book. The central argument is that indigenous young people's passage to adulthood is not guided by different actors as much as in the past; rather young people themselves now also form an integral part in this transition. In this process, rural-urban interactions play an important role due to the number of social, political, economic, and cultural relations between them. Parents and elderly people guide the transition of children to adolescence and from there to adulthood by passing on certain ways of doing things to their children. Today they increasingly want the young generation to learn how to interact in the contemporary world with a diversity of actors. In fact, in the process young people have become active agents, seeking out educational opportunities in urban areas, while looking to participate in indigenous politics, the youth movement and new youth culture, and the revival of shamanism, learning to speak and act for their communities in new types of human-to-human relations. The nation-state, via its educational system and contacts with non-Indians, has provided new tools for constructing a young person's agency.

The book moves through specific topics that form the substance for later chapters. Chapter 1 discusses the relations between Manchineri youths and the older kin in the reserve and the city, nonhuman actors (ancestors, plants, and animals), other indigenous groups, and non-Indians. It argues that a new diversity of actors can be found in the sociocosmology of Manchineri youths, especially urban residents and nonnatives, who now compose an essential part of the process of creating subjectivity. Chapter 2 contains an analysis of contemporary rites of passage to adulthood, reflecting both local and global changes and indigenous relations with new actors. The ethnography focuses especially on change and continuity in traditional puberty rituals, both in the reserve and in the city, and on attitudes to state education and current types of matrimony, both of which comprise alternative contemporary markers of social status, tasks, and roles. Young people especially value studying in urban areas where new knowledge can be embodied differently. This chapter argues that young people play an increasingly active role based on personal choices in their contemporary transition to adulthood. Chapter 3 continues the analysis of becoming an adult and examines shamanism, focusing specifically on Manchineri ayahuasca shamanism. It shows the role played by young people in shamanic practices and how shamanism provides knowledge about the community and the self, as well as creating new types of social networks. Chapter 4 explores ideas of the "city" and how indigenous people deal with alterity in their transitions between the reserve and the urban area. I argue that increased relations between the two environments have produced new types of forest-urban communities, where both the reserve and the city have their different potentials and areas of influence. Chapter 5 offers an analysis of young people's novel positions of responsibility, working as spokespeople and promoting intergroup relations, which are largely urban in practice. It shows how young men have gained much more power by taking on a range of new intermediary and representational roles in indigenous communities. Furthermore, the chapter illustrates how the attempt to make new alliances has been one of the main reasons for the growing generational gaps and rural-urban disparities. Chapter 6 focuses on how relatedness is being recreated by new practices of exchange, conviviality, and proximity between forest and urban areas, as well as strategical indigenousness and both new and "traditional" ritualism. It argues that new relations of trust are being built between indigenous urban and rural dwellers, generations, and indigenous groups through a new conceptualization of indigenous difference and producing indigenousness that has been taking its form in relation to the dominant society over recent years. The young generations in the cities, in particular, have grown closer to the people living in the reserve. Chapter 7 concludes with the new image of indigenous peoples to which young Indians have contributed and presents a novel form of being indigenous through youth cultures. It also discusses tensions, contradictions, and conflicts between elders and youths, and how these are managed or otherwise handled. It concludes that young Amazonian indigenous people perceive and negotiate these new social, cultural, and political situations. My analysis turns here to identity issues with the last two chapters considering contemporary indigenous identities and various ways of being an Indian.

This book is not only about the young generation, since it also includes the ideas of adults and elders and their past experiences. This helps reveal the generational tensions and different views encountered in the present. The social situations explored are those embodied by young people: rituals, schools, political negotiations, cultural events, communal meetings, and youth cultures. Young Indians have learned to recognize the opportunities available to them in different social situations, which are defined by the attitudes, gestures, representations, and languages in use. As the study will show, community members and even noncommunity members, particularly non-Indians, are not seen as homogeneous groups as such but as divided by diverse power relations stemming from different types of knowledge, skills, places of residence, and other elements that create prestige in different contexts. Young Indians' new knowledge and social contacts have resulted in the formation of new types of agency within different social environments.

The ethnography shows that the body is continually altering as Amazonian indigenous youths engage in schools, the ethnopolitical movement, shamanic practices, and so forth. Moreover, they also participate in so-called youth culture, contrary to the time when Indians passed from childhood to marriage and adulthood in a relatively short period of time. Thus the native youth have various native and nonnative bodies, enabling them to benefit from distinct social contexts and make new ethnic and interethnic relations. Apprehending the dominant society's view of indigenousness is an important factor in reshaping young people's experiences, but it is not passively adopted. This can be seen, for instance, in their new interactions with non-Indians and other Indians, as well as their new visibility. Moreover, it has encouraged new encounters between the native populations of the cities and reserves as well as the new image of Indians to emerge from these processes.

CHAPTER 1

The Sociocosmology of Amazonian Indigenous Youth

In this chapter we look at the social environment of Manchineri youths: the relations between young people and both their older kin in the reserve and the city as well as nonhuman beings and non-Manchineri people. This chapter creates a basis for understanding young people as an age group and how the different agencies, both human and nonhuman, employ different perspectives in the world, insofar as they embody different social and cultural environments in distinct ways. Here I shall discuss the experiences of social proximity in the native villages, looking at the different lifestyles of the Manchineri living in the Mamoadate reserve and those in the state capital, Rio Branco. I will then turn to the relations between young people and their ancestors, along with plant and animal spirits, and to their conceptions of the origin of the world as they apply to positioning the self within the web of relations. Finally, I will discuss changing positions vis-à-vis other indigenous groups and non-Indians. The main point in this chapter is that personhood is created in dynamic relations not only with community members and nonhumans but increasingly with other natives and different types of nonnatives.

Maklujine (Young People) and Kin in the Reserve and the City

For the Manchineri, interaction is associated with happiness, laughter, and generosity, whereas being at a distance from the kin—while traveling, for instance—is identified with sadness and longing. As a young man simply put it, he is happy when he sees his kin and sad when he is far away from them. The proximity among village members is constructed or deconstructed by social processes producing sociality. For many young people in the Mamoadate Indigenous Territory, the village exists as a unity within which they are surrounded by their family. The Mamoadate reserve is divided into nine villages—Extrema,

Lago Novo, Alves Rodrigues, Laranjeira, Cumaru, Água Preta, Santa Cruz, Jatobá, and Peri—as well as smaller settlements, such as Senegal. Some settlements, such as Santa Rosa, are situated outside the Mamoadate reserve. The urban centers closest to the indigenous territory are Rio Branco, Sena Madureira, and Assis Brasil. The locations of the largest villages and other locations mentioned in the study can be seen on the map in Figure 1.1.[1]

In each village, the sense of mutual trust and cooperation is built up through the continuous interaction with others that brings the community together. A person is viewed as part of a collective and as a complementary element in the social reality that organizes social experience. Numerous ethnographers have noted that in native Amazonian thought, something exists only insofar as it possesses a relationship to something else (Seeger, DaMatta, and Castro 1987; Vilaça 2002). Manchineri people are identifiable as humans through their relations with other community members.

One's social age defines ways of relating among the kin, since it determines people's expectations of others' actions as well as their own. Gender and age allocate tasks in different domains. Those adolescents who have begun to work with other men or women are called *maklujine* (youths).[2] They cannot play

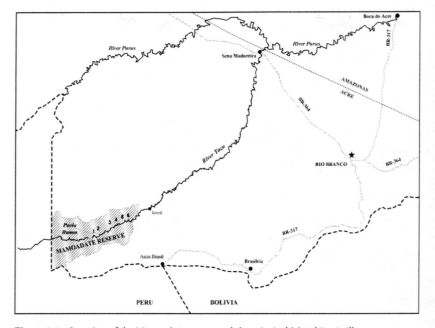

Figure 1.1 Location of the Mamoadate reserve and the principal Manchineri villages: (1) Extrema, (2) Lago Novo, (3) Laranjeira, (4) Santa Cruz, (5) Jatobá, (6) Peri

with children and wander around as their younger siblings do but must instead start to undertake typical gendered work at home and outside. During my research the elders and parents (*tsru yineru*—literally "big people") explained to me that young people are no longer considered children (*mturu*) when they are ready to do any kind of adult activity. This meant that they were now able to relate to other kin in an appropriate way, knowing their position in relation to every community member. Showing generosity to relatives and calling them by the correct kin terms, which will be presented shortly, compose the fundamental basis of personhood and adult agency. A young girl (*makloji*) is expected to carry out specific household tasks—for instance, she is to serve manioc beer to visitors and simply to control her actions and speaking with other people. A young man (*makluji*) hunts and works in the plantations. Unlike children, young people can prepare many of their own things, including food and some objects (baskets, brooms, nets, and so on), which was traditionally the way to start to live in their own house with a spouse and provide their family with food. One of the origin myths of the world, the story of the Tslatu, the cultural hero and ancestor, also tells how at one point Tslatu and his brothers passed from childhood to adulthood when they were able to make their own arrows and hunt. They thereby became full persons among others.

The daily life in the forest environment follows the rhythms of the sun, school, hunting, fishing, plantations, gatherings, rituals, and journeys where each person's age and sex determine different responsibilities. People in the villages wake up at sunrise (in the equatorial region, this remains basically the same time throughout the year, with the sun rising around 6 a.m. and daylight lasting until 6 p.m.) and consume the first cup of traditional manioc drink, *caiçuma* (*tepale in Manchineri*). Sexual difference is a fundamental dimension of social life and activities.[3] In the morning, the woman first lights a fire in a stove, prepares food, and brings water from the house's own spring. The young men and boys go hunting or fishing, or go to work in the plantations. Young women stay at home taking care of their children or younger siblings and performing household tasks. A young woman may accompany her sisters or mother to the manioc swiddens or to look for firewood for cooking, which they carry in baskets strapped to their foreheads. Even young teenage girls carry very heavy loads over long distances or transport their younger siblings when taking care of them. On their return the women prepare *caiçuma* for their families, clean the house, and do the laundry when necessary. They also help those elders without children living nearby or living alone. Unmarried girls may help in the house of an older sister who is already married and living in her own house. In Extrema village, I stayed in the house of a young couple, and the wife's nine-year-old sister would come to help her older sibling and act as company for her while the husband was away. She was also my companion wherever I went, and we had many laughs together.

In the afternoon, only women, children, and older people usually remain in the villages. Four times a week adolescents—mostly those who have not yet married—spend four or five hours in the village schools. There is also a class in the afternoon for more advanced students. The ratio of male to female students is roughly equal. Studying is not compulsory and those who want to work simply skip their class. Young adolescents already have many other tasks and responsibilities, unlike children, who, for instance, are often sent as messengers to nearby houses, since their social age allows them to move more freely beyond the social categories assigned to adolescents and adults.

When men return from working in the swiddens or from their hunting and fishing trips, they hand over any fish or game they may have killed—typically armadillo, brocket deer, monkey, tapir, tortoise, white-lipped peccary, paca, or birds such as tinamous—to their wives, who immediately start preparing the meal. If there are babies in the house, the men or those who have been in contact with animal spirits must bathe before meeting their smaller family members, since the smells of animals or other forest spirits, or even temporary proximity to them, can interact with those who have not formed their own personhood and harm their human forms. The Amazonian web of social relations is visibly or invisibly present in all actions.

Usually the game meat is sufficient for a few days, allowing men to work in the plantations on the other days, either clearing or planting them. Game animals are becoming more and more difficult to find, especially tapir and deer, owing to pollution and the settling of non-Indians closer to the indigenous land. Hunting and fishing trips may also last several days, during which boys travel together deeper into the forest or to lake areas. One of the characteristics of men's daily lives is the freedom to do things, such as go hunting or fishing, and return whenever they want, usually after they have found food. Sometimes the whole family goes fishing together and camps overnight by the lakes. However I heard people say that nowadays they rarely go on these long trips, since they have to attend school and there are now more visits from state officials, NGO staff, and missionaries.

In the late afternoon, shortly before sunset, the villages become livelier. Young people play football on a pitch cleared in the center of each settlement. The girls usually play first, sometimes against smaller boys, and then the young men play, while the girls stay to watch. People visit other houses to chat about the day's events and share and exchange food acquired from the forest. At relatives' homes, people are offered manioc beer or something to eat. The women who collect fruits and receive game from their husbands then distribute them to other women. There is a tendency to share forest produce (Overing 1992): game, fruits, and fish are exchanged within the immediate kin group.

Women often brought me bananas or some other food, and in return I would give them salt, sugar, rice, or something else I had brought with me and on which the families were running low. Once I was visiting some houses farther away from the village center with Ana Paula, the young wife of the small family with whom I was staying. When we passed a house whose men had just returned from a hunting trip, I was given a live turtle, which I then had to carry a long way home in my hands. At Ana Paula's house we already had fish that her husband had caught that same day and some game her mother had brought for us earlier. I asked Ana Paula what we should prepare to eat in the evening. Ana Paula laughed happily for a long time at my question and the situation. When it gets dark, people return to their houses, take a bath in the spring close to their house, and eat the food the women have prepared. Candles or gas lamps provide lighting, while a few houses use solar energy. By 8 or 9 p.m., people prepare for the night, couples and younger siblings sharing a hammock. People chat and tell stories until they fall asleep.

The different age groups of the same sex usually share the same spaces where different tasks are learned and shared. In all villages the proximity of the residential houses and the way they are divided into the spaces used for a variety of social activities are very similar, even if they differ in terms of their economic wealth and urban influences. There is usually an area for sleeping, plus a kitchen with a stove and dishes lining the walls. Some houses have just one room. The women's area is primarily the space close to the stove where manioc tubers are peeled and cooked, and the other food prepared. Children learn to skin game close to the habitations. A few houses also have a room to receive visitors, and most have a veranda for welcoming people with whom they wish to talk at length and offer something, usually manioc beer. As furniture there are usually a couple of handmade stools, which are given to respected visitors to sit on. It is easy to see who is visiting whom since the houses in each village are typically located within sight of each other, though some houses are located deeper in the forest (at most, twenty minutes away by foot).

In the center of the village, visible to everyone, are the communal buildings constructed with help from the government: schoolhouses, a hut for the VHF communications radio, a women's house used for making handicrafts (*Casa das Mulheres*),[4] a telephone booth, and sanitary facilities, although the last two items are seldom in working order. The establishment of an indigenous school is always one of the principal government actions confirming the settlement as an indigenous community. The first native teachers tried to pass on the little knowledge they had about writing and reading as a way of improving relations with the non-Indians. Since the end of the 1980s, education policies have recognized and promoted "indigenous cultures," and schools have consequently become the most important forums for defining and "recuperating" these cultures (see Weber 2006). The indigenous school may act as a sign, enhancing the dignity of the people in the village, as it shows their right to differentiated schooling. This is all in large contrast to the period of homogenizing state policies toward indigenous peoples—policies that ended quite recently in Brazil and, in fact, in all the nation-states of the Amazon region. The school buildings and the hut for radio communications are visited by all the community, though by elders less than others. Community houses differ from residential houses, because the local government's development projects and their non-Indian construction workers build them from wooden planks and other materials brought from the cities. The residential houses are transformed by men's physical strength from forest resources, including *paxiúba* wood for the timber framework and *ouricuri* or *jarina* palm leaves for the roof thatch.

The center of Jatobá village is also occupied by a Baptist church, founded by American missionaries of New Tribes Mission in Brazil (*Novas Tribos*) in the 1980s, where a service is held every Thursday and Sunday.[5] Some of the nearby houses owned by wealthier families also have tables and beds, reflecting the missionary influence. People in this village prefer to construct their houses from wooden boards, and young people are eager to have a house large enough to contain their own room. This shows a desire for independent ownership, rather than the need to mediate constantly with others. The fact that some villages are wealthier has also been a motive for jealousy. In the Mamoadate reserve, the increase in commodities purchased with the income from selling agricultural produce, salaries, or other remunerations has changed the dynamics of ownership and thus the relations of trust. Personal belongings, such as motors or chainsaws, are much desired as sources of economic power. They affect the constitution of sociality, since they are not shared in the same way as game and fruits. The industrialized goods most commonly purchased in nearby municipalities are salt, sugar, detergents, oil, candles, and ammunition. Like forest produce, these are shared only among close kin.

For the youths living in the Mamoadate reserve, relational proximity and being Manchineri is primarily constructed through social activities: working together, joking, speaking Manchineri, and eating Manchineri food. These practices "make bodies" and turn people into kin. Offering something to eat, especially fish or game, is still a form of producing kinship relations. One of the most important tasks young women have to learn is to serve visitors, especially their kin, serving elders, brothers or sisters-in-law, and potential partners differently according to their kin relation. This is a form of care, morality, and conviviality that young people learn. When somebody passes by a home, a woman from the house offers the traditional cassava drink from a huge bowl.

Generosity is important, and young wives dream of a house that has a separate room to welcome visitors. "To receive well" was one of the community's social norms. A similar standard is held among the Cashinahua: "Generosity with food and the capacity to feed others (as well as be fed) characterizes the construction of proper sociality and therefore of kinship itself" (McCallum 1997, 125).

If food or drink is not offered at a kin person's house, especially when traveling and food is a necessity, this failure to give anything is taken as an insult. A group of Manchineri once went to the neighboring village to play football and returned extremely downcast, despite winning the match. They were disappointed because they felt they had not been offered enough food by their hosts, especially meat and manioc drink. They themselves had fed players from the village in question generously with all kinds of food when the football match was held at their village, but they were resolved that the next time they would give them nothing. This event was discussed in the village for several days.

As in most indigenous Amazonian contexts, the Manchineri consider only game, fish, and traditional homemade cassava drink, *caiçuma* (*tepale*), to be "real food." When I was traveling to the village with a few Manchineri teachers returning from their education course, they were longing to drink *caiçuma*, which they had not consumed for a long time. This desire also showed that they wanted to see their relatives, especially their wives, who prepare *caiçuma* at home. Real food is produced within a web of relationships involving land, planting, and interacting with animals and other nonhumans and sharing the produce (Gow 1991; Lagrou 2001; Belaunde 2001). Consequently, for the Manchineri, these actions integrate people with their forest environment. The Manchineri give importance to speech in creating social relations and personhood. The addresses made through the use of language position the speakers relationally, such as the use of a kin term, a Manchineri nickname, a Portuguese name, or even a title marking a position of social responsibility title. A Manchineri name refers typically to some quality of the person (one that also makes his or her body or comes from the body). The name is usually given by elders, who receive the name from the spirits, and serves to strengthen the person's own spirit and qualities. Thus names locate young people in the social world. The name is part of the person in a material or substantial way, as suggested by the way in which the integration of social relations and subjects are represented in social bodies (Turner 1995; see also Crocker 1985). Subjective relations are both materialized and represented in bodily social activities. In the reserve people usually only use the Manchineri names of others. Portuguese names are given when filling out a newborn's birth certificate in the municipalities.

In addition to typical ways of addressing family members, such as one's mother, father, brother, sister, grandmother, and grandfather, there are other kin terms positioning people in the web of relationships. The mother's sister is called *nato*, while the father's sister is *shapa*, the mother's brother *koko*, and the father's brother *patu*. Young people already know how to address other community members. Cousins are also referred to in special terms: the youngest son of one's *patu* is called *nepuru* and the oldest *yeye*. They are like one's own brothers. A son of a *shapa*, *nato*, or *koko* is called *nanuru*. A daughter of a *patu*, *nato*, *koko*, and *shapa* is called *noyimlo*. Sister-in-law and brother-in-law, *mhuru*, *nanuru* or *panu*, are also common addresses and refer to potential marriage partners. Young people already know how to address their kin correctly, and the young men, for instance, already know that all sisters of the *nanuru* are their potential wives.[6] The Manchineri use the same kin terms for many of the animals mentioned in myths and often called by these terms in chants, too.

Greg Urban suggests that "kinship connections are a focus of public discourse precisely because they are not immediately accessible to the senses. In this sense, kinship is to be 'heard' and not seen" (1996, 81). But although he emphasizes the verticality of discourse, kinship is produced in various ways. The horizontal aspect between speakers is an important element. In fact, the Manchineri create equal social relationships between those involved in social actions by talking, while simultaneously positioning the speaker through the use of language. Sharing a discourse is a first step in establishing closer relations with someone, whatever the speaker's language or position. An appropriate social agent is cheerful and lively, and converses freely with his or her kin. For this, people also take forest medicines. If I fell quiet for any time, I was told "Talk, Cristina!" The Manchineri were highly appreciative of the fact that, in addition to visiting their houses and accepting their food, I talked with everybody and not just with those who had special responsibilities in the village. When I learned to speak more Manchineri, the new degree of proximity I gained with people was remarkable.

Generational relations also affect ways of speaking. Young Manchineri usually respect older people, and grandmothers are very tenderly called "grandma," *jiro*. Young people value the knowledge the elders pass on through everyday actions, especially those related to constantly present nonhuman beings. In terms of their ways of embodying knowledge, the schools have most changed the relations between the Manchineri generations. Elders sometimes visit the school buildings, which is also where the village meetings involving all community members take place. Sometimes elders are pushed more into the background and may even be treated disrespectfully. Some older people told me that their children or grandchildren go to pick up their pensions and immediately spend the money during the trip on things that the old person cannot enjoy. Those elders who can no longer move far from their houses find it especially difficult to act affirmatively within their own social environment. The things discussed by younger people—events relating to their visits to urban areas, for instance, may be foreign to them. Old people often remark on how young people have changed and are only interested in white people's things. Villages differ from each other in terms of their residents' abilities to speak Portuguese, their religion, their way of seeing the past and future of the village, and their economic wealth, all of which lead to different relations between the generations. Old people's knowledge is more valued in some villages than in others. Extrema is regarded as the most traditional settlement in the reserve, whereas the Baptist faith is practiced in Jatobá, and believers reject some traditional customs such as consuming *caiçuma* or the shamanic brew *ayahuasca*, as well as declining to perform the traditional dances. However, since the arrival of the American missionaries, all classes and church activities in Jatobá village have been given in Manchineri,[7] and only a few people speak Portuguese well. In other villages, various people are fluent in both languages, but as a whole the Manchineri language predominates over Portuguese. Residents of Jatobá are considered "believers" (*crentes*) and therefore as quiet and ungenerous people. I soon realized that their houses were kept closed, even when there were people inside, and lacked the terrace used by houses in other villages for social interaction. Thus religion is one of the most significant factors separating people: a form of negative social capital, in other words. It creates relatedness among some of the Manchineri insofar as it provides social control and recognition among those who have declared their faith in the church. But this has inhibited interaction with other villages and made some communal decisions more difficult. Among those baptized into the Catholic faith, no special interrelatedness stemming from their Christian faith was observable, since their religious affiliation did not affect social actions as strongly as Evangelical Baptism (cf. Opas 2008). A Catholic priest visits the other villages occasionally, but there are no church buildings. In general, living in close relationships is colored by rumors, gossip, and jealousy, just like in any other human community. Since everyone in the reserve knows everyone else, proximity has an ambivalent character. Sometimes this leads to conflicts, and a number of people have moved to other villages or even outside the Mamoadate Indigenous Territory in the wake of internal disputes. Young people in particular identify with their own villages, conceiving them as virtually autonomous settlements, and people living in neighboring villages are usually treated somewhat differently. The official name of the reserve is Mamoadate, but the word *village* (*poktshi* in Manchineri, *aldeia* in Portuguese) or the precise name of their settlement is more often used when referring to their home territory. Commenting on a teacher who was coming back to work in his own village, people said, "He went back to Extrema, he went back to his own land! (*Ele foi para Extrema, foi para a terra dele!*)" Population pressures have also led to an increase in the frequency of disputes between villages and a decline in mutual trust. For instance, people sharply criticized the visit made by hunters from the downriver villages to an area of forest close to the village farthest upriver where game is still found in abundance.

In spite of these internal unifying and diversifying relations, close relationships are still maintained with cousins, uncles, and aunts living in the same or other villages, especially when compared to relations with non-Manchineri. When I visited Peri village with some Manchineri visitors from another village, a young girl said that she was unable to remember the name of the owner of the house who was not present, since she only ever called her "aunt." It is also important to know people through bodily proximity, which involves knowing the qualities and substances of their bodies that could influence others. This shows what kind of person someone is. A girl commented about her deceased father, saying that she did not remember him well, as she could not even know what he was like physically. She did not even miss him, therefore. She had been unable to embody any substances and knowledge from her father and thus carried no memory of him.

Urban relatives are not as close as those living in Mamoadate since their work, houses, and foods are different and they rarely speak Manchineri. Neither are they missed, unlike close relatives when they are away traveling. For Amazonian peoples in general, living together is a decisive factor in forming kinship, and hence those living far away may be excluded from the universe of kin, turning into Others, or even non-Indians (Gow 1991; McCallum 1997; Belaunde 2001; Lagrou 2001). Comparing those living in the reserve with those in the city, we should note that from the perspective of the former, proximity and eating similar "real food" would make their bodies the same, meaning that it would make their "perspective" similar, too (cf. Viveiros de Castro 1996, 2002).

The difference from the Manchineri in the city has also become a more prominent topic of discussion in the reserves. The dissimilarity resides in the previously mentioned actions: their distinct way of life, diet, traditional knowledge, and use of language. Some people claimed that the Manchineri in the city are no longer really Manchineri. In the reserve, those who are not kin to some extent do not even exist since they are totally ignored, a fact shown by people not talking to them or giving them any food. In fact, even those Manchineri who live in the reserve and visit urban areas are frequently considered to be acting disrespectfully. For instance, an old man in Lago Novo village once yelled while drunk that one of the Manchineri settlements in Mamoadate cannot be called a village, since there are only a few houses and the people purportedly living there are actually always in the city, *na rua*. This may be taken to reflect the liminal character of visits to urban centers, when the person leaves the known, caring for kin and the communal values of relating to one another.

The Manchineri residing in the city were reproached for never or seldom coming back to visit the reserve. Moreover, those working for indigenous organizations are or have been accused of not contributing the people in Mamoadate and of earning money by exploiting the name of the community. The leader of the first officially recognized Manchineri village joined the first meetings of the regional indigenous movement in the 1980s. Eventually the Manchineri leader moved to the city with his large family and started to work for UNI. Campaigning for the demarcation of indigenous lands, new economic activities for communities who had once worked for the bosses, health care, and education programs consolidated the establishment of UNI-Acre. The indigenous movement emerged during a period of widespread cultural and political changes in Brazil. Indigenous families often moved to Rio Branco to accompany a father involved in the indigenous movement, in many cases leading to all family members becoming engaged in this new life of working for indigenous issues. Strong connections were forged with rubber tapper unions, the environmental movement, and the CPI-Acre, which helped train indigenous actors (Piedrafita Iglesias and Aquino 2005).

At first, the people in the village had expected, and still expect, the Manchineri living in the city—especially those working for indigenous organizations—to find financial support for the people in the reserve by "making projects" (*fazer projeto*). Other families have moved to Rio Branco in the wake of internal conflicts, such as the killing of a family member, but subsequently also become active in indigenous politics and are thus expected to provide some return for the reserve, too. Following new training courses for indigenous teachers and health agents, new policies, and the founding of the Manchineri organization, the interactions between the Manchineri in the urban and forest areas have increased, usually causing tensions.

It has been common for many of today's native peoples to decide to live in the urban centers for schooling, work, or just to learn about life in the cities. Those who have stayed in urban areas live in a very different environment from the Manchineri youths in the indigenous territory. They live far away from their relatives, since in the city their homes are scattered across distant neighborhoods. The outlying districts of Rio Branco are filled with the noise of cars, motorbikes, and blaring music. Usually just one main road leads to these districts, used by local buses, and then splits into smaller roads and tracks that are seldom accessible to vehicles. According to one Manchineri adolescent in Rio Branco, problems with their local neighborhoods include bad roads, poor sanitation and water distribution, and inadequate garbage disposal. But the living conditions are not as depressed as in some other *bairros*, where I also interviewed other native youths, such as the young Apurinã and Cashinahua. As the more outlying neighborhoods of Rio Branco are where incoming migrants tend to settle first, some of their inhabitants lack the necessary ID papers for work or school and are therefore unemployed and effectively excluded from the school system.[8] Some of my non-Indian Brazilian friends and colleagues regarded these districts as dangerous and had rarely visited them.

In Acre, according to my study, the migratory process of leaving the reserve for the city is very similar among all the young native people: before arriving in the state capital, Rio Branco, most had lived in smaller urban centers elsewhere in the state. Nearly all those who have migrated to Rio Branco first moved to the urban centers closer to the reserve or farms. Those who had moved directly to Rio Branco from the reserves had invariably accompanied a family member who had started to work for the indigenous organization in the state capital. Overall, only those who had maintained continuous contact with the reserve spoke Manchineri. Most of the Manchineri youths in Rio Branco had been born in the indigenous area or territories close to urban areas. The relocation of parents to the city is the main motive for migration among these adolescents. The second most common reason for moving is study. The reasons for migration given by those adolescents not born in Rio Branco were as follows: accompanying parents, studying, "temporary" residence, searching for employment, joining a husband, illness, and joining other relatives.

Urban neighborhoods initially become occupied by people referred to as *cariú*, the descendants of non-Indian rubber tappers, and later by the nonindigenous working class.[9] The urban elite is composed of migrants from southern states, their descendants, owners of ranchers, and educated whites. Most of them rarely differentiate the indigenous population from the stigma of *caboclos*, who are still seen as inferior (cf. Aquino 1977). The young Manchineri in cities have close relations with other Manchineri families in urban area, and their siblings and cousins usually make up their closest social circle. They still maintain their social proximity. However, this is also partially due to the prejudice experienced from their surrounding urban environment. For the indigenous youngsters, the social sphere of personal relations is experienced in the home and during the free time spent with their relatives. As in the villages, personhood is constructed by knowing everyone by their Manchineri name. The Manchineri kin terms that manifest the complexity of relational structures used in the reserve are not typically employed in the city. Manchineri families have usually lived in the city for a long time and often speak only in Portuguese. Their younger generations are familiar with the dominant society's language only. Just the families that have recently arrived from the reserve continue to speak Manchineri at home, like those residing in Assis Brasil, the municipality closest to the reserve.

In the city, the daily rhythm of indigenous youth is similar to the lives of other young urban residents: first thing in the morning, they take a shower, have breakfast, and catch a bus to school, which is usually located outside the district. If school classes are in the afternoon or the evening, the most popular daytime activity is watching television. During the afternoons and evenings, the unmarried Manchineri students, like their classmates, typically spend some hours after school in the city square or on the promenade, the Parque de Maternidade, a popular place to frequent in the evening and on weekends. People walk and jog there, sit on the park benches, play team games, or skateboard. The location includes a concert stage, the *Concha Acústica* (or "Acoustic Shell"), where some adolescents hang around even when no concerts are playing. The young Manchineri usually socialize in groups with their cousins or occasionally with other friends. Extracurricular activities may include computing and English courses run by private colleges, though only a few parents have the economic means to pay for their children to take these classes. Most young people, though, go straight home after lessons or work. Two of the Manchineri boys, living in Rio Branco at the time of my first field trips, practiced capoeira, and another boy, kung fu; all three had reached a very high level in their respective sports. Overall, taking on adult responsibilities is delayed since academic study is prolonged and finding employment difficult.[10] In urban areas, indigenous young people have more relations with other young people as an age group than in the reserve. In villages youngsters lack the same amount of spaces created for exclusive use by young people in urban areas. In cities, adult women and elderly people stay at home more and are less familiar with the areas frequented by young people, such as urban schools and other places where they "hang out."

In urban areas, social actions also take place within a system that goes beyond the boundaries of kinship relations to include a wide range of occupations, religions, ethnicities, classes, and more strongly marked age group divisions that imply complex relations of economic, cultural, and political power across a variety of social fields. On weekends adolescents often want to visit nightclubs, while a few boys are particularly keen to dance *forró*. Sometimes this behavior causes family disagreements and thus conflicts between the generations living in urban areas. Parents do not always let youths go out whenever they wish. Other family disputes involve the adoption of city fashions, as when the parents of two Manchineri girls admonished them for cutting their hair short. Their parents complained that in the village all girls wear their hair long.

The youths in the city regard themselves as members of indigenous communities who live in villages very different from urban areas and other kinds of rural settlement. The Manchineri youth living in the city identify with their original homeland, where the people's distinctive language, food, and practices remain strong. Today being a member of an indigenous community with different cultural traditions allows native youngsters to experience a kind of symbolic capital that other youngsters in urban areas lack. Although the youths were already accustomed to the typical food of the city, they often spoke about

Indian food (*comida do índio*) by which they meant cassava, game meat, and fish. The term *caboclo* was seldom heard and carried more negative connotations than the term *índio*.

As the reserve is situated far away from Rio Branco and reaching it requires a boat trip of several days and is very expensive, the youths have only ever visited the territory a few times in their life. Young Manchineri had rarely learned Manchineri oral history and only some of the youths could understand the Manchineri language, though they wanted to learn more. They were a little embarrassed about this fact but said that learning their history and language was very complicated since the urban parents of the Manchineri youngsters had been living in the city for a long time and their grandparents lived far away.

It should be remembered that when the parents of today's indigenous youths were younger, they were forced to avoid showing their indigenousness to non-Indians. They could not speak their own language in urban areas and wanted their children to learn the practices of the city so they would experience less prejudice. As young indigenous people became more interested in their past and attitudes toward the region's native peoples was changing, their parents started to be more open about their history. However, they had lost much of their ability to speak their indigenous languages. Some young Manchineri from the city view the reserve as an undeveloped or uncivilized place since the schooling there is inadequate. People in the reserve are regarded as different because they do not speak Portuguese well or fail to converse much with people from the city. According to a young Manchineri woman, who lived in Rio Branco, "They [people in the reserve] think that we are kind of lost in the world of the whites." However, some indigenous youngsters in the city believe that they are more interested in strengthening their culture than the young people in the reserve are. One girl said that it is only their work and studies that make it difficult for them to return to there. She added, though, that it would be difficult to live in the village, because there they would stand still. It would be difficult for the boys, since they are not used to hunting or other everyday activities of men in the reserve.

In the city, like most contemporary young urbanized people, members of the young generation of Manchineri rarely learn job skills from their parents. In the state capital, indigenous youths have greater access to social spaces independent of those occupied by adults. In the reserve, though, tasks are experienced and learned together with their mothers or fathers. For instance, Manchineri boys or girls wander together only near the village and their houses. Youths only ever live with other relatives. Younger men in the reserve go hunting or fishing in groups of older men and thus share many things with them. Even when they leave to hunt or fish alone, the forest is a place of personal relationships with the various nature spirits trying to maintain their social fabric with the community members. Thus the conceptual space of these young people, a universe where everyone is known by his or her personal qualities, is "larger."[11]

The city has more places for an individual to engage in social interaction—a social sphere in which everyone is parallel to everyone else, rather than complementary to them. The immediate family and other relatives residing in the city are not the only safety net, since there is a range of institutions—such as schools, political organizations, and leisure centers—which give rise to new social networks. Many native adolescents in the city remain close to indigenous groups. Being with other indigenous people usually means being in the social sphere of personalism—that is, being known by one's name and personal qualities. When at home or with indigenous families, the youngsters are positioned very differently than they would be in other social contexts. Young people often say that they "discuss things inside the family." Nevertheless, *family* does not refer exclusively to their parents' home or closest family: it usually indicates being with any family from the same indigenous group with whom a young person has close relations. Personhood is, however, to some extent limited to the sphere of the family, as only there are youths known through their relations to ancestors, parents, and siblings. In the city, a young indigenous person usually enters the sphere of the individual whenever he or she leaves home (cf. DaMatta [1979] 1991). This is a regular occurrence when youngsters leave for school or work, where similarities are found with non-Indians.

However, in some social environments or forms of employment, young people prefer to be labeled as indigenous since this may be advantageous. An indigenous background helped some Manchineri boys obtain part-time employment in an indigenous association, another boy in the indigenous sector of FUNASA (the National Health Foundation), and one girl at the museum of the *Casa dos Povos da Floresta*. In the city, those young people whose parents are involved in indigenous politics are able to observe up close how indigenousness is presented and articulated. Indigenous politics is thus one of the rare practices that is passed from parents to sons and daughters in urban areas.

The young Manchineri men often visit the reserve during the school holidays. The trip is physically arduous, and they were perhaps therefore more prepared than the girls given that sometimes the long journey from the closest municipality, Assis Brasil, to the Yaco River has to be undertaken on foot. The Manchineri girls were more interested in waiting for a chance to visit with government teams, who travel to the reserve with better transportation. Urban and rural young people display a special affinity with each other, marked in their own ways. During their visits to the reserve, adolescents eat the same kinds of food and share daily tasks and activities. One of the Manchineri young men living in the city taught the boys in the village how to perform capoeira sports, which he had learned in Rio Branco, while the boys from the reserve taught him how to speak the native language. He had some family members in the reserve, and five years after my first period of fieldwork he and his brother had moved to one of the villages.

The sense of their common past, conceptualized through the difference between the current and previous generations but also the continuity from time of the ancestors, unites the Manchineri both in the reserve and in the city. The myths of the past narrate a time that no longer exists—the era before the arrival of non-Indians. The time and life of the ancestors that people so enjoy narrating has an ambivalent character: on one hand, this period is valued as a time of powerful shamans and traditions, yet the ancestors were also living in a state of deprivation since they lacked the school education and commodities of today. For the youngsters in the reserve, the current generation is living in a period very different from that of their parents: they now have many new skills and are able to communicate and interact more with people outside the reserve. I was told about many differences in everyday practices—for instance, the fact that the previous generations never scrubbed a floor; they just used a broom. Sand was once used to wash dishes, whereas they now have soap and detergent. Furthermore, when I asked these youngsters to tell me one of their favorite stories, it was usually about how jaguars had killed many people in the past. They often added that their ancestors had lived in a state of ignorance deep in the jungle.[12]

However, the Manchineri young people feel they are living in a continuum with the past, not a discontinuity. Using Hannerz's (1997) argument that if flows are seen as continuities, then margins and limits are perceived as discontinuities, the Manchineri youth in the reserve do not feel like they are living on the margins. They view the world with their community as its center, especially in terms of the relations to the kin and nonhumans beings of the natural environment. The relations to the nonhuman beings and communal heroes have been reproduced since the time of ancestors.

Protectors, Advisors, and Followers

For the Manchineri, various nonhuman agents inhabit the forest, such as animal, plant and tree spirits, and even their so-called spirit masters. These nonhuman agents are usually invisible, though they are always real. A young girl from Extrema village once told me about a time she was collecting wood in the forest with her grandmother: growing weary, she had complained about how hard it was clambering up and down the forest hills with a heavy load. The grandmother replied that the hills of the forest are our father and mother. She probably wanted to show that even though life can be tough in the jungle, it is satisfying to live in a close relationship with the place where they have always lived and with whose nonhumans with whom they have maintained a special relationship. The Manchineri call many animals by kin terms, such as *yeye* (oldest brother) for jaguar, or *tote* (grandfather) for toucan.

Manchineri historicity—that is, their view of the past[13]—was formed by the narratives of certain ancestors regarding the origin of particular animals, beings, and things, including the fire, cassava, and birds. This provided young people with answers about their origins and their relations to previous generations and the forest beings. In the time of the ancient Manchineri (*tsrunni manxinerune*—literally "past adult and elder Manchineri") animals could speak, as described in ethnographies throughout indigenous Amazonia, and indeed they still appear in human form, including through shamanism.

According to one of the Manchineri origin myths, the story of Tslatu, also narrated by young people, a young woman once saw a snake in the field and said that were it a person, it would be her husband.[14] The snake appeared to the woman that night and they had a son. One day the woman left her son with her grandmother. She was rocking him in a hammock when he turned into a snake, which she threw in the fire. Then the snake turned into a boy again and he was crying. The river started to flood. The woman and her grandmother were given a little genipap tree to climb. As the river flooded, they tapped the tree to make it grow. They ate the fruits of the genipap. Soon the river was full. One day the water disappeared and the two women climbed down from the tree to the ground. They met a deer (*ksotheru*) and crossed the river. This usually marked the end of the story, though it continues with many subsequent events. Some young Manchineri people, especially those living in the remotest villages, were able to narrate the myth in detail. Those who knew the story rarely remembered the entire myth since it is very long and takes hours to narrate. However, young people usually mentioned the flooding, because the myth includes a deluge that destroyed everything and left just two women, *Yakoneru* and *Jweproneru*, as the only survivors. Those youngsters in the reserve who knew the story of the two women also said that the world and the first Manchineri began with a deluge.[15] Interestingly only two of the Manchineri adolescents living in Rio Branco—both of whom had come to the city just before their teens—knew this Manchineri story.

An old woman living in Santa Cruz, Juliana Fernandes, told me the story in all its detail: According to her version, when the flood had passed, the two women started to wander the earth. First, they met a brocket deer who helped them cross a river. The deer asked the older woman (Yakoneru) to have sexual intercourse in payment for his help. Then the women went looking for their relatives and met many beings—a manlike being called *shatsha*, an armadillo (*kshiwna*), a curassow (*hijeka*) "married" to an agouti (*pejri*), and a tinamou (*makokawa*)—who lived like people. Although the beings who the women met were like people, their way of living was in some sense strange to the women, and after these encounters, they decided to continue their journey. The women opted not to live with the beings, and thus reproduced their own type of bodies. The story continues, telling that after a meeting with a type of human man, the older woman became pregnant with Tslatu. The women continued their movement and arrived at a crossroads and took a path that led to the jaguars, who killed the old woman. The Manchineris' great teacher and ancestor Tslatu, then, emerged from her stomach. The story continues with the survival of the Tslatu. Later his brothers Hiplopineru and Reyonaneru were also born, and they began to avenge the death of their mother by tricking the jaguar in numerous ways. The brothers were highly intelligent. They passed on their knowledge to the Manchineri and then left this world.

Other origin myths also exist and in each of them the Manchineri learn something from animal, tree, or plant spirits. According to one of these myths, the first Manchineri people did not know how to make children. One day someone found a small boy living in a *samaúma* tree, and everyone was very happy. Other children were found later. They started to raise these little creatures. But they only had one eye. So the Manchineri had just one eye at first. Fortunately, later on, a man walking in the forest saw some monkeys engaging in sexual intercourse and thus learned how to make children with his wife. The children who were born had two eyes and all the villages gathered to celebrate the event. In the farthest villages from urban areas the younger generation still tells the story, but in the city none of the adolescents knew it.

As it is typical for Amazonian indigenous peoples, for the Manchineri, some elements of nature are also once human and have their own history vis-à-vis the people of today. In Mamoadate villages the origin of the moon was explained by the myth of a boy who turned into the astral body.[16] According to one of the versions narrated by a young man, a boy tried to sleep with his sister. The sister did not know who was coming to sleep with her at night. One night the sister put genipap on his face. He tried to wash away the stain, but the paint would not come off. When people discovered what had happened, the brother wondered what he could transform himself into. He thought, I'm going to be a star or hawk. He thought about all the possible beings and animals. Then he said, I shall be a moon. So he turned into the moon. He tied his neck and his head disappeared. After some time the moon appeared. Because of these events, even today people say that the moon has the genipap marks given to the boy by his sister. As revenge for his sister exposing him, the moon made all women menstruate. At the end of the myth, the young man said, "We always hear the old people tell these stories."

In Amerindian cosmologies, some plants, animals, and natural elements are considered persons and thus possess agency (Århem 1993; Viveiros de Castro 1996; Descola 2005). The most powerful animal spirits inhabiting the

Manchineri social cosmos are those of toucan, turkey vulture, parrot, frog, monkey, pink dolphin, otter, and tinamou. They are considered to live like humans, and their special qualities and behaviors can contribute to a person's health and strength. Certain animals can improve a person's flexibility, for instance, and thus help find a solution to difficult situations. There are also spirit masters that guide people, such as the mother of the moon, who appears as a beautiful woman. As Viveiros de Castro (1996) argues in his definition of perspectivism, these entities have their own bodies, personalities, and volitional and knowing capacities and see the world differently. The idea of perspectivism as defined by Viveiros de Castro has been taken as an attempt to theorize Amerindian social philosophies. However, as I shall discuss later, it is important to note the variety in Amazonian people's relations to both nonhuman beings and non-Indians.

Among community members, the youngsters openly recount their personal experiences of encounters with nonhuman beings, and these have an important value for the person's maturing process. The encounters take place in the forest, during the hallucinogenic visions, while dreaming, or when the person is alone. By contrast, when a mythic story is narrated, such as those describing the deluge and the birth of the moon, the youths always add that "old people tell it so" or "they said" (*Waneyhima*) it happened. They also begin by announcing, for instance, "My grandmother told me." According to Gow (1991, 60), this marks the story's authenticity. The same may have applied when the young Manchineri in the reserve said that their parents or grandparents tell them stories about how life was in the old times and about the forest animals, but that they themselves could not remember those stories. They wanted to attribute authorship to the elders who had closer experiences with the ancestors or nonhuman beings in question. However, as well as showing respect for their elders, storytelling was young people's way of remembering the *tsrunni manxinerune* and recreating it.[17] In the most isolated villages, myth telling was generally more animated, one of the reasons for this being that qualified indigenous teachers encourage multicultural education and have regular contacts with other native peoples. In the other villages, when I asked if they knew a specific story, such as that of the two women, the youths usually said yes and recounted at least one detail from the story. Some young people told me that their parents do not tell them the stories because their grandparents grew up on the rubber plantations and had consequently not passed on the stories to their parents. Sometimes, if the young people's parents were listening to our discussions, they would remark that they tell stories of the past, but their children do not bother listening. "I tell him stories, but he's not interested!"[18]

When the elder Manchineri told about the time of *tsrunni manxinerune*, they also wanted the young generation to understand the difference between the Manchineri and others, and how times had changed from the past. The eldest Manchineri had been born along the tributaries (or *igarapés*) of the upper Yaco River—namely, the Abismo, Mutum, and Paulo Ramos. Subsequently they experienced the period of hard work and debt bondage to rubber barons and colonizers (*seringalistas*) but maintained their dignity and identity. The elders wanted the young generation to appreciate more the struggle and difficult times the elders had passed through during the contact with the colonizers and the later work on their plantations. Although that time seemed distant to the young Manchineri, their relations with the forest environment were determined primarily by different nonhuman agencies who form a continuing part of the group's past and present. In some ways, young people were more interested in elder people's knowledge of how to live and deal with these nonhuman agencies than in learning the recent past of their elders.

Relationships with different nonhuman beings can be materialized voluntarily through chanting and through designs that can take the form of body paintings, artifacts, and shamanic visions. The designs appear with the help of the shamanic chants[19] in which forest or ancestor spirits are called by kinship terms and depicted in human forms and act like humans, including playing instruments. Nonhuman entities "arrive" and their designs can be visualized, which is when nonhuman knowledge becomes available. For instance, a frequently mentioned Manchineri ancestor, *Pwernokatu*, has his own geometric design that only becomes visible when the person is able to transform and produce his or her knowledge and form a relation with this spirit. *Pwernokatu* was a young man who miraculously received a long *koshma* robe with a beautiful geometric design. This design can appear in hallucinogenic visions alone, unaccompanied by any other spirit being. However, a young man also drew *Pwernokatu*'s design together with the *kajpomyolutu* spirit, which appeared as a small male figure, because this palm spirit had in fact helped bring the design of the ancestor. Designs accompanied by music make nonhuman entities present, reestablishing the balance between different entities as well as social networks and hierarchies between nonhumans and between nonhumans and humans. A shaman usually leads the shamanic ritual where this kind of interaction becomes possible.

The geometric designs are also the source of the patterns applied to cotton clothing, pottery, and the human body, though specific designs are used for particular purposes and objects.[20] Manchineri body paintings relate to the qualities and powers of certain beings and can also be used in curing. Lagrou (2007) has emphasized that designs are about relatedness, as they indicate the interdependence of different kinds of people. According to the Manchineri, the designs are activated especially through chanting, which materializes and "brings" them.

Young people knew the chants of different nonhuman beings for different uses, such as inducing hallucinogenic visions, curing, obtaining guidance, and dancing. The chants have remained potent spiritual representations, like the body paintings that depict various symbolically important animals, plants, and ancestors. The chants are also used for protection, for remembering someone, when traveling far away, or for receiving strength. For native peoples, music is an important means of opening up an imagined mythic world, as Hill (1993, 203) writes, by creating "cultural landscapes of rivers, peoples, and places." For the Manchineri living in the reserve and in urban areas, music is an important means of expressing the invisible worlds of protectors and creating relatedness, as will be explained in the next chapter on the transitions to adulthood and shamanism. In fact, especially in the cities, the forest spirits are now mainly encountered through shamanic practices, such as *ayahuasca* rituals.[21] These have their own restrictions on reifying nonhuman agents and their own specially allocated spaces in the Manchineri world.

In the reserve, young Manchineri people are given protective medicines concocted from different plants and trees. Through their substances and nonhuman agencies young people become stronger, find work less exhausting, and can trek for very long distances. The youngsters said that taking the natural medicines enables them to be healthy and cheerful. Women can work harder in the cassava plantations and carry heavier loads, while men encounter game and fish more quickly. Even during pregnancy, their mothers had taken certain types of medicine for their children to be born well. In the city finding the necessary plants is difficult. The medicines are usually liquid concoctions that elders or even young people themselves prepare a few days before taking them. They are drunk early in the morning and make the person vomit, purifying the body in the process.[22] Older boys who can already hunt alone try to strengthen or avoid relations with entities that change one's bodily substances, and thus agency— for instance, by the use of herbal medicines and controlling their interactions with women. The best hunters usually prefer to hunt alone. These men and hardworking women are also preferred as spouses.

Animal or plant spirits are usually encountered when a person is alone. The souls of dead people are also believed to wander during the night, and young Manchineri women in particular usually avoid walking alone in the dark. The past is made continuously present through the appearance of dead relatives. The souls of dead people are associated with natural phenomena, such as thunder bursts. Dead people are also believed to appear in dreams. Generally, dreams are a contact zone between spirits and human beings, allowing humans to receive signs that can guide their activities and decisions, such as whether it is propitious to set off on a journey or a hunting or fishing trip, or to predict what the community may face. In dreams, people may also acquire a better understanding of the teachings of animal or plant spirits that have appeared to them in the *ayahuasca* ritual. In this way, dreams can teach a person. I was also often told that in dreams you can see what is happening to absent relatives when they are traveling. What especially makes a person human is their close relationships with other humans (Vilaça 2002, 2005). Although the spirits of ancestors and nonhumans are one of the sources of Manchineri knowledge, adolescents are afraid of encountering them. Even the idea of mentioning the name of one of the most powerful nonhuman beings, *kajpomyolutu*, causes the speaker to whisper in a low voice. The human appearance of Amazonian spirits is well presented in the figures of the *kajpomyolutu*, which visibly appear as small persons, even though as nonhuman agents they have great physical powers and other superhuman qualities. The young men saw this figure in *ayahuasca* visions, which they subsequently depicted in their drawings. These drawings are not presented here since the youths preferred not to share this information with the majority of the non-Manchineri.

I shall take a deeper look at the *kajpomyolutu*, but I shall not touch on the information that I think the Manchineri would not wish to be told to a wider audience. The Manchineri say that the *kajpomyolutu* can be divided into three different groups according to their size, characteristics, and functions, and that both female and male spirits exist. The *kajpomyolutu* represent three palm trees and are spirit masters: the father of wind, the father of thunder, and the father of the forest.[23] The latter is regarded as a guardian of the forest and its animals, since he punishes those damaging the jungle through activities such as overhunting. In Portuguese, the same nonhuman agent is known throughout the region by the generic names *caboclinho* (*da mata*), the father of the forest (*pai da mata*), or even the mother of the forest, since sometimes the being appears as woman. Elsewhere in the Amazon, he is known as *sacharuna, curupira*, and *chullachaki*, as among the Amazonian mestizo populations (Regan 1983; Gow 1991; Luna 1986). This guardian of the forest is immensely strong and will even kill people if they do something he does not like. Young people claimed that you know when the father of the forest is close-by because he blows in his hands to make a sound like a whistle or a tinamou. A young man explained, "I have heard the *caboclinho da mata* many times. He blows in his hands. He is the size of this boy. He is like a person, like a boy. They say that he kills people. You know, my uncle met him. He came down with a fever. My father gave him medicine."

Young people said that sometimes the *kajpomyolutu* help hunters, leading them to places with an abundance of game, especially tapirs, which are difficult to catch. A hunter must usually make a deal with the father of the forest, agreeing to avoid the company of females, including his wife, and hunting only what is necessary. Young people also know well other ways to attract the father of the forest: you can speak to him by leaving tobacco. He passes on knowledge only if you respect him. One of the boys told me that it is difficult to negotiate with the father of the forest both because he can take one to his world forever and because one may die if he fails to follow the spirit's rules. For instance, I was also told that one of the boys who had made a deal with the father of the forest was now an excellent hunter. The father of the forest had asked the boy what he wanted to become. He said that he really would like to be a hunter, a man who kills game. Had the boy not made a deal with the nonhuman being, the latter would have killed the boy. Now he was able to hunt all kinds of game, finding peccaries and tortoises whenever he walked in the forest. But the father of the forest had told him that he should never become furious, or the boy would kill someone.

This particular nonhuman agent is widely feared and many young people told stories about how they had escaped the father of the forest by running away in panic after hearing him or after he had slapped them on their backs. Usually this happened after the people had done something wrong during their hunting trips, such as shooting badly. According to young people, an encounter with the father or mother of the forest may lead to mental disorders and sickness, as well as contacts with other forest spirits. Usually a person becomes sick first. If the cause is not discovered and the correct shamanic treatment not given, he or she will be lost. There was also secondhand information on these kinds of encounters that subsequently required shamanic cures, such as consuming the hallucinogenic *ayahuasca* drink. Two girls once had a discussion with me about this topic:

> We've never heard him [*kajpomyolutu*]. But once he affected my sister. We lived in a colony, and the jungle was very close [to the house], and he was blowing. If we hadn't prayed, she wouldn't be here today. My grandfather prayed for her. He took *ayahuasca* with her and he discovered that it was the *caboclinho*. When she walked alone, she became scared. Even at night, she wanted to sleep between us. Therefore my grandfather took *ayahuasca* with her. [He also discovered that] she had gone alone from here to over there [points into a house farther in the forest], and once she slept on the way. When she woke up, the *caboclinho* took her. My uncle took meat to him and the meat vanished . . . My brother also told me that when he was walking in the forest once, the *caboclinho* followed him blowing.

The narratives about the *kajpomyolutu* and other forest spirits that capture and harm people are related to morality, telling of those who would be taken by the *kajpomyolutu* and have to live in his (or her) abode, where the world would be seen from a different, nonhuman perspective. The narratives also illustrate the dangers of the forest.[24] Stories told by the youngsters, in which children were abducted, demonstrate the everyday risk that children and young people may become lost if they wander alone in the forest. But adolescent boys already at hunting age are more independent and can at least decide whether or not to make a deal with the *kajpomyolutu*. In the following tale, for instance, this happened after an adult man's encounter with the spirit: "When he [*kajpomyolutu*] is furious with us, he kills. I couldn't even run. He knocked over the village chief. He came along this path here, caught him and pushed him over. The chief ran but he [*kajpomyolutu*] went after him. A lightning storm arrived and with it heavy rain. He's like that. It was very dark rain, and a lot of lightning. [*Nothing happened to him?*][25] Nothing. He said that he just slammed into his back."

Sometimes it is difficult to know why the *kajpomyolutu* interacts with people, but the narratives are about his control and powers. In general, overhunting evokes anger of this nonhuman being. According to some of the younger Manchineri, such encounters also indicate that the spirit wants the contacted person to become a shaman or wants to offer him or her knowledge. These people should make a deal with the *kajpomyolutu,* as described above, which is also referred to as a "contract." However, owing to the obligations and conditions of the "contract," only a few people are willing to accept the approach. The same aspect of the powers of the forest beings applies to a huge jungle anaconda, a being known in the Peruvian Amazon as *sachamama*.[26] This is a big snake that lies underneath plants and trees. One story, for example, tells of a man who was alone in a forest once and suddenly wanted to stay there. He became insane, as he had started to behave like a nonhuman being and no longer saw the world as humans do. As we know from Viveiros de Castro (1996, 128), in Amerindian thought "the point of view is located in the body." The shaman later cured him and he decided not to become a shaman himself, even though he could now have sought contact with the anaconda. I was also often told that one of the present-day healers (all of whom are old men) from the most distant village had disappeared for a long period, but one day he had suddenly walked back out of the jungle. He was in a fairly good physical condition, though all his clothes had rotted away and he had acquired some kind of mental disorder. According to the adolescents, one of the *kajpomyolutu,* the mother of the forest (*mãe da mata*), had fed and taken care of him, and during this time he had learned many things about nature from her, such as healing skills. Since then, he has preferred to live by himself.

The young Manchineri people in the city had heard the name *caboclinho* and the being was usually pictured as a short man with one leg turned backward, a description that matches the nonhuman being widely known in the Amazon as *curupira*. When I asked the youths in the reserve if he had just one leg pointing forward, everyone said that both legs were to the front. None of the youths in the city told me about a personal encounter with the father of the forest, although some had heard about people who had met him.

[My father told me that] some Indians make a deal with him to hunt better. And they give him tobacco in exchange. Every week they give tobacco to the *caboclinho da mata*.

[*Tobacco?*] Tobacco and other things. It was my father's cousin it seems, who told [my father] that he had made a contract with the *caboclinho*. But one time the cousin failed to give anything to him, and the *caboclinho* was ready to take him. But he woke up. He woke up and he was in the middle of the jungle.

[*Did he return then?*] He returned home, normal. But the *caboclinho* was still ready to take him.

[*Could there be* caboclinhos *here?*] Only in the forest, I think. Here they no longer exist. Here people do not ask [for anything]; they just take the land without permission.

There was not much difference in the way young people and adults narrated their experiences of encountering nonhuman beings. Shamans and elders could certainly offer more detailed explanations of the encounters and their meanings. In contrast, in all the Manchineri villages, young people's explanations of the genesis of the many things in the world and its first people mixed "mythical," "Christian," and "Western scientific" elements. As an example, young people may explain thunder as the agency of the souls of dead Manchineri or through various kinds of "scientific" explanations—the belief that thunder means that it will rain or that vapor is heating the ground, for instance. The Manchineri adolescents in the city were more likely to use elements from the "scientific" worldview learned at school, an inclination evident in their explanations of the creation of the world, the moon, and thunder. But as well as using their knowledge of the natural sciences, they also drew on explanations from the Christian Genesis, as the elders do. In sum, exegesis also depends on the context in which the young person's narration is embedded. The source of the information is also mentioned to the listener, for example: "I am going to speak about geography now." Those youths who live in the reserve provide more detailed narratives about the past of their ancestors and the history of their environment and its nonhuman agencies, reflecting the specific oral history and knowledge of those localities. For all the Manchineri youngsters, nonhuman beings—animal, plant, and ancestor spirits—were considered to be "teachers" to the Manchineri. And occasionally they are presented to non-Manchineri.

Non-Manchineri

Among the young Indians, contacts with non-Indians have altered the way in which being in the world is understood.

For me the world was created like this, in my opinion. Like there is night and day, you know. For me [in the deep past there] only existed night, and so there were no other families or other ethnic groups. And in my view, as I live here in Extrema, only Extrema existed. The world really was enclosed like that.

[*How?*] We didn't see outside. I didn't think Jatobá existed. This moon shone down on Extrema alone and only my family existed. Today I already think that other villages and cities exist, other countries, and also the nation-state of Brazil. When I heard the name *Brazil* before, for me it didn't exist; it was like Peru, Bolivia, you know. For me, only what was here existed.

[*When did this change occur?*] When I started to think, when I started to study, you know. My teacher started to explain the names of the region's municipalities, like Mamoadate Indigenous Territory, those of the Upper Purus River, and that's how I discovered, through the Purus and Jurua basins, you see. And the municipalities of Acre, too. And I also learned that Rio Branco existed. I heard more about Rio Branco and I began to have contact with the city. Today we don't only talk about Assis [Brasil] and Sena [Madureira]; we talk about Boca do Acre, Cruzeiro [do Sul], and we already talk with them [via VHF radio], but not before. And in this way I began to discover that other municipalities exist, as well as other countries.

This snippet of conversation demonstrates that the relation to other indigenous groups and non-Indians gives meaning to the present situation of Manchineri adolescents. The community was thought to have always existed, and its relation to others was mainly focused on relations to nonhuman beings (such as the moon). In the past, other indigenous groups—many of them now extinct—were important trade partners and political allies for today's older community members.

In the summertime—that is, the dry season from June to October when the river is at its lowest—reaching the closest municipality, Assis Brasil, involves passing by the small settlement of Icuriã on the Yaco River, which is approximately a three-hour canoe trip from the nearest Manchineri village, Peri. Then the river level falls and fluvial transportation becomes difficult, meaning that canoes have to be pushed or even carried across some stretches. The farthest Manchineri village, Extrema, is one day's travel from Icuriã. The 50-mile (80-kilometer) distance from Icuriã to Assis Brasil is covered by foot or jeep. During the rainy season, the path becomes too muddy and the only means of transportation is by foot, a tough trek through hilly forest, lasting two to three days. In summertime, the path is accessible by jeep, meaning the journey from the river shore to Assis Brasil takes just two to three hours. Rio Branco, the state capital, is a five-hour drive from Assis Brasil (206 miles/331 kilometers). During the rainy season from November to April, the water level rises again and the river flow toward the nearest municipalities downriver is stronger. It then takes between six and twenty days to make the canoe trip to the other nearby municipality, Sena Madureira, from the reserve, depending on the size of outboard motor used on the canoe. These locations, roads, and rivers are all shown in Figure 1.1.

The young generation has been born during an era when relations with multiple actors are taken for granted. In contrast, a shaman from Extrema told me that before the demarcation of the Mamoadate Indigenous Territory, the Manchineri hardly ever saw non-Indians. When they worked in rubber tapping, just one of them would go to meet with an intermediary, who arrived with donkeys to take the rubber they had produced, leaving trade items for them in exchange. After the FUNAI reserved the area for the Indians by the Yaco River, the Manchineri moved higher up the river and farther away from the rubber plantations. At the time when Extrema village was founded, the only contact between the Manchineri and the outside world—albeit almost a daily occurrence—was via an airplane that brought supplies to the head of the FUNAI post and some tools for the Indians. But since the post's closure, the airplane has only come to the village to pick up seriously ill patients to take them to hospital. Several days' travel is needed to reach the municipality by any other means. Outboard motors for canoes were introduced only a decade ago and there are still only a few motors in each village. One of the Extrema village's shamans said that today he has seen many things—for instance, on a trip to Cruzeiro do Sul by airplane to attend an indigenous cultural meeting.[27] He even took his older children with him. He said, "It has changed a lot. Now we have rights. It's good because the kids know how to speak Portuguese and in our language."

The current young generation has mostly lived at a time when non-Manchineri visitors to the Mamoadate reserve have been rare: the direction of visits is more often from the villages to the outside than from the outside in. Since the group is highly endogamous and the reserve is closed off as a legally protected indigenous area, there is a fear of people arriving unexpectedly and thus a skeptical attitude to all outsiders prevails throughout the reserve. The Manchineri are afraid of those outsiders who invade their lands, such as drug traffickers or clandestine loggers. Beyond that, they seem to be suspicious that those non-Indians visiting the reserve from farther away are only interested in stealing their knowledge of medicinal plants and making money by using this knowledge in the cities. Previously the reserve was much more difficult to visit, and, to give an example, no academic researchers had been allowed to enter. I went to Mamoadate for the first time to attend the three-day meeting of Organization of All the Manchineri of the River Yaco (MAPKAHA), the Manchineri's recently established organization, held in Jatobá village. We heard that the people in the village had no idea that we were all coming. When I went alone there later on to begin my field studies, the Manchineri told me with evident satisfaction that they already knew I was coming.

Non-Indians are referred to as *payri*. They effectively remain "*não-parente*" ("nonkin"). Most nonindigenous visitors to the reserve are government officials, such as FUNASA employees, constructors for the infrastructural projects being implemented by the government, or NGO workers. Their visits—nowadays more frequent—have changed the everyday rhythm of the villages considerably. Meetings are mostly held in the biggest villages or those closest to the urban centers, and other villagers travel to these locations. The Jatobá schoolteacher said he used to have more time to go fishing on the lakes in the summer or to visit other villages. Now he cannot leave because more people visit them than before and he has to receive them all. He also has his schoolteaching work. People from another village had invited him to give some advanced lessons there and the secretary of education gave him permission to go, but the people in his own village would not let him. People also complained that the officials and NGO workers stay for only a short time in the village, meaning they have no real idea of what life is like in Mamoadate. Nor do the Manchineri have the chance to talk to them at length. They are already used to government officials arriving at the villages by speedboat, quickly interviewing the chief of the village, and leaving. The Manchineri seem to like people who are calm, adapt to their own pace of life, and explain things carefully. Many of these government officials coming from the city have little knowledge about Indians or intercultural sensitivity. Fortunately, some local government officials, NGO workers, and consultants do seem to have abandoned the colonialist attitudes and have learned from the mistakes of the government's previous projects. Nonetheless, the Manchineri remain suspicious of new plans and projects implemented on their lands. As a young boy explained to me, they no longer trust people who come to the village to present a project for the reserve, since experience has shown that what the visitors promise during their visits never materializes in the reserve. They summon all the people in the village to assemble, hold a meeting, and talk a lot, but nothing changes. Typically nothing more is heard from these visitors, meaning they are all accused of being liars. On the other hand, although the young Manchineri are skeptical about outsiders, for them important information and knowledge come from the outside, especially from nonnatives and cities (cf. Gow 1991, 235; Vilaça [1999] 2007; Kelly 2011). Hence the encounters with non-Indian institutions and organizations are crucial. For instance, referring to the training courses in the city, an agroforestry agent remarked, "The more contact we have with the whites, the more we'll be able to improve our work."

Generally, the Manchineri are content with the people who pass knowledge and information on to them. Young people are often named as intermediaries between the non-Manchineri and other community members. Some younger

people also aspire to more contacts with "outsiders." Some construction workers and male NGO staff told me how young unmarried girls regularly came
to visit the houses where they were lodged and openly expressed their willingness to have a short affair with them. Young Manchineri men looked more for
conversations with these visitors, but in the cities, when far from their families
and when drunk at parties, they also looked for nonindigenous women. However, this seemed to be more part of the behavior learned from other indigenous
groups or the attitudes of non-Indians of eroticizing and exoticizing native men
as good lovers. Few Ashaninka and Cashinahua men had married white women.

Personal relations between youngsters living in Mamoadate and non-Indians
are still rare, and the encounters tend to be limited to short communications
between those living on the route to urban centers and indigenous officials.
The social and cultural border between "here" and "there" is maintained by
the rare social contacts and interactions with non-Manchineri. But it is not
only territorial distance that causes differentiation; linguistic, economic, and
cultural barriers also create social boundaries. I was constantly asked, "How do
you do this?" and told that "*we* do or speak like this." The whites remain "the
Other" since there is no giving, sharing, or talking. For the Manchineri, one of
the main differences with non-Indians is their food. For Amazonian people in
general, food plays a significant role in the construction of social relations.[28] In
Mamoadate I was told that a government consultant, who had come to evalu-
ate the situation of the indigenous territory, was "miserable" because he did not
eat meat. As another example, the natives' way of eating with their hands while
sitting on the floor reveals different ways of regulating the body and maintains
the division between "us" and "them."

During the last days of my first long-term stay in the reserve, I was told
that although they were now eating with me, this was not their usual practice.
I remembered that at the beginning of my stay in the reserve, I was given food
first while people looked on as I ate. My assumption at the time was that they
were not hungry. In fact, they did not want to eat at the same time as me. Later,
while we were eating *pataraska* together one time (fish roasted in banana leaf in
typical Manchineri style), an older woman said that they do not usually eat with
whites, because white people say that their food is inadequate (*não presta*) and
this makes them ashamed. When I visited another house with the same woman
one day, she told me that the owner of the house was embarrassed because she
only had Manchineri fish soup to offer me. But since I liked the soup, she was
delighted.

However, even though I ate the same food as the Manchineri when in
Mamoadate, I was often called *"payri"* or "Cristina," since there are still many
other criteria identifying the Other. For the Manchineri, *payri* is someone who
is fundamentally different, someone who does not live with the Manchineri.

It refers to anyone non-Indian, whether living in Rio de Janeiro, Manaus, Rio Branco, or Sena Madureira or anyone mestizo, white, or black. Young mothers liked to scare their children by saying that if they did not behave, the *payri* (referring to myself as "the white person") would be very angry. Likewise, when I visited houses in Jatobá, the children did not dare to enter the same room but peered curiously through the chinks in the wall. I was also asked to explain what the benefit of my study would be for the Manchineri. Young people in particular have become more aware of the historical events and situations experienced by their ancestors.

For the people in the reserve, the clearest representatives of the "Other" are those whites they meet in the cities, *na rua* (literally, "in the street"). When the Manchineri are outside the reserve, they do not expect to be offered food by "whites"—people who do not even give away water for free, as young people often noted. Moreover, for many of the young Manchineri, respect and calmness are essential qualities differentiating them from non-Indians. While in one of the villages, I saw pictures of the singers Madonna and Michael Jackson on the cover of a young man's wallet and asked him who they were. His answer was simply "people from the city." It is interesting that he did not say that they were *payri*, non-Indians. Thus when the Manchineri say that someone is from the city, they mean that the person is from the other world of which the Manchineri are no part. They do not know about natural medicines and do not respect nature. The Manchineri may have closer relations with some of these people living in rural areas closer to the reserve: at least they can stop at their houses and exchange the news.

The closest people to the Manchineri are the other Yine groups in Peru, though some adolescents had only visited their Diamante village, one of the Yine *comunidades nativas* on the Madre de Dios. In fact, two older men had moved from the Peruvian Yine communities to Brazil in the 1980s. *Yine* means "humans" (*yineru*) and they are formed by different ancestral groups, *manxineru* being one of them. The idea that the Manchineri once constituted the same indigenous group with the Yine of Peru seems to be increasingly important, providing an idea of ethnic belonging even more pronounced than that of many other indigenous groups in Acre or Brazil. It also offers a new tool for obtaining international cooperation.

Indians from other groups are called *kajitu*. Even though the Manchineri share the same indigenous reserve with the Yaminahua, whose villages are located on the lower course of the Yaco River, the two ethnic groups communicate little. The Yaminahua, especially those in the nearest villages in the reserve, sometimes visit the Manchineri to use the radio or conduct trade, such as buying domestic animals. They eat different food, like caimans, and have different cultural traits: for example, they never use the *koshma*, a long cotton robe often used by the Manchineri.

However, the Yaminahua are known by their individual names, contrary to the so-called uncontacted Indians living in the region, the Mashco-Piro, who occasionally leave trails in isolated areas of the reserve close to the Peruvian border. These *isolados* leave these tracks when on the move, especially in summertime looking for the eggs of *tracajá* turtles. They are considered to be "wild Indians" (*índios bravos*), a term reminiscent of the Urubamba Yine attitude toward so-called uncivilized forest Indians who do not speak Spanish and are illiterate (cf. Gow 1991, 85–89).

Manchineri adolescents and young adults living in the reserve have met many of the other indigenous groups in the region's municipalities (principally Sena Madureira and Rio Branco) and on training courses, as well as at political and cultural meetings of local indigenous peoples. These events provide an opportunity to reflect on the differences between indigenous groups as well as the differences to nonnatives. People from other indigenous groups are occasionally called kin (*parentes*), whatever their ethnicity. This, though, only occurs in certain contexts and when certain discourses are involved. The case is similar for many other native peoples: Jackson (1995), for example, also emphasizes that the word *brothers*, referring to the different language groups among the Tukano, was used solely in pan-Indian discourse, whereas among the same group the same term had negative connotations. A young Manchineri woman who was taking part on a national training course for indigenous health agents, organized by FUNASA in Brasilia, said the following about her visit in 2005:

[*Did you meet up with other indigenous groups?*] Other kin—relatives since they are other Indians. But we only got to talk during the lunch break . . . I said that I'm from Acre. They said that they were from the region. And they asked me whether I was Manchineri. And I said that I was. I think they know more than us. There was one who knew about computers and how to put [a slide] on a wall. They spoke in their native language and used a computer and they read it out to us . . . I heard him talking, asking questions to those organizing the course . . .

But I don't think they have much culture left. Because they walk around very well dressed, with a ring in their ears . . . They already have mobile phones which they walk around with . . . They live almost entirely in the city. They travel when they are asked. They spend their life wandering.

As this interview extract shows, Indians from other groups are regarded as kin in many interethnic contexts, but when compared to "us" these Indians living in the city are no longer indigenous. They may have new knowledge, but they have lost their indigenous differences. When other indigenous people are called *kajitu*, which could thus also translate as *parente*, we can see that the term refers to potential affinity. Gow (2001, 305) notes that the meaning of *kajitu* for the Piro has changed over time from the Inca state officials to its current meaning of "white people."

At regional level, young Manchineri have noted similarities with the Arawak-speaking Apurinã and Ashaninka, especially in terms of the proximity between their language and that of the Apurinã, as well as the shared use of *ayahuasca*. Many other groups, such as the Cashinahua, also consume shamanic drink. For the youngsters, these meetings provide important opportunities to meet up and increase their awareness of the local history of indigenous groups. Indigenous political and cultural meetings and training courses, which have increased in number over recent years, allow native peoples to become more aware of their differences and to express them in new ways. These events are the ideal moments to use traditional costumes, ritual body paintings, and native objects—such as handmade bags, necklaces, and bracelets—with the symbolism of each group, connecting them to the nonhuman beings specific to their culture. They also bring together Indians from the remote indigenous territories and the city. What has changed is the relationship to third parties—non-Indians and other Indians—especially in terms of power. Turner (1991) has argued that the Kayapo turned from cosmology to culturalism when they started to see themselves through their own cultural differences from others.

For many young Manchineri city dwellers, the other Indians living in the city are usually regarded as similar insofar as they share a common third party, the nonnatives. In the city, friendships with nonindigenous adolescents are still rare or limited to school. The school is also, though, usually the first institution where they experience prejudice. However, the indigenous youngsters who had arrived in the city long ago did say that the situation was worse in the past. Many people were afraid of them and would avoid talking to them: "It was difficult to meet someone," as a young Manchineri man said. In 2003, when I had one of the first conversations with indigenous youths in Rio Branco, a young Manchineri girl, Soleane, who had been living most of her life in in Rio Branco, told about her experiences of non-Indians in the city:

> With them [non-Indian]---alone---they don't tease me anymore. They tease us when there are lots of us, you see. They say we're sons of Indians. That we're from the forest. Sometimes there's no point in saying anything. They speak from a distance, showing off.
>
> [*Did this happen when you were alone?*] Once at school. A teacher said that I was absent since it was my day, the Indian Day [*dia do índio*]. Absent since I'd gone to the jungle. My friend told me ---.
>
> [*Are you afraid of anything?*] Of the people who don't know us. Who want to harm us. Like when he [an Indian][29] was burnt in Brasilia. He was sleeping on a

bench---. Sometimes this makes you afraid of people. But we are already used to it. And we answer if someone asks. I say the truth. I'm not embarrassed to speak.[30]

Even a young woman living in the reserve said that she had been called *caboclo* by a white person in the town, and she had said to the person that she could take the person to the court. In fact, many young indigenous youth seem to have put their heads up. When I asked in the city, "How do you feel here [in the city]?" The answers of a young Manchineri woman, Alessandra, living in Rio Branco was

> Sometimes good, sometimes bad. Bad because there is prejudice against indigenous peoples. We feel bad. Sometimes good because we're studying and it is good to learn, since one day, who knows, we shall be able to defend our rights. There are already many Indians defending [our rights].
> [*What is this prejudice like?*] There are people who don't like Indians.
> [*How do they show it?*] When we pass by, they say, "Ah, Indians, Indians are vagrants." I was with my sister and she said to a man, "Don't you know that's called prejudice?!"---And he fell silent.
> [*What was it like before?*] Before it was worse, since we didn't know our rights to the same extent and the Constitution of the Indian has now been created. We still want more things, because before we didn't know what our rights were. And now there are people who want to defend these rights and it is much better. Both whites and Indians are working towards the same objectives: education and health. They too. But there are still people who see us as animals. From now on many things will change.

As these conversations show, the urban youths have become aware that they possess certain rights.

In the city, the young Manchineri have closer relations with other native adolescents in the city than with non-Indian youths. Some young Manchineri even told me that their indigenous origin was usually unknown to anyone else at their school. They felt that it was not the right context to make their indigenous difference explicit, since school was a space for equal opportunities (here in education) with other Brazilians.[31] Their best friends were often their cousins or people from other indigenous groups. However, shamanic rituals and some other social environments, such as youth cultures, have united young people with non-Indians, as I discuss in the following chapters.

In this chapter we have seen that in the social universe occupied by young indigenous people, positioning oneself as similar or different decreases or increases other differences and similarities, not only in relations with nonhumans but also between different human perspectives in the world. "Others" can become "us" if they have a common opposite. Thus the other group may be opposed or it may be jointly opposed to a common opposite (Viveiros de Castro 2002; Lagrou 2001). This becomes particularly evident when we observe the attempts by young Manchineri, especially in the city, to identify with their kin in the reserve in some situations and with non-Manchineri in others. Everyday social processes in constructing kin relations separate the Manchineri in the city from those living in the reserve and vice versa. From the point of view of those living in the reserve, there is a decrease in real humanness when one relocates from a village and its community to other groups.

For both the youths, in the reserve and those in the city, "they" and "we" vary according to the context in which the person is acting. As Rosaldo (1989, 87) argues, "The view of an authentic culture as an autonomous internally coherent universe no longer seems tenable in the postcolonial world. Neither 'we' nor 'they' are as self-contained and homogenous as we/they once appeared." Indigenous adolescents' ways of speaking about "us" and "them" are formed and shaped in changing situations, which must be understood within their different contexts and relations with the dominant society and other native groups. The community members in rural and urban areas have become closer owing to a new sense of relatedness as a group opposed to a common third party: other Indians and non-Indians. This is a topic discussed in the following chapters. Moreover, the sense of community changes to include all the Manchineri (both in the city and in the reserve), or only those in the reserve, or just those in the same village. As my study revealed, different levels of similarity and proximity are also experienced in relation to other indigenous groups and to *payri* (white people) depending on their urban or rural emphasis and the knowledge that people wish to embody. As discussed in the following chapters, non-Manchineri and Manchineri, along with the different age groups, are related differently in altering contexts. Learning to interact within the contemporary diversity of human perspectives forms the main passage from adolescence to adulthood, involving elders, parents, adults, and other younger people in embodying new knowledge, which is what I shall discuss in the next chapter.

CHAPTER 2

Ritual Passages from Soft to Firm

In the previous chapter, we saw that the relations among community members, nonhuman agencies, and the non-Manchineri shape a web of connections in which young Manchineri people strive to form their subjectivity. This chapter focuses on contemporary ritualistic transitions that prepare indigenous youths to strengthen their position, body, and knowledge in relation to others and to learn about themselves as actors in the world: a transition to adulthood. In the first section I discuss young Manchineri experiences of the traditional puberty ritual in different villages within the reserve and in the city. The ethnography shows both continuation and change, reflecting the relationship to a changing forest environment and the new social contexts within which young people act. The second section examines schooling, one of the most important contemporary rites of passage, marking the person's embodiment of knowledge in a novel system largely designed by the state. Finally I turn to new types of matrimony and shifts in the assignment of gender tasks, roles, and social status. The main message of this chapter is that young people themselves have taken an active role in strengthening their bodies and minds and in structuring their own learning processes.

The Puberty Rite

Generally speaking, initiation during puberty has been one of the most significant ritual performances in non-Western societies, marking the transition to adulthood through the person's acquisition of new tasks, roles, and social status. Many art forms and sacred chants have formed an important part of these rituals, since they turn a child into a human adult within the generational lines. Bodily changes at puberty are the sign of a person's transition to a new social status. The Manchineri call the change from childhood to preadulthood *ralixatka*, meaning "to finish" or "to terminate," a term that can also be used for completing any kind of work (e.g., to finish writing). This is related to the completion of a child's body: for a girl, this happens during her first menstrual periods, while for a boys the change occurs when his voice breaks. For this reason, the transition to adulthood takes place not at a set age but when the person is physically mature. Puberty has a significant meaning for the youths in the reserve and for their explanation of their own life course. They would say about certain events that they took place before or after they had "grown up." At first I was surprised when a boy or a girl told me exactly where and when they were "formed"—for instance, "I was formed in Extrema" (*Eu me formei na Extrema*).[1] I asked, "How?" "I grew up."

A lengthy puberty ritual still marks the Manchineri girls' transition to *makluji* (being a "youth" or "young adult"). This status is in stark contrast to the earlier period, when they were called *mturu*, "children." The elders explained to me that the young person's body must be controlled at puberty since the body is then soft (*poptshi* in Manchineri, *mole* in Portuguese). This refers to a girl's first menses or the moment when a boy's voice is breaking. During rubber production and the work for the bosses, Manchineri parents continued instructing their children to observe the diets and behavioral restrictions during this phase in which their bodies were changing. Today, though, the elders worry that the bodies of young people are weaker than before. In the past their bodies were much more carefully controlled, meaning that they became stronger and lived longer without becoming ill.

The most elaborate rituals are practiced in the two villages farthest from the urban centers, Extrema and Lago Novo. The girl's puberty ritual is called *hapijihlu*, referring to her menstrual blood. Some young women also referred to their initiation ritual as "when I was painted," since the ritual ends with the painting of her body with Manchineri geometric designs. During the ritual, the body is controlled and secluded in various ways. The structure of the *hapijihlu* rite, its moral codes, and the physical regulations imposed on the girl vary between different villages, but all these actions still empower both the girl and the people closest to her. During the period when the young person's body is thought to be at its softest and in the process of change, the person may become very weak, even close to death. The Manchineri girls who have passed through the ritual are usually deemed to be stronger. The family's organization of the communal festivity to celebrate the girl's passage also shows their generosity. Hence the girl is then in an even better position to marry an important young man or even to be selected for a position of responsibility in the community.

The girl's puberty ritual begins as soon as the first menstruation is noticed. If the girl is to be secluded, she is separated from the community and the rest of her family inside her parents' house: there she remains lying in a hammock, which is suspended close to the roof or in a corner of the house invisible to other people. She may have contact with her mother or an elder woman who takes care of her. The beginning of seclusion is referred to as "my mother lifted me up." It indicates the intense physical regulation of the girl's body, since the girl has to stay still in her hammock. During her menstrual period, all she is allowed to drink is a green banana porridge, three times a day. The various behavioral and alimentary restrictions applied during the girl's ritual illustrate ideas about sameness and difference between forest beings and humans, as well as the immediate relations between them.

In Amazonia, human agency is typically constructed by increasing the inter-relatedness of the community members and negating certain nonhuman powers during the period when the human body is undergoing change. A body is a distinctive factor, socially fabricated by naming, painting, and piercing, and by forming ceremonial groups that show its central position for human existence and human thinking. Bodily modifications have been associated in particu-lar with childbirth, puberty, shamanic initiation, sickness, death, mourning, or killing an enemy, since it is during these moments that relationships with others are reestablished (Seeger, DaMatta, and Castro 1987; Viveiros de Castro 1987; Conklin 2001; Vilaça 2002). The changing body has to be protected from energies coming from the outside—a process that defines personhood. Consequently, these are events when a person has the most instable identity and they have typically involved moments of seclusion from other people.

In general for many indigenous people, at puberty the changing body is vulnerable to spirits and thus to permanent modifications, since it is passing through a phase of physical transformations (indicated by the girl's first men-struation or the boy's voice breaking). Among the Manchineri, this could be seen when a young woman, Ana Paula, told me that because she had tried to study during her puberty seclusion in a hammock, her eyesight has already become poor. She was only told later that you should not read during this period because you can ruin your eyesight. She said that were her mother to have seen her reading, she would have been angry. However, the softness of the body at puberty is common to male bodies, too, when their voice is breaking. This is the main male corporeal change for the Manchineri and for many other Amazonian indigenous groups. The control of the human body, both male and female, and the accompanying restrictions highlight the importance of the fabrication of social relations at the time of puberty in order to produce a certain kind of human body and avoid its transformation into nonkin. Only such control ensures a person's protection, youthfulness, and strength.

After her menstruation, the girl takes a bath with special leaves early in the morning, and her father or a hunter from the village hunts for monkey (*macaco cairara*), which is subsequently prepared and cooked for her to eat. This first food, monkey, is eaten using the right side of her body only. Over the following month until her next period, the girl still has to remain at home, although she can move outside if she stays close to the house. If she does walk around near the house, she has to wear a cloth on her head. Otherwise bird excrement may fall on her hair, turning it white when she gets older. The girl also has to stick to eating lean fish without swollen bellies in order to avoid developing the same trait. She cannot eat fruits since snakes like them and the girl could be bitten by one as a consequence. Moreover she can only scratch herself using a kind of wooden hook (*gancho*) since scratching with her nails would leave lifelong streaks on her skin or on her child's. If the hook breaks before the girl is painted, the girl's life will be short. The whole community knows the threats facing the person if the regulations are not followed. Human corporeality is produced in many different ways. For instance, red cords are also tied at the girl's joints—knees, ankles, arms, and elbows—and she wears them over the ensuing months in order to induce muscle growth.

Throughout their puberty seclusion, during their first menstrual period, and for a month after, the young women are in a phase of "liminality" that marks them off from social space-time and everyday conduct.[2] Manchineri adolescents in puberty are in a marginal state, located between the community and the liminal condition primarily inhabited by animals and spirits. Thus, then their agency can be affected easily by other agencies. It is precisely during the events of their puberty ritual that people typically experience selfhood and all personal codes are abolished, as in many other rites of passage. Eliade ([1959]

Figure 2.1   A girl with a hook and a scarf in front of her house (Extrema village)

2004), for instance, noted that among certain tribes in Australia, novices have to lie down to illustrate that they are symbolically dead, a phase that symbolizes completion. Victor Turner (1969) argued that novices during initiation rituals are typically passive, humble, and submissive to the rules, because they communicate with the sacred objects and ritual symbols. He called this marginal state "betwixt and between," which involves an intensive period of isolation and autonomy. Van Gennep ([1909] 1960) defined this first stage of rites of passage as *separation*, followed by *transition* and *incorporation*.

For the Manchineri, when the bodily changes at puberty have passed, the young person ruptures the certainty provided by dependent relationships with his or her immediate family and the safety net they provide. The adolescent turns from a liminal being into a full person and member of the community. As Fabian (1992, 32) has written, "Essentially, all Bororo boys must 'die' in order to be culturally reborn as adults privy to a complex set of rights and responsibilities." The separation leads to conceiving the distinctiveness of society as a space of moral norms and the person as a member of that community with personal resources. That is forming and firming one's agency. As DaMatta (2000) explains, liminality has a positive and communal character, since the experience of individuality and isolation always concludes with a return to society and a transformation of the person into one more component in a network of social relationships.

Painting the girl and holding a festival involving the whole community usually mark the end of seclusion and confinement. The festival—as the transitional phase of this rite of passage to adulthood—is thus completed by the onset of the person's incorporation of her new status. On the day of the festival, two older women take the girl into the forest, where they cover her entire body in designs using a paint made from genipap fruit, and cut her hair, cutting her fringe for the first time. Evanuzia explains how this moment can determine the girl's life as a woman of the community in many other ways:

> When the old woman paints, you have to stay quiet, since their stick is really thin, and if that breaks, we shall not live long. We have to use a hook to scratch ourselves, before we're painted—or else scratching leaves striped scars on the skin. And when the girl gives birth to a baby, he or she would have stripes, too. [*And the festival?*] We can dance. We are all painted. Our hair is cut at the front and the back. You cannot have your hair cut before you are painted. You wear a cloth on your head to avoid the vulture shitting on it.

The women in the house laughed at Evanuzia's last sentence.

The body decorations painted on the girl's body imitate the skins of animals, like a tortoise (*knoya*) painted on the legs to induce resistance and a boa constrictor (*himnu*) painted on her body to bring wisdom and protection. The elders told me that those who had lived a very long life had been painted by the image of one of the Manchineri ancestors, *Hoyakalu*, who had reached a very great age and also translates as the Christian "God." However, knowledge of the specific initiation designs is disappearing and thus any kind of Manchineri patterns are used in some villages, although painting still has the same main overall objective: to prevent attacks by predators, snakes, and diseases. Designs are applied using a fine stick, meaning the painter has to be highly skilled. If the genipap paint runs out while applying the body painting to the girl, her life will end quickly. The girls said that because of the paintings, they "don't get ill" "no snakes have bitten" them. This can be seen as activating "the powers of different bodies" (Viveiros de Castro 1996), since the paintings are "clothes" of certain entities that enable the "wearer" to act like these animals or spirit beings. Hence in addition to the regulation of the body, body painting is one of the primary ways to interact with the nonhuman animal agents of the forest.

In addition to being fabricated in relation to forest spirits, the body is also formed by strengthening the relations with community members: at the end of the ritual the community as a whole joins the "formed" girl. The festivity organized for her and the community starts when the painted girl, dressed only in a red bra and skirt, arrives at the site of the ritual with the old women. This is when the girl becomes a woman, her female beauty observable by everyone. When the girl appears to the public at the site of the festival, her body is presented to others: she emerges from the forest with few clothes and her fringe cut to reveal her face clearly. One of the most important functions of the festivity is to show others that the girl is "cleaned" and no longer "vulnerable." For the community, the safe maturation to adulthood still ensures and protects its supply of future healthy members, especially girls for boys to marry. Gow (2001) writes that when the Piro girl is painted and shown to the guests, she actually transforms from a mythical being into her human form, the connection between the myth of the anaconda and history being constructed in the process.[3]

In the Manchineri puberty festivity, the girl first of all drinks manioc beer from a huge bowl with the eldest man of the community. After this ritual opening, her duty is to serve manioc beer to everyone, leaving the young men until last. The same order applies to dancing: first she dances with the old men and later with the younger boys. She can also start from the men who are the most hard working in the community, "in order to live long," as the mother of one girl said. The qualities of certain community members are transmitted to the girl in the ritual, paying her an honor. Ana Paula recalled her ritual with pride:

> I arrived [at the festival location] and gave manioc beer to the old man and those who know [things] and are not lazy, and to those to whom I was supposed to give [manioc beer] and drink with them. The old people and the workers. Not with

those boys. And then I had to give some to the young people. I drank manioc beer with an old man from here, who has since died. And also another deceased man, who lived in Lago Novo.

[*What happened then?*] My grandfather sang when the manioc beer was being distributed. That I do remember. He sang in Manchineri---for me to live for many years and to endure longer, not to become ill before old age. Just like my grandmother. She is alive even today.

[*Then the festivity started?*] Dances from our culture, as people say, and then the festivity started. From 3 p.m. until 5 p.m. and then there was a white people's festival, as people say.

[*With whom did you dance first?*] With the old man.

[*Were you drunk?*] Aha. And the old people say that when you dance with the elders, you live for a long time. Then I danced with the boys.

[*Was everybody there?*] Everyone. Even my uncle, he helped.

Acenilda from Lago Novo village also explained how she was "taken back" to her community: "When the blood had stopped running, she [grandmother] took me [down from the hammock]. 'Now you are going to descend,' she said. On the eighth week, the blood returned and I had to lie down again. She told me that the bleeding had stopped, and I was going to descend. 'Let's go to the forest.' I went with my aunts. And she tied me like this [she shows her arms and legs]. They finished painting me and told me to go. The men drank strong manioc beer and there was a festivity." Sharing things with elders is conceived to make young people essentially more like them. The interrelatedness of generations and the skills and qualities that the adults and elders pass on to the young are made visible in the ritual.

Nevertheless, the Manchineri girls' remarks during the interviews show that the situation was embarrassing at first for the girls entering the festival locale, as they still felt too shy to appear alone. Only afterward did they really enjoy the festival. Ana Paula recalls her day of festivity: "I arrived back home. It was there [points to the place] at the spring, where I saw my face. I was embarrassed to arrive covered in painted designs. I thought they would tease me. And I went to the spring [to wash away the paint], but it didn't come off . . . I was wearing just a red bra and shorts. I was embarrassed because I always use a skirt, and [I was] in little shorts—I was embarrassed."

Moreover, the girl recalled how the seclusion had been difficult for her, since she felt hungry and separated from others. For the first time she had to cease all the everyday tasks that she usually performed with her sisters. "It's like being ill," the girls said. Although the girl follows the rules for her own sake, they also reflect her position in the generational lines, and she is glad to receive support from the community, which comes together during the festival. "Everybody was close-by" was how the girls often pictured their experience. The older girls were very proud to talk about their ritual and said, "This is our tradition," and, "This is our culture." The girls especially liked the festival part of the ritual. When I asked what they thought about it, they usually replied, "I was very happy. There were many people, lots of manioc beer," or, "I liked it." There was plenty of food, and guests became drunk on the strong manioc beer, *caiçuma forte*, fermented over a long period. The girl is "the festival hostess" (*a dona da festa*) and effectively runs it (*É ela que manda a festa*).

Formerly, songs telling of the beings or ancestors who lived a long life were sung for "graduating" girls. Music is an important spiritual expression for the Manchineri, relating them to certain types of beings and their qualities. Afterward, as in other village festivals, a popular style of Brazilian country music, *forró*, is played, which the adolescents call "white music" (*música do branco*), and this dance music indicates that people are gathered together to celebrate. From now on the girl can eat any kind of food. The drawings made by the girls showing their puberty festival revealed the most important people for them during the event: usually an old woman painting them, an old man drinking and sharing manioc beer with them, other people nearby, and themselves in the center painted in Manchineri boa constrictor designs and wearing red clothes.

The festivity was seldom held in the villages downriver, a fact that can also be connected to the changes in the natural environment (such as decrease in the

Figure 2.2   Andreia's drawing depicting her puberty festival (Extrema village)

amount of game available locally, new social contacts, and changing uncertainties). In Santa Cruz, most girls interviewed went into seclusion at the time of their first menses, but few were subsequently painted or had any festival held for them. The importance of older women in transmitting knowledge and thus in forming the girl's body was still evident in the ritual. These elder women made the red strings and scarves for the girl to wear. If the girl was to be painted, this would also take place inside a house, not in the forest as in the past. For those girls for whom a festivity had been organized, the presence of the community was what they most liked in their process of "becoming a woman." The experience of continuity between the generations was important for the young women. Even the girls who had not passed through the ritual said that they would have liked to have participated in it.

In the evangelized Jatobá village, the food intake of some girls was controlled during their first menstruation and they ceased their daily tasks to lie down. Later on, a small festival was held among their families where nonalcoholic cassava drink was served. The woman is important, as serving the manioc drink showed the family's productivity. The teacher from this village said that they had stopped holding the lengthy ritual because they had no time for it. During the period of the rubber plantations, they had to work intensively and there was no time for prolonged fasting. In some ways, they now seem to be in the same situation: the leader of Jatobá village told me that they cannot afford to miss five days' work. He also said that they realized that nothing untoward happens nowadays if the ritual is not held, even though, he added, in the past a young person really did die if all the regulations were not followed. However, I heard that many girls had also fasted while on the rubber plantations. The change had probably occurred following their encounters with missionaries and the local non-Indian population, which have undoubtedly affected the importance attached by the community to its own typical practices.

In Extrema and Lago Novo villages, the farthest ones from the urban centers, all the girls I interviewed had passed through seclusion and fasting, but older girls said that the younger girls had not followed all the regulations they themselves had in the recent past. For instance, they explained, the younger girls now walk far from their home and talk with other people, since the older women do not keep an eye on them all the time. Some girls even eat fruit and run. However, many girls still use red cords around their knees, ankles, arms, and elbows for months to strengthen their muscles and wear a cloth on their heads to have the strength to perform many different tasks, old and new.

In Extrema, a father with many daughters said that the ritual is not practiced with every girl, since there is too much work to be done for them to be able to prepare the festival for the rapidly expanding population. He also criticized his own people, saying that they value only the things of "white men, instead of their own culture." It should also be borne in mind that the resources for obtaining forest food for the feast are now more limited owing to the more polluted and overexploited natural environment. In fact, only the most prestigious families organized the festivity in the past. This is a crucial factor, since generosity is a fundamental characteristic of Amerindian festivities and their sponsors.[4] Alliances are especially rematerialized when people from other villages are invited to celebrate the girl's emergence from seclusion.

The different forms assumed by the puberty ritual are an important way of increasing and decreasing the relations between certain entities, forest beings, ancestors, community members, and the white. In the cosmological web of connections young person's relations to others are regarded differently as empowering or depressing, and thus the relations between agencies are either avoided or nurtured. In Amazonia, this construction of personhood includes the idea that the person must have a certain kind of body that is socially shaped through relations to others. Gender roles especially are made visible and same-sex generational lines are explicitly connected. As "the festival hostess," the Manchineri girl still displays her new role as a woman by offering food and manioc beer to others. At the festival, a young girl accepts that she has grown up and reached adulthood, since now she can work in and for the community. "Then I was ready to help my mother" and "[The ritual helped me] to help other people," as two of the girls put it. In this way, the formation of gender becomes a central issue, along with the impact of gender on social fabrication. The sexual difference in a girl's social life and activities will follow her from now on. Ana Paula explained how happy she had been that the ritual had been held for her: "Before I formed [the body], I wanted to be formed since I had seen others undergo the same, and I said, 'Mum, one day I shall.' I wanted to be formed. And I was very happy. And when I see my daughter growing up, I shall want to do the same thing for her as my mother did for me."

The older Manchineri women, who play an important role throughout the seclusion period and during the festivity, tell the girl what the women of their community must do and have done traditionally to become healthy, beautiful women. The girl's mother usually prepares the manioc beer for the festival, an act that can be regarded as the transmission of a woman's role to her daughter with the creation of new social networks. An older woman is the only one who can take close care of the girl being "formed," since she herself no longer menstruates. Many cultures indeed conceive women who have passed the menopause to be no longer completely female (Héritier 1996). According to Gow (2001), three Piro female generations are united in the girl's puberty ritual, which symbolizes the woman's life through different cycles: as a young girl, as an adult woman, and as an elderly woman. He also suggests that the girl's ritual demonstrates control over three fluids: blood, manioc beer, and paint. The girl has to control her internal bodily flow of menstrual blood; the mother who prepares the drink for the festivity demonstrates women's control over manioc beer; and the old women who paint the girl show their control over maternity. Among the Manchineri, the relationship with the male members of the community at the festivity also enhances the girl's longevity and the community's continuity and fertility, as the oldest man and the best hunter of the community drink the first bowl of manioc beer with the girl.

For the Cashinahua, infant baptism, the *nixpu pima* ritual, held for boys and girls alike, forms a vital part of the group's dualistic cosmology: it makes the children into women and men, embodied selves opposed to free-floating images and spirits. The child is ready for *nixpu pima* when he or she acquires permanent teeth, a criterion applicable therefore to both sexes. During the *nixpu pima* ritual, children's bodies are in transformation and thus open to receiving the instruction of adults, who prepare them for their gender-based tasks and roles, as well as their interactions with spirits. Later on, the Cashinahua girl's first menses leads to a period of seclusion and fasting during which female agency is produced, since the girl learns to weave (Lagrou 2007; McCallum 2001).

Older Manchineri people told me that, in the past, boys also went into seclusion and followed a strict diet when their voices started to break. This was followed by guidance from a hunter on the use of traditional hunters' herbal remedies and drugs, as well as learning to hit a target with an arrow on the first shot. Along the same lines, Matteson (1965) wrote that when Piro (Yine) boys' voices started to change, they passed through seclusion and were given herbal remedies to ingest, taught how to make a bow and arrows, and then trained until they could shoot a small, lean fish in the eye. Today, the Manchineri boys at puberty are advised not to carry heavy loads, since it is believed that during this phase the skin of their stomach or nerves could break. Surprisingly, a 24-year-old young man living in the Lago Novo village, Euclides, told me that he had also passed a lengthy ritual process when his voice was breaking. He, too, was painted and a festival was held for him. His explanation of his puberty ritual was very similar to the ones held for the girls. His grandfather had guided him during his seclusion period and painted his body afterward, making him a member of his male kin. Euclides also reckoned that he had never been pursued by any animal or even heard any predators or spirits in the forest because of the ritual. In his drawing, he illustrated his grandfather collecting fruits from the genipap tree for the body paint, him being painted, manioc beer, the people dancing, and the protector spirit of Manchineri festivities, *Paho*, made from leaves.

In order to understand the meaning of the ritual, we need to take into account its significance for both girls and boys, processes of firming one's agency, and the natural and social environment they live. According to the youths in the

Figure 2.3   Euclides's drawing depicting the day of his puberty festival (Lago Novo village)

reserve, the aim of the ritual for both sexes is to enable a long life, health, stamina, and protection from harmful forest spirits and animals. Performing the puberty ritual also helps prevent the girl's hair from turning white too soon or her skin from blemishing, factors, along with the examples mentioned previously, that can be considered to relate to Manchineri aesthetics. A balance with the forest spirits is achieved by establishing controlled relations with them (see Vilaça 2002). These relations are fabricated via a variety of different methods, either to produce sameness with some animals (such as monkeys and tortoises) or to avoid similarity (such as fish with big bellies). Manchineri girls and young women said that the ritual had protected them from snake bites or other kinds of harm from animals and that they have strong bodies, allowing them to do heavy physical work. The boys themselves said that the old men in the village are still strong and have enjoyed a long life, precisely because they had undergone the ritual. Thus, the ritual continued the lines of generations of reproducing the essences of the "ancient people" (*tsrunni yineru*).

Vilaça (2002) argues that kinship in Amerindian communities is fashioned at those times when a person is receiving a new identity by individualizing him or her from "the undifferentiated universe of subjectivities" of people, animals, and spirits. The aim is to make the person human and prevent him or her from turning into an animal or nonhuman being. The changing body is at risk and therefore must be protected from outside agencies, both human and nonhuman

(Belaunde 2001; Vilaça 2002). In the most distant Manchineri villages from urban areas, the parents' actions are also conceived to influence unborn and newborn babies in various ways until they have received a name and are breast-feeding. The father of a small baby should not cut trees or kill snakes because their spirits would harm the infant through the many invisible relations between the parents, forest spirits, and babies. Puberty ends this period, making young people's bodies stronger, but people have to produce their humanness constantly through different corporeal everyday actions. Moreover, the link between human and nonhuman perspectives has to be continually recreated given human dependency on the natural environment and its resources.

In the past, the puberty ritual prepared Manchineri girls for work in the gardens and at home. The more complex versions of the puberty ritual are practiced in the most remote villages where the agencies of the forest environment still form the "vital other," as people interact with the spirits of animals, plants, trees, and other entities encountered during their everyday activities. The rituals influence how the body forms gendered strength, and the gendered roles established in the process serve as a basis for livelihood closely related with the natural environment, hunting, and agricultural success. The ritual practice is less elaborated the farther downriver one goes (toward the urban centers) where the forest environment is also becoming ever more inhabited by other subjectivities: nonnatives. Here people from nearby farms live closer to the reserve and the encounters with them are more frequent. Power derives not only from the spirit world but also from people outside the community.

Menstrual blood in particular symbolizes a transformation of new life forms and opening of proximity to nonhumans that can pose threats to the community, meaning that the behavior of menstruating women is strictly controlled, in part for their own sake. This also explains why female pubescence in general is still heavily controlled among the Manchineri, and in general usually more so than male puberty. For young Manchineri girls, menstrual blood is mostly associated with danger. As Arlene remarked about her ritual, "It is bad, the blood of humans, isn't it? I told my mum [about the menstruation] and she suspended a hammock for me. I stayed lying in it and went several days without eating anything. Only *mingau* [porridge]." Control of the first menses—with which Manchineri associate corporeal softness—has been the most ceremonially marked bodily transformation in many cultures the world over.[5] In fact, in all Manchineri villages, any woman who is menstruating must still avoid touching hunters or their hunting weapons, or walking in areas where game is found. Otherwise the hunters will experience bad luck. Women's bodies have to be controlled in particular because of their menses, conceived to be more transformative than blood in general, its mere proximity capable of transforming objects and beings.

On the one hand, blood is reminiscent of the dangerous animal nature opposite to humanity (Vilaça 2005). Similar to anomalous animals, the changing human body at puberty is often associated with strong emotions and has occupied an important place in Amerindian symbolic systems. In the Manchineri cosmos, elders told me that blood once had such an important meaning that some boys had lain in their hammocks while their sisters were "changing." This can be explained by the threat that the sister's menstrual blood poses for the brother's development as a hunter. McCallum (2001, 53) notes of the Cashinahua, "Menstrual blood, like other bodily substances, links humans to spirits, because it makes the separation between the human domain and spirit domain begin to break down. Its smell makes a path from one domain to the other and makes normally invisible humans visible to the spirits." The Manchineri youths also still connect menstruating girls and women with the birth of the moon, as made explicit in one of their myths.[6]

On the other hand, blood has a liminal essence due to its vitality for life, health, resistance, and growth (Conklin 2001). The substance of blood is an important aspect of life and has also been considered a vehicle for memory, learning, and communication (Belaunde 2005). Indeed the red clothes given to a Manchineri girl to wear during the festival can be seen to symbolize the fact that the blood is now under control. The body symbolization helps reinforce the community's interrelatedness.[7]

Still today, when the girls have passed through the transformative phase of their first menstrual periods, they become more powerful and protected persons. Besides being able to take on the tasks typical to women, the control of their female bodies at puberty also affords them specific powers for many other new processes using their bodies. Today young indigenous people, even girls, are required to learn various other skills, such as writing, reading, and knowledge of Portuguese, since they sometimes have to travel to nearby municipalities for health care or to purchase commodities essential to contemporary life. Various items have to be obtained in the municipalities, including, for instance, medicines, detergents, and ammunition, and the Manchineri are obliged to look for alternative ways of earning cash income for these goods.

The boys' ritual practice is vanishing, since their responsibilities are now less directly related to the forest environment and, as I shall discuss in Chapter 5, young Manchineri men act more and more as spokesmen of the community. In villages with more contact with the urban centers, the boys have also begun to look for employment in the towns and cities, given that the forest is no longer able to offer a livelihood due to overhunting and exploitative fishing, as well as the effects of ranching and agricultural activities in nearby areas. This may also explain an interesting detail I heard in one of the villages concerning the girl's festival. In Santa Cruz, Arlene told me that a boy had been responsible for serving the manioc beer during the festival. She also depicted him with a bowl of manioc beer in her drawing. The importance and dominance of young men in the area of new responsibilities may thus explain why the young man was the person serving manioc beer in the girl's festival in one of the villages closer to the urban areas.

Although not all parents are able or willing to organize the ritual and the festivity, some adolescents have a strong wish to experience it. The attitudes of the girls living in urban areas in particular reflect this desire. In the state capital, only two Manchineri female adolescents said that they had undergone the traditional girls' initiation ritual. They had asked an elderly Manchineri woman to paint them. The other girls stated that they had not undergone the ritual because they had left the village before they started menstruating or they had been born in Rio Branco. The two girls, who now wanted to experience being painted as the girls in the reserve during their ritual, had moved to the city while they were infants, at one and three years of age respectively, and had not visited Mamoadate since, though they were in contact with people from the reserve. When I first talked to the girls in 2003, one of them told me that her mother had wanted to hold the ritual for her, but the girl refused, saying it belonged to the past. Two years later, both had changed their minds. When asked now about being painted in the city, one of the girls, Alessandra, said,

> She [the old woman who painted the girls] said that it was a painting for a woman. She said that she had used the design of the tortoise in the painting. When a girl becomes a woman, she has a spirit and the design used on the body is a representation of it. She brought genipap and *ayahuasca* from the village. They baptized the son of a relative using *ayahuasca*. They drank it and told his name in *ayahuasca*. He [the baby's father] said he could not adapt to life in the city and he went back to the village.
>
> When my cousin [the old woman] came, I asked her to paint me. She said that since I would not be painted in the village, she would paint me with a different stick to have a different spirit, a different form of thinking. Since people are painted with a stick. She painted my cousin, too. And she said that we had to be painted with different sticks, since we have different spirits.

The girls in the city acted in different spaces and performed different tasks than the girls in the city. However, the ritual was a source of power for the girls by enabling them to receive more personal capacities and protection. In addition to protecting the community from harmful spirits, the ritual strengthens Manchineri identity, and the special body painting is an expression of the social world to which the girls belong. Furthermore, for the girls, the sense of community is a sense of place that leads to the construction of the self as a Manchineri person through the ritual painting and its display in the city. This offers a new way of understanding the traditional puberty ritual in urban areas where it is increasingly performed to mark the social boundaries and agency—in other words, what it is to be Manchineri—rather than to manipulate and control the external powers to which society as a whole is exposed by the open boundaries of the female body (during puberty).

On the other hand, though, we still have to deal with the construction of cultural categories and the risks that certain things pose for the community. As ethnographers working with Amazonian peoples have argued previously, the fabrication of the body and the sociality embedded in the body both dynamically create personhood, since they locate people within the social system (Gow 1991; Conklin and Morgan 1996; Belaunde 2001; McCallum 2001; Overing 2003). The Manchineri girls' interpretations of the ritual in the city show that it positions them in the social world by molding their bodies and minds—that is, their identities.

As we have seen, in the urban context, the special body designs painted at puberty not only represent the nonhuman strength sought by a young person but also relate to the initiate's personality and support its development. Hence the two girls in Rio Branco had to be painted with different sticks and different designs. These procedures also involve locating the youngster within the social network of his or her community.

Even though the puberty ritual was no longer held in urban areas in its traditional form, since the rite does not respond to the local environment and the cosmology of those Manchineri who have lived in the city for a long time, it still allows people to form their identities: to learn about themselves, their own social group, and their personal qualities. It may provide solutions to the difficulties faced by contemporary indigenous youngsters, problems that today are more personal and psychological in kind.

The personal choice to undergo the ritual was also expressed by Cashinahua youths. Among the Cashinahua, the puberty ritual lasting various days, *nixpu pima*, is also organized in a few villages. A 20-year-old Cashinahua young man, Fabiano, who was living in the city and had passed through the ritual, told me about it:

> I thought it was good. I passed the baptism. My teeth were not approved in the baptism [i.e., painted by the *nixpu* plant]. I want to do more, I want to teach those who are growing up now and will do the baptism in the future. And I think it's interesting for them to have this rite of passage in our community.
>
> *Why is it important for youngsters to undergo the* nixpu pima *ritual?* Every youth thinks differently. For me, this puberty ritual was a very important step in becoming an adult. And also for dealing with bad things. It allows us to separate bad and good things—to know the myths, to see the sun and sky, and to see your

way of life. Whether it's going to be long or not. So it's a kind of rite of passage for the children, who are going to learn many things. And they stay lying in their hammocks for five days. And I think that at that moment I understood how to maintain my culture and what is ours.

His younger brother, 17 years old, also from the Jordão region and now living in the city, said that he would still like to participate in the *nixpu pima* initiation ritual, since it would have a strong meaning for him. He felt he would receive important powers and insights into his own existence: "I want to have a longer life, a healthy body, strong blood, a pure spirit, you know. To have better memory, luck, thought. It [the ritual] is good."

In particular, many Amazonian native youths looking to take on new positions of responsibility hoped to gain spiritual guidance, protection, and knowledge through the rituals. Moreover, puberty rituals are still essential as a time for learning new human skills and the responsibilities that make people human. In Chapter 5 I shall return to these roles, which increasingly involve knowledge of the group's history and its traditional practices, materializing indigenousness in a diverse range of encounters.

Participating in state education is one of the new rites of passage during which young people learn to control their bodies: they have to participate in classes for several hours at a time, speak only when asked, sit down quietly, and eat at the set time. Gow (2001) notes that since the 1980s, the festivals of the Native Community, which are usually school openings or other white people's festivities, have replaced the performance of the girls' initiation ritual among the Piro of the Urubamba River. According to Gow, for the Piro, school education offers capacities to defend themselves against enslavement by whites, while shamanic knowledge defends them from forest and river demons. In this view, the increase in a woman's capacity to act with new actors in the world through education may have led to a decrease in the control of the female body. Studying as a new form of seclusion will be examined in more detail in the next section.

Schooling

During my first months in the reserve, many young Manchineri people came to ask me the meaning of words like *project* (*projeto*), *biodiversity* (*biodiversidade*), *biopiracy* (*biopirataria*), *budget* (*orçamento*), *globalization* (*globalização*), and even *indigenous* (*indígena*). I realized that these were strange words for them but that these were precisely the terms that public authorities and NGO staff working with native populations like to use. Soon afterward I was even invited to give a short course in the school village on how to produce a document and write a letter to state officials. The young people told me about a state official who had come to the village to collect information for a report on livelihoods in the reserve. The official had distributed forms to the people of the village and asked them to fill them in. One of the boys said that he did not even understand what the official meant by the word *form* (*formulário*). Moreover, on this form they were asked about their nutrition, kinship relations, and other words unfamiliar to them. The boy from the village said he ended up deciding to write nothing. The questionnaire was for the local government to know the current dietary situation of the families in the reserve. Difficult concepts also appeared in their talk of "sustainable development" and "the preservation of natural resources" without any explanation of the terms. They were not part of the vocabulary used in the reserve, even if their ideas would actually be very familiar. The young people and the community greatly appreciated the fact that I helped explain difficult words and the meaning of new concepts.

For Manchineri, new knowledge is not an external discourse to be memorized but something to be lived. The body learns and acquires knowledge through its contact with the external world (see, for example, McCallum 1996; Rosengren 2006). This knowledge is built in relations with others, with other subjectivities. Learning what is knowledge per se changes the body, and the body can reveal what it knows. The body learns and thus changes constantly.

Learning to do math and to read and write in Portuguese are still the main objectives of schooling at present. All the schools located in nine of the reserve's villages are authorized to provide basic education by Manchineri teachers until the fourth grade. The teacher at the Jatobá school has already been authorized to provide classes up to the completion of compulsory education in the eighth grade. In Brazil, schooling has been one of the most significant achievements of the indigenous movement, and "differentiated education" is a right of indigenous peoples guaranteed in the 1988 Constitution as well as in various decrees.[8] Indigenous education has valued indigenous cultures and knowledge in a new way and given indigenous peoples new possibilities for relating to non-Indian knowledge (Monte 1996; Silva and Ferreira 2001; Dalmolin 2004; Collet Gouvêa 2006; Weber 2006; Rival 2002). In Acre's indigenous schools (*escolas indígenas*), most teachers have already been trained by indigenous teacher training courses, but many have only basic levels of schooling, achieved while living temporarily outside the reserve. The training courses also include administrative or organizational skills related to indigenous education.

The Manchineri youngsters, especially those in the reserve, felt that they were living at a time when they needed much more information to understand the processes affecting their lives and taking place outside their reserve. Hence they require new knowledge and language skills, distinct from those of their parents, in order to negotiate successfully with others, such as public authorities. One problem that surfaced in all the villages was the lack of explanations for laws and difficult concepts, and a general inability to communicate effectively with nonnatives. As a young Manchineri man, Alberico, said to me in 2005, they

> don't have information on how to do things and we don't know how to look for it. The other issue is health care: we don't know how to obtain something, and we don't know how to produce a document, to make it official so that we could send it to the governor, or what do you call it—an NGO, or to an organization. We don't know how to make a document. But in the future we'll know how to do this, and we'll improve things in the indigenous reserve—how to send a document to FUNAI, the CPI, UNI, and the education secretary. We are going to get improvements.

In the past a collective way of life made young people ready to achieve their social realization as a person by acting in accordance with criteria specific to their social age. Now social situations are constantly changing. Native societies have not lived and do not live in isolation: globalization and development have brought them into contact with new situations where they have to acquire new skills to negotiate. Today, literacy is an important part of growing up: it marks maturity, and the community reinforces the conditions for this process in adolescence. Since the world has become more complicated and the needs of native society have changed, it seems clear that new forms of "training" are required to prepare young native people for the world.

The oldest of my interviewees, especially young women, had not learned to read and write because such abilities were not needed in the recent past. As a young father of small children remarked,

> For my mother, education came from the forest. She was brought up in the period when there was no school or anything. Now we have started to study, she says that it does not give me anything. But we now know that it is useful for many things. *Do you learn many things in the forest, too?* Yes, in a forest you learn many things, but people don't learn their rights. The old people have lots of knowledge about the plants and jungle, and in the school you learn what kinds of tree and jungle these are. The jungle is the Indians' science. At school we not only have knowledge, there is now more knowledge of the jungle and more tradition, culture, and also written knowledge to help ensure our future. So they can say that their father died but left them everything.
> *Is it important to study to live well?* For me to be educated and for us to learn these studies, to know---because we could do many things, Cristina. I could learn to work with a computer. That's one example of the work we could do. And to study more objects little by little. Soon it will be important for us to study computing.

Intellectual aspirations are one instrument for social reorganization, and the schools offer a source of power and a means of controlling the contemporary period of change and uncertainty. In the most distant village, Extrema, all the young people speak Portuguese, since their parents have lived in the colonies outside the reserve and the head of the FUNAI post resided in their village for almost a decade. However, everyone speaks Manchineri among themselves, except for a few families who moved to the reserve later and had been living close to white people in the neighboring region. By contrast, nearly all young interviewees in the other villages said that they have a problem expressing what they think in Portuguese. This is especially difficult when representatives of governmental and NGO officials arrive at their villages and they are unable to pass on their own point of view and opinions. A young man who had already been to the city many times to negotiate with authorities, and had sometimes spent longer periods in the city, provided a good summary of the thoughts of young people: "[It is important] to study in order to lead and take care of my group. We face so many problems in this world, I think that without studies we are nothing. A person without studies is like a dog. I know that our aim is to study. This is my dream."

For this young man, education has a liberating dimension because it can help alleviate the problems now faced by indigenous peoples; at the same time, a literate person can assume special tasks in the community, as happened in his case. The dream of studying held by most youngsters, both in the city and in the reserve, demonstrates that adequate education is today a kind of cultural norm that is taken for granted. Lacking certain skills and practices, such as understanding new Portuguese words, the adolescents remain vulnerable to being dominated by others, especially whites, and thus to being considered subhuman. As discussions with public authorities in Mamoadate are today more frequent, as are their own trips to the municipalities, it is even more important to be able to communicate in Portuguese. Studying is directly related to the accumulation of symbolic capital.

Manchineri youngsters' desires to study are linked to the state and local politics, as well as historical events, since they believe that education can free them from the paternalist treatment of indigenous peoples and allow them to gain more independence and active agency. In the youths' opinion, the school should offer the skills needed to produce a kind of cultural capital that liberates them from ignorance and makes freedom from social exclusion possible. Articulation through the Manchineri's own voices enables this freedom: as Hall (1992) argues, articulation is an essential link between the field of power and ideologies, enabling a politics of representation that works to change the relations between positions at the margins and the center. Through their cultural capitals, the adolescents benefit from the new opportunity to act as indigenous people due to their logic of practice, in Bourdieu's sense,[9] and use and look for these new ideas. The school has its own *habitus*, distinct from the youth's *habitus* in the jungle, in the home, or during rituals and forms a main part of learning the new practices of non-Indian (cf. Bourdieu [1979] 1984). The school sets its own behavioral codes and supplies a different set of references.[10] Before the pupils attend classes, they always take a bath and change into fresh clean clothes, usually a T-shirt distributed freely by the local government. Teachers call students by their Portuguese names instead of the Manchineri names typically used in the community. I even once saw a girl put on high heel shoes before leaving for school, despite the fact that she had to cross the muddy field of the village.

However, Manchineri students in the reserve usually study for no more than a few years. They generally leave school between the ages of 15 and 20. Early marriages and pregnancies also hinder young girls in particular from studying. The girls drop out of school when they become pregnant and rarely return later. However, many girls participated in the classes given for more advanced levels. The young people of both sexes had noticed, however, that at schools they could learn to defend themselves through new knowledge, especially that related to the non-Indians, as well as to transmit their difference as indigenous peoples. Those who had participated in the "indigenous cultural meeting" of the state, for instance, said that they were ashamed to have performed their traditional dances dressed only in T-shirts and shorts, since other groups had worn many decorations, straw skirts, *koshmas*, or woven clothes. In contrast to other indigenous groups, they also had few craftwork objects to exhibit and sell. The comments made by one boy later—namely, that he had been drinking alcohol throughout the whole festival—may be precisely due to these negative experiences. Nowadays young people are more aware that if they do not ask elders about myths and how to make craftwork, for instance, this knowledge could be lost forever. Now the elders are actually regarded as the village "libraries." Previously, old people were rarely asked about oral history, making them apparently unwilling to speak about things that nobody was interested in.

On the other hand, village schools are in a way places "to learn to be Indian." In the villages that have applied well-functioning, differentiated indigenous education, the school has encouraged the learning of indigenous history, medicine, and language in a more systematized way, using its own methods (cf. Weber 2006). The trained teachers have also been encouraged to do their own research into indigenous language, chants, plants, and myths. But there are some teachers who have been away from the reserve for a long time, and they rarely speak Manchineri, which itself impedes any concrete development of multicultural and bilingual education. Moreover, nearly all the school material is still available in Portuguese only and its content is very distant from the social, cultural, and economic realities of the indigenous reserves. With the help of the local indi-genist organization CPI-Acre, their sponsors, and the local secretary of educa-tion, qualified Manchineri teachers have produced a first reader book, a book of myths, and geography and mathematics textbooks in Manchineri. Nevertheless, their use is limited because there are not enough copies for all the schools in the reserve, especially of the first reader books. The latter texts were also made without proper linguistic assistance for the Manchineri authors. Other books, and a few school materials, are sent by the secretary of education and are used more frequently. However, teachers themselves have noted that only part of the state school material can be used, such as the biology textbooks on Brazil's other regions, since their content is not applicable to the lived worlds of their pupils. Indigenous schools still need to reflect on how to apply different forms of learning, pedagogies, worldviews, values, knowledge, and methods in their multicultural and local curricular and educational plans. Overall, the question of multicultural education is a complicated one for the Manchineri, since there are many things to be learned at the same time: the content and the frame.

In my conversations with indigenous youth, a desire to study in the city was a very common theme. In order to continue their studies, Manchineri pupils have to journey to the municipalities, though in Jatobá the teacher was autho-rized to give classes up to the fourth grade. Currently, therefore, some young people told me that they want to study in a municipality and dream eagerly about obtaining a scholarship. Youngsters in their reserve aspired to know about laws, their rights, local indigenous authorities, organizations, and social move-ments in the cities. Almost all these adolescents said that they would return to the reserve and that they would teach other students in the future.

Studying, especially outside the reserve, is a new rite of passage for the reserve's young people, in which they learn skills important for their commu-nity's autonomy. It is a short-term sacrifice: it involves a seclusion from the community similar to the stages in other rites of passage, when the person has to live temporarily in anonymity and is usually physically separated from the rest of the community. The young person has to go through his or her own process of solitude and elaborate a new personal identity as someone living between two locations: the place of origin where social actions and the present location are constructed. Gow (2001) has also argued that, for the Piro (Yine), secondary schools in particular are new forms of puberty seclusion. This more recent seclusion involves Piro pupils dedicating themselves to studying and is celebrated in the *fiestas de la Comunidad Nativa*, community festivals that focus on the school and schoolchildren. Like the girls' festival, they celebrate knowl-edge and transformation (into white people rather than jaguars), while they are also a moment for drunkenness, music, and sexual desire.[11] There are no school festivals as such among the Manchineri: their schools are a kind of sacred place where people can acquire valuable knowledge. Schools are also spaces used for village meetings, where a newly acquired *habitus* can be embodied.

In general, the native youngsters in the cities face numerous difficulties in entering schools and attending the classes. The matriculation fee has to be paid, while school shirts, books, and other school materials have to be acquired. FUNAI provides some indigenous students with a small grant, but usually the financial support is only enough to buy a few notebooks. So far more than five Manchineri men from the reserve have been studying in the nearest municipality, Assis Brasil. One of them explained how he had been working on a farm whose owner one day asked whether he wanted to study. The owner had suggested a school in Assis Brasil and since the young man had earned some money, he was able to buy the necessary materials, such as pencils and notebooks. In general, all these young Manchineri people—as is common for adolescents coming from Indian reserves—had encountered a reality in the city very different from what they had imagined. They were forced to reside in underdeveloped neighborhoods without adequate sustenance, facing a series of difficulties. Before starting the classes, one of these young men had managed to purchase new clothes for the school, including brand new Bermuda shorts. However, his teacher had not allowed him to attend the class without long trousers. He had not known they were compulsory at school. The next day he returned to discuss the problem with the owner of the farm and he managed to obtain appropriate clothing. Even so, the boy said that his earnings from the farm work were soon spent in the municipality, his classmates teased him at first because he could not speak Portuguese, and simply going to school was dangerous. Once three men had attacked him unprovoked. Thereafter, he was too frightened to walk alone in the street. The Manchineri young men told me that over time they had become a little more used to the different way of life in the municipality. However, one of the young men's mothers came to take him back to the reserve, explaining that "it isn't good to be away from one's family for a long time." Afterward, though, the boy regretted that he had not stayed on, since he would have probably managed to finish the compulsory school in Assis Brasil.

Young indigenous people's parents often have a different view of education in the cities. This was even more apparent in the views of indigenous officials. According to the federal secretary of indigenous peoples in Acre, the knowledge of indigenous youths in the city about the ways of being, doing, and thinking of their indigenous communities depends on their parents. Talking about the education of indigenous youths in the city, he said,

> You only learn traditional things with people in the village, because there is a river, jungle, dances, everything is there. Here [in the city], none of that is possible. If a [young Indian] is born here [in the city], he will grow up here. However

much I may know [about the things in the village], there is no way of transferring it to him. If he wants to contribute [to the community], he has to become well educated. But if I send him to a village, he won't even know how to plant a swidden. And who would he be able to depend on?

He also said that urban study would only be successful if the native communities could control the studies of young people in the city and their education could be planned beforehand according to each community's needs. Anyone studying in the city should, he argued, become a professional in the areas of health care, agroforestry, or law in order to help their communities achieve their goals. If the youths are not properly prepared for this, he said, they will end up staying in areas where they interact with people whose influence could prove negative. The village leaders should also tell their villages what the cities and city life are like.

Many people emphasized the importance of "learning two sides of the world," though. Indigenous groups have different strategies for this. When I talked to a Cashinahua *pajé*, or shaman, who had come to Rio Branco for medical treatment, and to a leader working in UNI, they each emphasized that their young people have to learn both their culture and nonindigenous culture in order to learn who they are and from where they come. They added that people cannot change the fact they are Indian, since they cannot be something different from what they are. These two things must be lived in new ways. Two Cashinahua boys with whom the shaman had a close relationship moved to São Paulo and Rio de Janeiro to learn about the urban forests. Their activities have made the Cashinahua renowned as knowledgeable people among a much wider Brazilian public. In Central Brazil, the Xavante have also created their own method of educating their young for interactions with the contemporary world. They formed a group of boys who spent a long period living with Brazilian white families learning Portuguese and the ways in which the dominant society functions. The young Xavante men returned to the community and took over many important positions as community spokesmen. The Xavante elders had designed this strategy deliberately (see Belisário 2007).

By participating in the national school system in the cities, indigenous youths in Acre show that they, like other young people, are trying to master knowledge that will allow them to cope in the global world. Saying that they are in the city for their studies is acceptable to other city dwellers, who are also trying to obtain education. But entering the non-Indian school system is difficult, as already described regarding the Manchineris' attempts to study in Assis Brasil. In Rio Branco young people from different ethnic groups explained that obtaining school materials depends on how much money you have available.

Had they obtained a scholarship, they could have studied for more time and with more of an objective.

As another example from urban area, in Rio Branco an Apurinã boy, Wallace, told me about his problems on arriving in the city:

> Everything [was a problem]. We did not know how to walk in the city. I arrived first and got lost in the city. I didn't know how to take a bus and to pull that thing there [to stop the bus]. It was all shameful—and we were often really hungry—we are used to plenty, you don't have to buy anything. But here you have to buy everything. First I went to look for my cousin who was at my uncle's house. I spent one month there. It was very difficult—I was often very hungry. Then when he [points to his brother] arrived here, we started to live by ourselves. For breakfast, there was no coffee, only biscuits and water . . . We didn't want to stay here. At FUNAI they asked us, 'Why don't you go to the village?' But there we would have stood still . . . We suffered a lot. Now we are almost winning. We are gaining, not losing . . . And it was our neighbor who saved us from death. This was very painful for us.

Usually the student's entire family comes to the city, and since study takes more time than expected, they create a new life there. Some people end up staying in the city. A young Apurinã woman, Regina, who had arrived in Rio Branco with her grandmother at the age of 13 in order to study and never left. She no longer wanted to return to her village, though she intended to visit during the school holidays. When asked how she felt when she came to Rio Branco, she said, "First I felt a little bit bad and wanted to go back, but I didn't know how. If I returned, I would have lost one year's study. But after some time, I got used to being here. And now I have already been here six years."

The Manchineri adolescents living in the city for a long time also complained about the difficulty of entering the education system. In fact, most individual problems encountered by the Manchineri adolescents in Rio Branco are related to studying, such as enrolling at schools, economic difficulties in taking all courses combined with the costs of private classes (such as computing), and difficulties in finding employment. A young Manchineri woman—a single mother with three small children living in Rio Branco—tried to embark on a new way of life by taking school classes in the city. She had tried to obtain temporary work while studying but had problems finding someone to take care of her children. She said that her only reason for being in the city was her studies. Over recent years, the ethnicity of indigenous people has facilitated access to schooling following the introduction of quotas for indigenous students in higher education. Two Manchineri girls and a Manchineri boy have started to study in private and federal universities with the help of scholarships. For the Manchineri in the reserve, this option is extremely difficult since they lack the required level of basic education to apply for such scholarships. Moreover, they also lack the necessary contacts with indigenous organizations capable of passing on information concerning these possibilities. These opportunities include the dominant society's funding for cultural preservation projects, as well as environmental protection and services for indigenous peoples. Three Manchineri teachers in their thirties have received a scholarship to study at the local university and now spend half the year away from their villages.

In the city, Manchineri adolescents have already embodied lots of knowledge that does not directly relate to their lived worlds. In the city, education has become an even more highly regarded virtue, since it increases the person's cultural capital. This cultural capital exists as symbolic capital: recognized and legitimated competence.[12] The newly acquired knowledge is not as functionally oriented as in the reserve, where knowledge is valued only if it can be practically applied and adequately adapted to the reality of their communities. Studying in the city has become a question of investing in the future, contrary to acquiring knowledge that can be directly used in practice. The knowledge made available through education is not necessarily needed in the present. In recent years, the national development policies implemented by Brazil's federal governments have boosted the value of education, meaning only some manual and physical work can be obtained without school qualifications. Usually the youngsters in the city are already looking for employment, or planning to do so, and are thus acquiring education with paid work in mind. Their dream is to become lawyers, as two boys stated, or to work in journalism, agronomy, medicine, business administration, or civil engineering. One young Manchineri woman said that she was going to study media studies and that her thesis would be on communication in indigenous languages. She was planning a project for the village where her father had been living, which even included plans to found a new museum of indigenous peoples. Many young people said that it is important for them to be able to help their ethnic group in the reserve by working for them.

However, these wishes change over time, as is typical for young people who are still in the process of discovering their own personality. One boy had earlier said that he wanted to live in the village, too, but now planned to take the entrance exam for military service, which is quite well paid. Another young Manchineri man, who had said earlier that he would work in the reserve, one year later stated that, if he really wanted to help his people, it would be better for him to work in the city rather than return to the reserve. Just as people are related through the body, such as when they are sharing food, eating, working, and speaking, so they want to construct new social relationships through their knowledge and new skills. In new types of interacting, new skills are needed, but they also give the person self-confidence and enhance the process of constructing personal histories and self-development.

According to many young people, even those in the reserve, differentiated indigenous education that takes into account linguistic, cultural, spiritual, and pedagogical differences, does not represent a "global" form of education that nonnatives have created in order to empower them. Consequently, Indians see education as a source of alterity vis-à-vis the non-Indians, as I have discussed earlier. The biggest motive for migration stated by all native adolescents residing in Rio Branco was study. Recently, study has provided a rational basis for many life situations in Latin America. Contrary to the period from the 1950s to 1970s, it is not only employment that is driving native people to head to Brazil's urban centers. As we know from the earlier urban migration processes of the Pankararu and Terena, indigenous men looked for jobs on construction sites, while women sought work as domestic servants. However, attempts to achieve better education are still allied to economic and social motives, such as to secure a better education and gain access to adequate health services. Today, education is perceived as a means of improving one's livelihood. Only educated Indians know how to look for benefits and negotiate with authorities. For the native population, as well as allowing them to improve their lives economically, education is a key factor in ensuring cultural reinforcement. It can help make indigenous people more independent and offer them better cultural, social, and political possibilities.

In general, migrants in Latin America tend to be young people seeking further education, while the number returning to rural areas later has decreased, one of the factors behind the new rural problems in general (Gilbert [1994] 1998). In Rio Branco many native adolescents had come to the city with expectations of enrolling at a public school. In the city, though, they actually faced a whole series of economic, social, and cultural problems. Usually young Indians arrive without any savings and have to find employment in order to pay for their studies and living expenses. This fact, compounded with other difficulties, means that they end up postponing their studies. Another problem experienced by young indigenous people in urban areas is early abandonment of school. After staying in Rio Branco for a while, some young people said it was easier for them to achieve some basic education in the reserve than try to enroll at a school in the city.

Studying in the city, even if temporarily, affords a person special prestige. He or she may acquire a new status: that of an educated person who through a learning process has acquired new ways to embody the world among the nonnatives as well as carry out new tasks in their indigenous communities. As Gomes (2000, 172) suggests, "those who acquire the urban experience and later decide to return to their lands come with a deeper knowledge of the society that oppresses them and pressures them to live constantly in search of cultural defenses for their survival." For instance, many young men who had already studied in the municipality, even if only for a short time, currently hold positions of responsibility within the community or posts representing the Manchineri in indigenous organizations. They were able to take on these posts as they knew Portuguese and were familiar with the new practices. Another young man who had moved to Rio Branco after his father was murdered was able to enter school at the beginning of the 1990s and went on to work for UNI and FUNAI, later becoming a general coordinator for the Coordinator of the Indigenous Organizations of the Amazon Basin (COICA) for a short while.

The wish to study in cities is not only related to schooling: the young Manchineri people in the reserve wanted to learn how to behave with whites and how to speak correctly, a desire that appeared many times in their narratives. In order to act in different contexts, they wanted to learn two cultures, their own and that of the whites. Cardoso de Oliveira (1968) already noted some decades ago that Terena youngsters wanted to learn the rules for good behavior in urban spaces.[13] This can be seen as a desire to acquire the etiquette and bodily practices needed in interethnic relations.[14] For the Manchineri, transitions between the village and city are about learning what the outside world was like, and for this they want opportunities to learn just by watching and observing, mirroring the way in which they become skilled in their own techniques, such as those connected to hunting and agriculture. A young Manchineri man, Amauri, explained this form of learning: "Like fishing—here we have our own way of fishing while whites know a new way. Here we know things in our own way. But today [in the city] there are traffic lights and those streetlights. In the city it is different. There are places for people to cross and stop. For me at least, it was strange." This is "learning two sides of the world," as another youth described learning how to live in the cities.

Matrimony and Parenthood

The early adolescent years are a time of flirting, playing, teasing, and first loves. This was readily observable, but the young people did not want to talk about it and would usually even deny that they had a relationship with someone if it was not yet steady. Hard workers, good speakers, and good hunters attract girls, who see that the man is capable of bringing home food.[15] Manchineri couples typically make the first closer contact in *forró* parties organized at somebody's house or school, and this may be followed by meetings alone in the forest outside the village. In the *forró* parties music is played from a sound system or someone plays guitar, and strong manioc beer and alcohol are consumed. These gatherings are usually held to celebrate an anniversary or a visit. As jealousy is quite common, serious confrontations have broken out over recent years, especially in *forró* parties where people get drunk. One of these festivities even led to a young

Manchineri girl being killed by another young woman. *Forró* dances are also a place for the adolescents from neighboring villages to meet.

The boys especially use shamanic techniques to make a particular girl attracted to them, such as the use of *ayahuasca* and natural remedies. These natural "love medicines" make them good speakers and outgoing persons, and make women attracted to men. An older man in Jatobá, an evangelist, told me he was afraid that the boys who take *ayahuasca* could use it for the wrong purposes—for sorcery and for making girls fall in love with them. The girls also use the natural medicines in order to catch the attention of notable boys. Moreover, as girls especially insist, in *ayahuasca* rituals it is possible "to see your future partner."

As is typical in many Amazonian native societies, no special ritual marks marriage, contrary to the life-cycle phases involving body transformations. However, matrimony changes the life of the young person the most perhaps, since it is one of the markers of full membership of the community. Marriage means that a girl and boy start to live together, and the girl usually becomes pregnant soon after. From then on, the couple starts to learn to take care of their own household and family. The majority of Manchineri youngsters in the reserve are already in a conjugal relationship, whereas only one third of urban youngsters in the same age band are married. Hence becoming a full member of society, belonging to the adult world because one is married and has children, occurs earlier in Mamoadate than in the city. The same applies, therefore, to constructing a household. Only those young couples who have children and live in their own house can be regarded as adult women (*suxi*) and adult men (*heji*)—adults (*tsru yineru*) of their community. This can take some years after the couple has begun to live together and share the same hammock in the girl's parents' house. The conduct of the couple changes, however, the moment they are acknowledged as partners. I remember when I returned to Brazil and met a shaman from Extrema village on the street of Assis Brasil with other Manchineri people. I told him that I was now married, since I lived with my boyfriend. He was surprised because he felt my way of moving and talking with people was the same as before.

The Manchineri population in the Mamoadate reserve has remained homogeneous, because intermarriages with non-Manchineri are unusual and, when they do occur, they usually end in separation. Only Manchineri boys are married with other indigenous groups or non-Indians. The girls of the Mamoadate Indigenous Territory get married roughly between the ages of 14 and 17, and boys between the ages of 15 and 18. Today girls marry later than they did thirty years ago. In the past girls would get married around the age of 10 or 11. In general, marriages are monogamous: divorces occur, but these are rare.

The Manchineri youngsters in the city complained that it was difficult to find a Manchineri spouse. At the time of my fieldwork one Manchineri young man was married to a non-Indian woman and two young men were married to indigenous spouses, although neither was Manchineri. One of the spouses was a Cashinahua woman from Acre, while the other was Pankararu. Like the Manchineri adolescents in the city, the young people in the reserve prefer to choose their partners independently, while a number of young couples had themselves asked their parents to authorize their relationship. Some marriages, however, are still arranged by fathers. If both fathers accept the marriage, the boy is allowed to live at the home of his father-in-law. The girl was often brought to the boy's house and the boy was at that moment told how he should treat his new wife with respect. The parents used to be responsible for looking for a companion for their children. Today the young people are themselves encouraged to find a person they want to marry, though parents may also advise them in this quest.

In the Amazon region, native marriage rules have traditionally been highly sophisticated owing to the complex system of kinship relations (see, for example, Rivière 1984; Kensinger 1984). Traditionally marriage takes place between cross-cousins: the daughter marries the son of her father's sister (*nanuru*), and the son marries the daughter of his mother's brother (*noyimlo*). Among the Manchineri, it seems that the ancient subgroups of the contemporary Manchineri and Yine, the *nerus*, have influenced the choice of partner, but today kinship rules are rarely applied. However, it is still common for the elders or grandparents to prevent marriages. For instance, the uncle of a young man, almost 30 years old at the time, had prevented him from marrying the girl he wanted. According to the uncle, the girl's family was not as important as their own. The young man was from a family that had taken over the chiefdom in the past. He moved out of the reserve and married a non-Manchineri girl. These cases are not frequent, unlike so-called wife stealing, which also occurs among the neighboring groups. As one example, one night while I was in Mamoadate, all the people from the family I was staying with were woken by the sound of a father chasing his daughter outside the house: she had eloped with a boy from another village. The father was furious, since he did not want the girl to stay with this particular boy. Later on I heard that the girl had returned to her father's house but fled again to the boy's village. In fact, the girl has not visited her original village since this incident.

Although kin relations no longer have much influence over marriage rules, young couples in the reserve still stay at the girl's parents' house first and the son-in-law works for the girl's family's sustenance. It can be noted that matrimony leads to conducting bride service at the bride's home, a form of bridewealth to be paid, common also among other Amazonian Indians and *cariú* rubber tappers. As in many other Amazonian communities, the son-in-law must help the girl's father in various tasks, such as opening and clearing swiddens, hunting, and bringing meat to his mother-in-law at the beginning of the marriage (Rivière 1984). Moreover, among the Manchineri a son-in-law is not allowed to talk directly to his mother-in-law or father-in-law as a mark of respect. This can be seen as a form of care typical to Amazonian conviviality. The youths said that this rule no longer applied "owing to the contact with white people." However, young people did say there were many situations in which the practice was observed. A young male teacher said that his mother-in-law did not talk to him, not even when she participated in the classes he gave to adults. The father of a girl also explained that he did not talk to his son-in-law directly. When they went hunting, he would tell other people where to go to wait for the animals to arrive, and the son-in-law would overhear. In urban areas, these rules of respect rarely apply. The freeing up of the dialogue between the husband and his wife's parents may indicate a change not only in the formation of male autonomy (Rivière 1984) but also in the manipulation of human forces, since it is no longer food alone that satisfies the needs of the girl's family. Education and paid employment are also required. Moreover, the role of women is less controlled, as shown in the decline in the girls' ritual and its new meanings. The youths in the city usually live at their parents' houses until they get married, but as economic conditions are more difficult now, making it harder to do things such as obtain the construction material needed to build their own home, couples stay at their parents' home for longer and often even live with the husband's family.

Couples form independent social units only when both the man and woman have managed to develop the skills appropriate to their gender. Until the young woman learns her household tasks, such as cooking and serving food, her mother is more present in her actions, including preparing *caiçuma* for the couple. When the husband has managed to clear and plant his own swiddens, and the latter are already producing crops, the couple may build their house. The materials used in building houses—*paxiúba* wood and *ouricuri* palm leaves for the roof thatch—must be brought from the forest. The houses and swiddens of young couples are situated next to those of the girl's parents. Gow (1991) has remarked that the garden and house among the Piro are exclusively properties of a husband-and-wife couple. Unmarried people never own them. Moreover, these spaces of house and garden are human settlements in the jungle created by a man and his wife, and thus belong to them as a result of their activities within them. Clearing a plantation and the site for a house in the forest using just a machete and an axe is hard work; so, too, is the burning and clearing of land for a swidden. Native societies have transmitted knowledge through socialized human body techniques, and the young men are usually already familiar with these tasks since they have accompanied their fathers, older brothers, and cousins, but the real apprenticeship begins when they get married. Young married men are equivalent to professional carpenters, hunters, and agriculturists. Young women are gardeners, household managers, and child raisers, and are responsible for numerous other tasks learned in their homes and within the community. In the city, the couples have to learn other tasks and skills that ensure their livelihood—namely, finding employment.

If a couple does not have a baby soon after starting to live together, it is taken as a bad sign and may even be considered evidence of sorcery. Among my interviewees living in Mamoadate, nearly two thirds have a baby. Among them are a few single-parent girls, single either because the baby's father had left or because the girl had wanted a separation. Generally speaking, children help their families and are therefore welcome, even if they mean more work. However, for today's adolescents, two to four children was considered an appropriate number. Some girls already knew about the use of contraceptives, though owing to their expense, their use was uncommon or so irregular they had no effect. Families of young parents were very close units, and parents were proud of their small families. I especially saw how young fathers expressed their pride and care for their children and wives. For instance, whereas in Europe adolescents might design the name of their favorite bands on their school books, the young Manchineri fathers drew the names of their children and wife.

Girls attend school classes only until they get married and have children. From then on they have to work at home, as one young Manchineri girl told

Figure 2.4 Proud young mother with her first baby (Santa Cruz village)

me when I met her for the second time: she had already started to live with her husband and had given birth to a baby. She said that her life had changed now that she had to wash her husband's clothes and prepare food and *caiçuma*. There was no time to study. According to her, being single is the ideal time to wander around visiting places and to study. For many young women, the family is more important; so, too, is the continuance of everyday routines, such as raising children and working in the plantations, while also enjoying the close company of relatives. In some senses, therefore, it is also true for Manchineri girls that the wife and husband have a complementary relationship, and the women regard their position as mother and wife as more essential, producing sociality at home (McCallum 2010). For example, one girl, who had not studied and was illiterate, said that for her the most important things are her children, her house, and good health. Some young women still do not know how to spell their name or tell their age. Also, as Gow (1991) has shown, young Piro men preferred to start working for money in the lumber business to study. Moreover, according to Gow, young people—both boys and girls—are often driven by the sexual desire that makes them want to start a family, something that for them seemed more important than starting secondary school. The scenario is similar for Manchineri youngsters, since sexuality and marriage usually put an end to their education, though they seldom leave their reserve to look for employment. Their difficulties and problems are also economic, since they cannot afford to study outside the reserve, and social, because the state does not provide further education in their own reserve. However, it is important to note that many Manchineri girls wanted to study more, and many Manchineri boys and girls study at schools and act in interethnic relations, as I shall discuss in Chapter 5.

Among my interviewees in the city, only a few young men and women had children. Even though some were more than twenty years old, most did not want to marry or have children before they finished compulsory education and started to earn their own money. For them their closest unit was their families, and they still enjoyed more individuality in contrast to the youths in the reserve, whose closest unit comprised their young spouse and children. Matrimony raises an interesting question concerning the current transition to adulthood among Amazonian youths. Today, the shift to adulthood is complex and many of those who are already married or have children are not considered adults yet since they are still learning new skills. It is not the only passage to full adulthood. In the city, preparations may take place over many years before marriage and parenthood occur: for example, literacy skills are needed to find employment and thus the financial means to sustain a young family.

In this chapter we have seen that the Manchineri adolescents' passage to adulthood is linked to the construction of personal and group identity through their own personal experiences and encounters with "others" and the self. The experiences and knowledge are offered by the community and by many other agents preparing young indigenous people to act in the modern world. However, young people themselves have also role in that process. Embodied knowledge is linked to issues of power. When the perspective of the non-Manchineri "others" (especially non-Indians) is difficult to adopt, a feeling of ignorance and uncertainty arises, along with the sense of being unable to control the things directly affecting one's own life. In these cases, young people lack the tools and resources to do the things they want. This learning is not limited solely to school studies. Some young people spend more time becoming familiar with interethnic networks or even dedicate themselves to shamanism and thus prefer to postpone their marriage.

Following the argument presented here, the Amazonian contemporary rites of passage activate a mode of differentiation within the human body. However, previous works have limited this idea to the observation that, in constructing humanity, Amerindians differentiate their bodies by differentiating their perspectives from animals and spirits (Viveiros de Castro 1996; Belaunde 2001; Vilaça 2002, 2005). Thus nonhuman relations have been emphasized. By contrast, today's Amazonian indigenous youths are increasingly made ready for human-to-human relations.

Marking the stage of bodily changes is found among many peoples across the world, especially in hunter-gatherer societies that depend on the natural environment and the human body's close relationship to it. For those young Manchineri Indians and their families living in the reserves, the performance of body regulation (seclusion) and body painting at puberty still carry importance, because the traditional ritual stills provide the main means of intervening in the forest environment during puberty. It fabricates the relations to the spirit world and gender roles related to certain kinds of environments. But today this transitional state and its associations with the unknown also forms their identities as a certain kind of people and thus nurtures the relations between kin and the web of various beings that cause feelings of uncertainty. The current puberty rituals performed for some young people make visible the moral values of the community, strengthening its communal and personal identity. They still make young people firm and strong by preparing them to interrelate with the unknown.

Since there are more social agents and the constructed power relations are more complex, learning about the social situations created by different powers is important. There are new actors whose existence cannot be ignored. New demands and social roles push native youths into a new kind of insecurity, and schooling provides them with new tools to deal with these problems. Today education is the principal means for ensuring the safe maturation of young people almost globally. For young Amazonian Indians, humanity is no longer opposed solely to the nonhuman agents of the forest environment but also to particular cultural "deficits," such as illiteracy or ignorance of one's own indigenous background and oral history, meaning the person is incapable of acting appropriately in the contemporary social fields found in their own village and the urban centers.

Generally speaking, the older generation and their knowledge have come to be identified with more specific areas such as shamanism, craftwork, and oral history, which the dominant society has also come to value as indigenous or traditional knowledge. In the next chapters I examine other important issues in the transition to adulthood, in particular shamanic practices and the transitions between the reserve and urban areas. This results in a later transition to matrimony and adulthood. In terms of contemporary native adolescence, youth today covers the whole period during which subjectivity emerges and interacts with new entities.

CHAPTER 3

Creativity in Shamanic Practices

S hamanic practices provide a vital source of knowledge for a young adult's personal maturity. In this chapter the ethnographic examples are taken from *ayahuasca* shamanism. The primary subjective experiences related to shamanism occur in youth, and shamanic practices contribute to construcing personhood and agency. In the second section, after exploring the use of *ayahuasca* among the Manchineri, so-called *kamalampi* rituals, I look at shamanic practices as a contact area between community members and nonhuman beings, as well as increasingly between other indigenous groups and non-Indians, also taking into account power relations. Young indigenous people in the Acre region have contributed to new types of interactions between Indians and non-Indians through the development of new networks based on the practice of shamanism. The cultural creativity of Amazonian indigenous communities is especially visible in shamanic practices that are used as new social reference points and allow the personal encounters with various human and nonhuman actors.

Ayahuasca Shamanism

For the Manchineri, the *ayahuasca* ritual is the main form of shamanism and of their communal ritual in general. They call the *ayahuasca* brew *kamalampi* and it is used in collective rituals as a way of receiving spiritual guidance, protection, knowledge from the spirits, and cures. The survey of the ethnographic literature shows that *ayahuasca* ritual has been one of the most important spiritual and healing rituals for centuries among many peoples of southwestern and northwestern Amazonia. It is a primary means of learning about the nonhuman world, providing knowledge that subsequently helps in the practice of everyday life (Reichel- Dolmatoff 1975; Gow 1991; Lagrou 2007). Shamanism also offers answers to existential questions. According to older Manchineri people, in earlier times everybody had to learn some knowledge from the spirits in order to develop "basic skills" in healing. People negotiate with nonhumans constantly in everyday actions. Also in Evangelical Manchineri village, a young boy explained to me that if someone picks up any fruit, the person first has to ask the master of the tree for a permission to take them. Overing (1988) has already shown that learning shamanic practices is an essential part of growing up. This learning is related to experiences of selfhood that the Manchineri adolescents gain when they hunt alone in the jungle, take the shamanic *kamalampi* liquid or powerful natural medicines, such as *sanango*. Through the use of these substances, young people experience the power of nonhumans and being alone.

McCallum (2001) has suggested that when Cashinahua boys learn to hunt, they start to take *ayahuasca* (*nixi pae* in Cashinahua) seriously as a part of the construction of male agency. As Kensinger (1973, 13) wrote concerning the Cashinahua use of *ayahuasca*, "the Cashinahua drink *ayahuasca* in order to learn about things, persons, and events, removed from them by time and/or space which could affect either the society as whole or its individual members." Among the Manchineri, the *kamalampi* ritual is becoming a more important symbolic means of encountering the nonhuman agents. A young man in the village closest to the urbanized area of his reserve depicted the situation: "There are people who don't take *ayahuasca* because they lack the necessary knowledge. The people who take it are usually those from Extrema [the remotest village from urban areas], where I managed to learn the gist of it enough for me to consume *ayahuasca* here. Today we take *ayahuasca*. And now we're learning its music."

For many young Manchineri themselves, the *kamalampi* ritual helps in decisions and in "learning things," as the youngsters put it. According to them, the brew helps show the participant which way he or she should proceed and foresee the future in general: for instance, whether the person is about to take a position in the community, or whether one should dedicate oneself to a shamanic or political career, and so forth. A Manchineri boy currently living in the city explained this apprenticeship as follows when we discussed how he took *ayahuasca* with his uncle: "My uncle always comes here . . . He always teaches us. We learn and maybe one day when we need it, you know. We learn like that and it stays in our memory. Since we cannot go and spread out in the world." However, the youngsters often claimed that one can learn some shamanic skills from other people, but the really important knowledge only comes from the spirits. Learning from the spirits is not limited exclusively to shamans. According to Lagrou (2001), in Cashinahua communities, it is the adults' responsibility to guide children through the variety of perceptions related to nonhumans and the emotions and activities they experience in the process, so that they can form the human identity of *Huni Kui*, "true people." In the past, Manchineri shamans also used other plants, such as *kanaxiro*, *kahniu*, and *foni*, which elicit very strong hallucinogenic visions. In Acre the *ayahuasca* beverage is also commonly known as *cipó* ("vine"), or *daime*, as it is called and consumed today by nonnatives in the Santo Daime churches.[1]

In the reserve, *kamalampi* is most frequently taken in the village farthest from the urban centers, Extrema. Young people in the reserve take the shamanic drink for the first time when they are between 11 and 19 years old, and in the city when they are little older, most of the young people having already reached 18 at least. A very small portion of the *kamalampi* brew is even given to children, since it is believed to be good for them to get used to the substance from an early age, as well as for its immediate healing effects. Even younger boys know how to prepare *ayahuasca*: this process involves collecting vines (Latin name *Banisteriopsis caapi*), leaves of different plants (*Psycotria viridis*), and the special herbs and roots used by the Manchineri and then boiling the brew for several hours. In the city, the difficulty resides in obtaining *ayahuasca*: usually the only way is via relatives coming from the reserve or from the Santo Daime churches.

In the reserve, the *kamalampi* ritual starts in the evening when the village becomes quieter, and children and other people not participating in the ritual are already asleep. The *kamalampi* ritual is usually held in a house, on its terrace, in the forest, or on a river beach. The brew also continues to be taken in urban areas, where everything takes place in a very similar form. The difference is that the ritual is usually held on Friday and Saturday nights when the youngsters do not have to go to school or work the next day, whereas in the reserve there are no typical or specific days for the ritual.

The ritual created opens up its own sacred time and space through the performance of certain practices. Especially in the city, the *ayahuasca* ritual is spatially and socially organized. Sacralization is achieved by creating a visible place for a specific use and behavior. As in any religious ritual, therefore, there are specific objects, roles, and informal conventions determining the participants' actions, all of which mark out a ritual space. A special speech form—chatting quietly as one arrives at the location—is one of the ways of marking the ritualistic space and time.[2] It takes a while before the atmosphere has settled down and everyone is present and has found a comfortable place in a circle, sitting down or lying outstretched on the floor or in a hammock. The ritual offers a place and time for encountering the power of timelessness and formlessness that tends to be excluded from everyday life, where experience is normally categorized and controlled in the script of events. The ritual drink is placed in a pot in the middle, and the leader of the ritual—who is the best singer, a shaman, or an older person—usually serves a cup to those wishing to take it, the quantity given according to their perceived ability and resistance. The men typically smoke a pipe or cigarette while waiting for the *kamalampi* to take effect.

Figure 3.1 Drawing by a Manchineri boy showing the *ayahuasca* ritual (Extrema village)

When the leader of the ritual feels the initial effects of the plant take hold, he starts singing the shamanic chants, which are songs of the spirit of *kamalampi*, along with certain plant, nature, and animal spirits that are now called. The other people remain silent.[3] The singer controls the encounter with the spirit world through music, singing chants that materialize certain nonhumans and alternately invigorating or calming the hallucinations. The visions are also said to be dependent on the ritual's chant leader. The shamans are specialists of *kamalampi* songs, since they know a variety of different chants and how to use them. They themselves have learned directly "from the spirits" or from other people. In some indigenous communities only shamans use *ayahuasca* and they tell about the encounter with the spirits by singing to the others. However, among the Manchineri, other participants can also sing and the ritual leader can even ask others to perform a chant. Anyone capable of singing an appropriate song is clearly in control, meaning singing can be seen as an exercise of ritual power.

As in the reserve, young people in the city have also assumed important roles in *ayahuasca* rituals and are interested in strengthening Manchineri spirituality. Currently some young Manchineri boys are actively looking for knowledge of new songs. Nevertheless, the young participants asked the older ones for permission to sing a song.[4] Although there are many young people who take part in the *ayahuasca* ritual, none of them has spent a long time in the forest alone, as shamanic apprentices did in the more distant past. Manchineri shamans in particular consume *ayahuasca* individually to cure illnesses, since they are able to see the cause of the sickness during the hallucinogenic visions. However, other people also take it for various reasons. Among the Manchineri, shamanic practices do not necessarily imply learning the skills of a healer, though the shamans can also cure people collectively.

Music is a central aspect of the ritual. The ritual chanting usually attracts the forest animals, which have traditionally played a central role in Manchineri mythology, or other nonhumans, such as the mother spirit of *kamalampi* herself, who works through the substance of the drink. The chants materialize and thus facilitate the appearance of nonhumans and encourage them to transmit their knowledge and protection. The mother spirit of *kamalampi* or the other spirits who are "summoned" can cure the person under the influence of the drink "by themselves," or they can "show" how to do certain things, what has caused certain events, and the real essences of entities. According to young people in the reserve, each animal and plant has its own song and if a participant learns it, he or she learns the animal's or plant's secret. Under a *kamalampi* effect, one can suddenly "receive" a teaching from an animal or plant spirit and thus use its power in one's own life. The chants help the person "see" a certain nonhuman that is called in kin terms (such as "grandfather toucan") and consequently enable him or her to receive its powers. They therefore work as spells and charms similar to those used by shamans in various other parts of the world. In general terms, as Seeger (1987, 7) noted while studying the musicality of the Suyá, "music transcends time, space, and existential levels of reality. It affects humans, spirits, animals and those hard-to-imagine beings in between." Hill (1993, 202) argues that native singing opens up two social places connected through the music: the outer space of spirits, which comprises horizontal space, and the human world, which comprises vertical space. He writes, "Mystification, or transforming the powerful sounds of language music into mythic speech, is a miniaturizing process, an inscription of the macrocosmic creation of natural species into the microcosm of individual human bodies."

In general, chants help someone see the animals, who actually see themselves as humans, as persons and to learn from this metamorphosis. As Viveiros de Castro (1996) has argued, this consists of a change in perspective: in Amerindian cosmologies, shamans adopt the perspective of animals and see the world from the animal's or spirit's intentionality and their normally invisible "human" viewpoint. Thus the process is not the same as traveling to other worlds. For the Manchineri, the *kamalampi* ritual enables any prepared person to engage with this alien viewpoint by absorbing a shamanic substance into the body. Moreover, the Manchineri usually mix *kamalampi* with other sacred plants referred to as *kamaleji*. This mixture facilitates visions because certain plants and animals have their own *kamaleji*s and when they are taken their qualities can be seen. "All animals have their own secret," as a young Manchineri man explained.

The *kamalampi* ritual generates an intersubjective field in which things that are normally invisible (the spirit world) become visible. Although they are always real, not mere hallucinations,[5] the ritual is a special state of being, in terms of both the quality of the perceiver and the context of perception as a corporeal experience. Shamanic chants are deeply rooted in Manchineri history, and singing them is an important way of creating and maintaining the Manchineri identity and ethnic boundaries, since it sets limits for the people to recognize themselves as certain kinds of beings, while separating them from others on the basis of their possession of a specific kind of humanity and particular ethnic differences. As well as the types of visions already described, seeing an ancestor or a recently deceased relative is fairly common. According to Hill (1993), shamanic language evokes mythic beings, landscapes, and places, and connects them to both historical time and the present. Therefore, music creates special bonds between the participants. Ethnicity and musical traditions are strongly linked for the Manchineri, given that their style of singing is highly distinctive compared with those of other indigenous peoples of the region.[6] Moreover, sharing similar visions and experiences, provoked by the shamanic plant and the music, is especially effective in cultivating trust between the participants. For the Manchineri, this is how they encounter the past, just as they do through dreaming. Music can also enable the maintenance and continuity of knowledge shared by the community members, as ethnomusicologists have explored (see Connell and Gibson 2003).

Besides the shamans and other participants, the *kamalampi* rituals usually also include participants who do not consume the psychoactive plants. Whole indigenous families are typically present when some family members, usually men, are due to take *kamalampi*. Even babies and children attend. The same occurs in the city, and the event is equally important for the young native people who live in distant suburbs and far away from each other. The *kamalampi* ritual offers a space to meet other community members and to listen to their own language and ritual chants, which are usually about ancestors and forest spirits with their own histories. It therefore links the native participants to non-humans, past beings, and places that may prove dangerous if not adequately separated from daily routines. In the city, since the ritual is usually held on the occasion of an important visit from one of the villages, it can also unite native groups from both the urban and rural areas. Shamanic experiences help bind participants to the community and the cosmos as complementary dimensions.

In the reserve, people who had taken *kamalampi* generally said that taking it allowed them to "see better" or to "see everything," meaning that the user can see spirits, the future, and distant relatives, and generally has a better vision of things and the world. It was compared to the television images that young people had seen in the towns (*na rua*). Two girls told me, for instance, that *ayahuasca* is like television since it even allows them to see their future boyfriends, things from cities, as well as all those animals that come and cure someone who is ill. The positive effects increase as the user becomes more experienced. According to the youngsters, the positive sides of *ayahuasca* experiences are that "it shows everything," "it helps us to understand, [to see] what will happen and supports us to find the path for us to travel on," and "when we want to see something, she shows us." For the young Manchineri, seeing their future partner is especially important, as well as learning how to attract her or him. However, pure pleasure is not an idea present in Manchineri *kamalampi* rituals. Similarly, among the Tukano for instance, *caapi* is not used for hedonistic purposes but is strictly ritualized (Reichel-Dolmatoff 1975).

Nonhumans appearing in the shamanic visions may also tell how to harm someone through the use of sorcery. All animals have good and bad qualities, and thus may teach how to protect life as well as how to destroy it. The adolescents themselves declared that they were uninterested in learning sorcery techniques. One of the boys had seen a peccary in his hallucination, which could have taught its secret to him. The boy did not want to know, since he would have learned something bad: how to harm people with a spell.

In the reserve, some young people of both sexes explained that they did not want to consume *kamalampi* owing to the altered state of consciousness produced and the visions of the spirit world. People say that the *kamalampi* mother spirit only gives visions to those to whom she wishes (the spirits may not appear at all) or she may only induce horrifying visions.[7] Girls in particular are afraid of these frightening visions, believing that they may even lose their minds when they take the shamanic drink, a danger that was usually given as a reason for not taking the drug. When asked if they had taken *kamalampi*, a typical answer from both sexes was simply, "I'm afraid to take it."

Both in the reserve and in the city, certain preparations are required to ensure that a positive effect is obtained from the shamanic plants. These include avoiding the consumption of salt, alcohol, and greasy food or having sexual intercourse a few days before and after taking the drug. Otherwise, the spirits that appear may turn out to be evil. Failure to observe these recommendations can result in nasty visions or the person becoming queasy and sick. Nevertheless, during the ritual, the participant has to concentrate and wait for any phases of nausea and vomiting to pass, only then discovering what the female spirit of the *kamalampi* has to teach. *Kamalampi* possesses an ambivalent character, therefore: it is fascinating, admired, and feared.

Control of the person's food intake, including fasting, sexual abstinence, and controlling bodily behavior, has been described as archetypical techniques of sacrifice and purification (Paden 1988). Different food and behavioral prohibitions typically work to ensure the separation of those things classified as sacred.[8] Obeying the rules seems to be even harder in the city, since there the person has to renounce many comforts. Manchineri youngsters regard this temporary renunciation as physically and psychologically difficult since it requires special willpower. During *kamalampi* rituals the user has to temporarily renounce various symbolic capitals, such as those related to education, employment, kin relation, or his or her economic capital. On the other hand, this may mean an increase in traditional values and morality. One of the young Manchineri men said to me that when he experienced the plant, it had no effect on him. He explained that he could not see anything because he had lived among the white population. But then he began to have closer relations with his Manchineri cousin and started to discover more about his culture, learning the Manchineri language and ritual chants, which he now found very beautiful. Likewise, two boys in the reserve told me that when they took *ayahuasca* for the first time, they had tried unsuccessfully to see Jesus and the devil. Only when they had taken more did they learn what *ayahuasca* is about and then were generally able to experience the hallucinatory visions.

The *kamalampi* rituals have a special relationship to morality and social control. In the ritual, sexuality and desires are thought to cause feelings of guilt and prompt confessions. By controlling and limiting the use of the body, certain kinds of behavior are shown to be bad for the community. Consequently, young people are habituated from an early age to understanding that their acts are both controlled and punished. The Manchineri youngsters also say that not everybody is capable of experiencing visions. Especially the first time, adolescents rarely have any visions, which, they say, derives from the fact they possess little knowledge of the spirit world. Thus some people have to take it more often and slowly learn what *ayahuasca* actually involves.

Overall, the adolescents in the city said that the experience of starting to consume *ayahuasca* or to participate in these meetings marked a turning point in their lives. In the *kamalampi* ritual, experiences of selfhood precede experiences of new personhood. This is related to the experience of the other world as a sense of wholeness and unity, because the social, economic, and cultural codes of difference typical to everyday life no longer define the participants.[9] Although personal histories affect their experiences, participants "meet" spirits alone, even when in the company of other members of the community. It can be compared to the separation phase of rites of passage, when the subject is in the temporary state of liminality.

Ayahuasca experiences can give an elated feeling despite any drunkenness and discomfort the brew may cause. This experience may generate self-confidence, since once the feelings of fear have passed—a prominent factor, especially for novices—the participant gains a sensation of strength. After this phase, the person has a triumphal feeling of "returning" to the community. Especially during the nocturnal moments of the *kamalampi* rituals, liminality is real and offers experiences of being beyond time as well as being autonomous from the group. As DaMatta (2000) has argued, this liminality has a positive and communal character, insofar as the experience of individuality and isolation always concludes with a return to society and the transformation of the person into one component within a network of social relationships. For the Manchineri, *kamalampi* causes a feeling of inner wholeness, as well as a balance between humans and between humans and the spirit world, an equilibrium that for them is essential to health. Persons are redefined by his or her relations to others. Moreover, for some Manchineri people, fortune-telling, the treatment of illnesses, and the practice of sorcery can maintain complementary and balanced relationships with the nonhuman world. The ritual is one of the most significant contexts in which social capital is produced between the kin. Nevertheless, the participants are not completely equal, since certain hierarchical roles are observed in the ritual.

Talk about individual experiences is an essential part of the ritual. In the reserve, young people were even more active than other age groups in recounting their *ayahuasca* experiences to the elders, who were able to offer explanations, since the visions usually involve ancestors and mythical beings. Similarly, Reichel-Dolmatoff (1975) suggests that, for the Tukano, the experiences induced by *caapi* (their name for *ayahuasca*) are collective in kind insofar as the visions are later discussed by everyone. These are ritualistic conversations that increase trust between the ritual's participants. Urban (1996, 220) has written similarly about the discourses relating to dreams found in Amerindian communities, noting that telling of bad dreams amounts to sharing the fear with others, who respond by showing that the dreamer is not alone and isolated but part of the group: "Sociability and fear are opposed because the fear is linked in part to isolation, disconnectedness." This return to the shared everyday world is equally apparent among the Manchineri. When the hallucinogenic effects have passed, either in the middle of the ritual when more *kamalampi* is served or at its end, the participants talk about topics relating to the kin, politics, village life—including confidential matters—and discuss new solutions. I see this as an important means of organizing information collectively and creating relations between things and events. Likewise the ritualistic conversations in the city after the hallucinations are an important means of sharing information and discussing life in general. The young people express their deepest feelings, crying and happy to be close to their relatives. The conversations certainly offer good tools for the youths to cope with the problems of their lived worlds as they acquire more knowledge of themselves, their oral history, and their place in the world.

Moreover, during the ritual, participants are required to act in accordance with social roles, a fact that legitimates social order. New cultural capital acquired in the ritual, such as spiritual expertise, can be converted into social capital, since it promotes new social networks among their own indigenous group, in the city and village, and with nonindigenous people who are interested in native spirituality (see Virtanen 2009a). The rituals are important encounters for creating social and cultural capital by becoming a spiritual expert: hence the rituals offer important means for personal development and the transition to the adulthood.

Shamanic practices involving contact with nonhuman beings enable young people to appropriate the symbolic power of their native communities, providing them with an empowering sense of certainty in defining their distinctiveness vis-à-vis the dominant society or other Indians. In the case of native populations living in urban areas inhabited by a multitude of different social and indigenous groups, both these aspects become extremely important. Shamanic practices can be a key means of identifying and marking things as different. They relate to hunting, agriculture, and fishing, as well as many other daily activities performed by both sexes, as well as being linked to nonhuman beings and knowledge of the jungle.

In urban areas, when the native youths gather with their family members in rituals, these events provide the space to construct an embodied indigenous identity, at least temporarily. Many traditional practices constitute their own liminal spaces and phases, allowing them to reorganize the current social situation. Everyday behavior is ideally controlled in ritual, such as the demand for silence in shamanic rituals, and other socially internalized prohibitions and rules mark the entry into the temporary and liminal space of the sacred (Anttonen 2000). They provide the younger generation with the chance to construct their selfhood and consequently with a feeling of belonging to a community that maintains certain differences.

Furthermore, in the urban area, the experiences involved in attending the event appeared to increase the community feeling between people with indigenous backgrounds. As Gupta and Ferguson ([1997] 2001) have suggested, cultural differences should be understood in relation to space and power: within this analytic framework, taking the psychoactive drink in shamanic rituals can be understood in terms of power relations and the attempt to make a difference to the surrounding physical and social environment. As an example, once when I was invited to a *kamalampi* ritual in one of the distant neighborhoods of Rio Branco, the event was held at a location where music is played far into Friday and Saturday night. In the early evening, the sound of *forró* entered the house of the Manchineri family living there from the nearby street, audible even with the windows and doors closed. While we were in the living room, electronic sounds also came from the next room where a Manchineri boy was playing computer games. Thus the ritual is spatially constructed and gaining control of space is part of the process.[10] In the city, it produces difference and enables the acquisition of space for the self and the group. Despite the noise, those taking part in the *kamalampi* ritual were able to construct their own sacred space through acts of ritualization. The lights were switched off and the boy from the next room joined the ceremonial group later. Like on the reserve, the ritual has its own special, recognized rules of how it should proceed, as well as its own roles, sacred objects, and pace. These objects and the ritual setting of the people involved were depicted in the Manchineri drawings of the ritual as performed in both the reserve and the city: the musical instruments, pipe and *ayahuasca* pot, as well as the people sitting quietly. The contents of the ayahuasca visions of youths living in the city shed light on the forest-related reality that is normally invisible in the urban context, as can be seen in the following drawing by a Manchineri boy of his visions. The boy depicted various nonhumans from the Manchineri cosmos and his brother curing him in the foreground.

Shamanic visions and music carry images of the shared past that can guide, control, and instruct the young person vis-à-vis his or her actions in the present. Importing chants and the use of *ayahuasca* in the urban context is easier than staging the big ritual dances, for example, and chants offer a special sphere

Figure 3.2 Drawing by a Manchineri boy of *ayahuasca* visions experienced in the suburb of Rio Branco

of communication and symbolic representation. For Hill (2003), shamanic practices among Venezuelan Arawak speakers are processes of "'remembering' the world, or repopulating the world of the living with an imagined community of mythic and deceased beings so that the past is not forgotten or reified into a dead, external thing." Common means of achieving this liminal state are music and the mythic and spiritual landscapes it creates. The same applies to other artistic and spiritual practices and expressions that afford the possibility of reordering social structure. They enable the embodiment of the "viewpoint" of ancestors, the dead, and other nonhumans, each with its different *habitus*.[11] This embodied viewpoint is provoked in a very strong way by the consumption of the shamanic brew.

Today the encounter with nonhumans and a shamanic experience that enables feelings of unity with something superior and capable of enabling the young person to organize thoughts, emotions, and memories is extremely important for indigenous youths (Virtanen 2009a). Especially in the city, becoming familiar with shamanism is fundamental when young people are searching for answers for their own identity and personal development. State education, for instance, does not answer all their questions. Furthermore, participants in shamanic practices felt that by adopting certain dispositions, they could affect the future. Interactions with nonhumans may open a different set of methods for the young person to respond to the world. The same is demonstrated in the opinions of a young Cashinahua woman living in Rio Branco concerning the consumption of *ayahuasca*: "It can be very good for us, too. Your behavior can improve or get worse. For me it was really good . . . We see some things. And it is more or less—I think it is good. I want to take a little bit more—to see how my mind is. How it should be. And it improved me a lot. This way of thinking of people." A young Cashinahua man told me how he felt when he knew that he was going to take *cipó*: "The first time I felt a little bit nervous, but when I took it, I was willing to take it. And I knew that I would see images of good things passing in front of me, my life. I saw some things. I saw what would happen to my relatives, everything. I took it because I wanted to see my future, my family, my community, and my evolution. How I would be in the future." A young boy living in Extrema village told me that once when he was taking *ayahuasca* in Rio Branco (it was one of his first times), his vision made him understand that he had to return to the village soon and continue the practice of *ayahuasca* there. The same young man later said that he was now aspiring to become a shaman, and his preferred place for a ritual was in a silent, deep jungle: "I am willing to take [*ayahuasca*] in the forest, but my father takes it here [at home]. So we don't take it [in the jungle], and we cannot take it deep in the forest. [*Why is it better to take ayahuasca in the forest?*] Because all the forest animals come to talk to us. And it is better to take it in the jungle, far away from here."

A close bond with the forest environment was important for a ritual setting. One boy who was doing military service in Rio Branco (but had previously lived all his life in the most remote village), had taken *ayahuasca* in the city and said that the experience was very different, owing to the noise of the radio, stereos, and people constantly moving around. When I asked him to depict his *ayahuasca* experience, he drew his latest vision in the city and showed merely "noise." In the drawing the noise had clear borders and was thus also spiritualized as an element of the city. The young man said that taking *ayahuasca* in the village is different, since from 8 p.m. onward everything is quiet, broken only by the sound of a few animals.

In order to increase deeper shamanic powers, one of training procedures is the continuous consumption of psychoactive plants living in the wild, which enables visions of the spirit world and the observation of certain rules. One of the problems may be that in today's world, there are many more things (or comforts) for the initiate to renounce. One of the Manchineri elders said that although it is still possible to become a shaman today, the person has to abandon "everything that belongs to the whites." He said that there were no longer any powerful shamans because contemporary adolescents consider the shamanic training too difficult. For Manchineri, becoming a shaman can also occur in a more involuntarily way: for example, when the person becomes enchanted and later guided by a spirit of the forest.

However, there were a couple of boys in the most outlying villages who aspired to become shamans and were ready to undertake the training. After various conversations, for instance, the son of the shaman told me that his dream was to become a shaman, too. This was said in a low voice, since it requires renunciation and a lot of respect toward elders and the spirit world. Later his elder brother also told me that a great shaman, already dead, had noticed his brother's potential to become a shaman. The shaman had already taught him some things and had even given him a few supernatural items "not from this world." These were a long white robe (*koshma*) and a shining bow and arrow. The brother told me that he had seen all this while he and his brother were taking *kamalampi*. Now his younger brother should put into practice what he had learned and walk around armed, since many people were jealous of his powers. The elders had already told me earlier that a special set of bow and arrows were the main "instruments" used by the shaman in ancient times as they helped ward off harmful forces. These objects are typical of shamans in many parts of the world and have also been used for sending spirits and spells (along with other objects such as drums, masks, headdresses, sticks, and the shaman's attire). The novice's brother told me that he himself did not want to become a shaman, since there are always other shamans with a better knowledge of the spirit world, and these like to provoke less experienced shamans through sorcery attacks that cause illness. Sorcery attacks are today common in interethnic politics. I asked if his younger brother was not afraid of the powers he would encounter and learn. He said that his brother was not frightened. A few young men also rarely talked to me face to face as they were working with a certain spirit. Usually they were the best hunters.

The shaman trainee has to spend time in the jungle, learning through direct contact with the forest spirits and eating nothing but cassava, plus a kind of banana porridge and smoked game and fish prepared by an older woman. Along with these obligations, people also focused on the abstentions involved in becoming a shaman: a person has to be isolated from others. Increasing shamanic knowledge in the urban areas is regarded as difficult. In the city, his diet is typically spicy food with garlic, beef, bread, sweet drinks, and coffee. However, one boy, who lived in the city, often consumed *ayahuasca* and tried to dedicate his life to learning shamanic techniques. He also explained that he has a close relationship with the forest environment: "Since I began to train to be a *kahontshi*, I have had to learn about nature. The forest is our mother, she gives us medicines. In the jungle, I feel good, healthy, more energetic. I don't know if she feels good with me! [Laughs.]"

In the past, young women were unable to take any active part in shamanic practices owing to their menstruation and the threat posed to connecting with the nonhuman world. The spirits controlled the success of hunting and agriculture, but communities are no longer dependent solely on these practices. Both sexes are needed when it comes to transmitting oral history and indigenous identity. Traditionally women take less *ayahuasca* since it is not their role to communicate with the spirit world, with the exception of women who have gone through menopause, who may become experts in *ayahuasca* chants. Again this can be explained by menstruation and the danger posed by the woman to the spirit world.[12] A few older Manchineri women in Extrema village are excellent singers. Some fathers do not want their children to take *ayahuasca* since they believe they are not ready for it; this is especially the case with girls. I never heard young girls sing in *kamalampi* rituals, but two girls, one living in the reserve and the other in Rio Branco, told me that they had suddenly learned an *ayahuasca* chant during the ritual, although they could not recall the ritual itself. This may be proof that the social norms dictating women's positions are about to change in response to the new roles performed by women—for example, as health agents and representatives of women. This has also affected the way in which they practice shamanism. Today *kampalampi* rituals are increasingly shared with women and even Indians of other groups and non-Indians.

Shamanic Practices as a Social Reference

For both the Manchineri and the Cashinahua, *ayahuasca* rituals are the most common form of shamanism. Among the Apurinã, for instance, these techniques are connected to the use of herbal medicines such as *rapé*, which was used by most of the young males in my study. In fact, the existence of nonhumans who become visible in shamanism is present in many indigenous activities. They are also present in the worldview of the Amazonian region's so-called traditional peoples, many rubber tappers and river dwellers.[13] The *ayahuasca* churches, such as Santo Daime, have also begun to share some of this knowledge on nonhumans.

In the city, participation in *ayahuasca* rituals can be seen as a statement of the person's native identity and even religiosity. The young people regard *ayahuasca* as something truly their own, a part of their culture, and they even mentioned that *ayahuasca* should be called by its Manchineri name, *kamalampi*. They argued various times that taking *ayahuasca* forms the basis of their religious practice as a people and that they therefore wish to continue performing the ancient ritual. "The religion of the Indian is *ayahuasca*." In the city, young Manchineri said that one of the objectives of the young leader who usually ran the ritual in Rio Branco was for the adolescents to learn about their own form of spirituality. When I met a Manchineri boy at the Youth Forum held in Rio Branco in 2005, he announced in the workshop on racism that his religion was *ayahuasca* after the workshop coordinator had asked about the participants' religious beliefs. This was a very strong manifestation of his own values and principles. Two young men even declared their wish to construct a house in the reserve village as a place to take *ayahuasca* and invite other people to attend.

Indigenous youths in urban areas often gather together and their shamanic traditions connect them. Even non-Indians, both men and women, are occasionally invited to take *ayahuasca*. A Manchineri young man explained this to me: "[*Who do you take (ayahuasca) with here (in the city)?*] Some people who are friends. The people who we want to share with."

The young indigenous men especially have started to lead these shamanic sessions, and nonnatives are becoming more and more interested in experiencing native spirituality. The *ayahuasca* sessions take place at youths' homes, friends' houses, or in distant places surrounded by the forest environment. Young Indians usually came prepared for the events carrying ritual objects such as their headdresses, musical instruments, snuff, or traditional clothes. A Manchineri man in Rio Branco once showed me a special *kushma* he had designed for when he consumes *ayahuasca*, covered in beautiful traditional painted designs.

Those nonnatives who are invited to the ritual events are usually interested in indigenous philosophy. Hence the cultural capital of the native adolescents accumulated in shamanism, including knowledge of spiritual matters, medicinal plants, and healing practices, can enable new friendships and respectful relations that offer symbolic capital for indigenous young people. Non-Indians are, however, invited only if closer relations already exist between them. The non-Indians are usually representatives of nongovernmental organizations, artists, and male or female government officials, and the indigenous population usually respect these nonnative activists and experts as contributors to the work of recovering and documenting indigenous practices, music, iconography, and mythologies. Many local, national, and even international musicians have made contacts with indigenous people who are renowned chanters or create their own music, and these contacts have offered the indigenous youngsters the chance to travel to other cities and sometimes other countries. However, the ritual is not open to all, and some indigenous families do not want to share the ritual with others. But for those who are willing to share their knowledge and way of thinking, getting involved with shamanic practices and rituals offers an opportunity to engage in a new encounter beyond ethnic and urban boundaries, since it can also be a field of interaction between other indigenous groups and non-Indians. These nonnatives are also educated people who usually belong to the middle class or already have a higher social status—people with whom the indigenous youngsters would not otherwise have the opportunity to interact. Hence the new social networks that are sometimes constructed can extend beyond the established class, rural-urban, gender, and ethnic boundaries, since the ritual group may be extremely mixed: members of the participant's own family, people from other indigenous groups, and nonindigenous people.

The encounters with nonhuman beings with their own personal histories embedded in the mythologies of indigenous peoples generate informal relations between the actors involved in shamanic practices, based on sharing a similar cosmology. This causes a strong psychological feeling of reciprocity between people who can understand and believe in the same nonhuman beings and phenomena. Even in urban areas, the same animal and plant masters still ensure good health—that is, good physical and mental health. Young native people in reserves and cities still share similar beliefs of forest beings as purveyors of guidance and learning, for instance for curing. Nevertheless the difference is that in the rural context where people are more dependent on the forest and thus on climatic and seasonal conditions, for instance, shamanic practices still center on negotiations with game animal masters and other beings considered as the owners of the forest. Music is a significant element in creating shared experiences. As Stokes (1994, 5) suggests, music negotiates and transforms hierarchies of place: "I would argue therefore that music is socially meaningful not entirely but largely because it provides means by which people recognize identities and places, and the boundaries which separate them."

In shamanism, knowledge and experiences are spatially shared in a special way with others. Like the native youths, these nonindigenous participants seek to establish favorable personal relations with the same nonhuman beings and their curing elements. Shamanism is therefore a new type of encounter that crosses the participants' social boundaries (such as those of class and ethnicity), and even social elites may experience the power relations between nonhumans and humans. Symbols used in shamanic practices connect people to what is mostly invisible in their day-to-day activities. Thus the group of people practicing shamanism has its own rules and predictability. However, as mentioned, the nonnatives can act in a way that is not anticipated for the native participants.

For young people, the traditional means of receiving *ayahuasca* teachings has not changed, given that the same methods are used to prepare the body for its separation from the spirit. The aim is a temporal phase of a timeless ritual process and this is only achieved by certain behavioral regulations. The prohibitions on the user's conduct before, during, and after the *ayahuasca* ritual mark out sacred space and time. By controlling one's own actions and body in a specific way, certain things are made visible, as well as their special value and sacredness. The increase in shamanism can be linked, I think, to the attempt to control the contemporary world. The community's shamans and spiritual leaders are ascetics of a kind who set new norms and rules for behavior. As authors working within the structuralist tradition have argued, in any culture, a renouncer "shows to his fellow companions the fragility and arbitrariness of their conventions, thus creating the possibility of a 'reinvention' of society amid the hierarchized world of authority in which he presently lives" (DaMatta [1979] 1991, 212). Becoming a spiritual expert, therefore, still attracts some young people even though it is a marginal way of life. Shamanic practices create exclusive bonds between participants due to their observance of the same rules, such as those relating to diet. In fact, when the world becomes more complicated, these rules impose very strong limits on everyday life and thus shamanism offers alternative mental models and places for feelings that go beyond social differences.

The body produced in shamanism differs from the body in an everyday context, since at a personal level the shamanic practices allow young people to leave behind the responsibilities and roles needed in contemporary society, especially in urban areas. It excludes, for instance, the categorization in terms of the social prerogatives that living in society establishes. This is the socially produced social space in which religious ideas and practices "allow [the] group to live with the imposed order, to challenge it with a nonracist narrative, and to transcend it by allowing something different and more just to be imagined" (Knott 2005, 165). Knowledge of the forest environment; indigenous ways of curing, stories, and beliefs; and the history of the indigenous group manifested in shamanism make shamanic practices a forum for acquiring indigenous knowledge. This cultural capital is distinct from the so-called scientific knowledge provided by state education and may be acknowledged as cultural capital by Indians and non-Indians alike. Enhancing this cultural capital also reinforces social capital since it may lead to being treated positively in various contexts. Shamanic knowledge and other forms of ethnic and social capital accumulable in shamanism play an important role in today's ethnopolitical movement, forming legitimate actors among indigenous groups. In addition, they can also create special bonding and relations with other indigenous peoples and nonnatives, producing social networks, friendships, and prestigious relationships. However, these networks may also separate themselves from others, meaning that the production of social capital among the people involved is limited to the ritual sphere only.

To some extent the shamanic space allows native adolescents to experience even more things than they could elsewhere. Globally speaking, entertainment has become increasingly materialized and related to consumption. As a consequence, the limited financial resources of young indigenous people can prevent them from engaging in the activities they would really like to pursue. Shamanic rituals can offer new feelings, even "supernatural" experiences. However, they are not about entertainment per se: instead, these practices represent the domain of the sacred. I prefer not to discuss New Age shamanism here, therefore, because the native shamanic practices remain rather closed to nonnatives and attempt to adhere to the way they have been practiced in the past. Undoubtedly there is a production of new forms, since new musical instruments and chants have become increasingly incorporated. But these must be seen as merely new means to alter the states of consciousness that can be achieved by using different rhythms, sounds, prayers, and spells. Academic studies of authenticity and musical tastes (distinctions) have shown that authenticity is constructed in relation to how it is perceived; that is, the way in which artistic productions are consumed (Connell and Gibson 2003). Here what matters is the experience of continuity between the community and the nonhuman beings that represent ancestors and the jungle.

However, shamanism also has its own power struggles, especially where authenticity is concerned. For instance, after *ayahuasca* rituals, nonnative participants are sometimes criticized for not being quiet or still enough. However, some people do follow the behavior of the Indians, which is very different from the way the plant is taken, for instance, in the Santo Daime churches frequented by many people from Acre. This especially happens when interethnic shamanic rituals are practiced at the homes of Indians or other spaces demarcated as indigenous, such as their training courses and urban political and cultural meetings. These events assemble people from different indigenous groups, usually along with nonnatives. They bestow shamanic fame on the indigenous people organizing the event, even if a singer from another indigenous group takes the floor during the ceremony.

Some young Cashinahua men have even made contacts with people from other states interested in alternative healing techniques and neoshamanism. Two Cashinahua young men started to offer *ayahuasca* sessions for nonnatives in Brazil's largest cities and now participate in the exchange of shamanic knowledge.[14] They were criticized, though, for sharing their sacred knowledge with outsiders. In Rio Branco they had already been invited to the homes of non-Indians to take *ayahuasca* and to conduct the ritual. The two young men were becoming more experienced in dealing with the nonhumans familiar to their communities but were also interested in learning new techniques from others. In these ritual spaces, nonnatives typically introduce other religious aspects, such as chants, other substances, and musical instruments. Once a young Cashinahua man said that he was not disturbed by the other spiritual methods that had been used but was sad nonetheless that others had also introduced new spirit agencies into the ritual because he had already called his master spirit to lead the visions.

Urban centers have also been important in terms of strengthening the performance of the *ayahuasca* ritual, since interethnic contacts have encouraged indigenous peoples to value and respect their own ways of relating to the world, including shamanism. Nevertheless, the musical repertoire has changed and some new elements have been incorporated under the influence of urban centers and other peoples. Various *ayahuasca* songs used today were learned in the municipalities during the interethnic *ayahuasca* rituals held, for instance, during the courses run for indigenous teachers or at cultural events. The new songs are seldom derived from other indigenous groups, but are more often from the Santo Daime church, widespread throughout Acre. Lyrics in the indigenous languages have replaced the Portuguese words, but the melody remains the same. The younger generation, especially young men who may lead the shamanic practices, also make use of some new instruments like guitars. Previously the Manchineri used only the *tromba* (an instrument made of a bow and string, held in the mouth and played with the fingers), flutes, and drums. Young people in particular have introduced these new influences, although they actively seek out the instruction of the elders. Among many groups, though, the *ayahuasca* ritual has still not been absorbed into nonindigenous practices to the same extent as among the mestizo populations of urban Peru and Ecuador, for instance.[15] The ritual also remains very different from the ceremonies performed in the Santo Daime churches.

Although urban centers are places for reinforcing the interaction between indigenous peoples, the origin of shamanic knowledge resides in the forest where the strongest experiences can be obtained.[16] Nonhuman beings are located in new social places that are activated in the cognitive maps of the young people in certain ritualized urban situations. In the social context of shamanism, different nonhuman forest beings are important social actors and materialize with their own capitals and *habitus*. They are truly seen by human beings only when the latter take *ayahuasca*, when they appear in their human form. In addition, the functions of these nonhuman beings have changed: for young people, they do not play a significant role in curing or hunting alone in the forest but in receiving inner wisdom and better self-knowledge, as well as offering a confidential space to establish new networks. In addition to linking the environment, the past, and the present, singing is an important way of expressing feelings, making it an eminently creative activity (Seeger 1987).

Moreover, *ayahuasca* shamanism offers a way to examine the essences of other participants, and shamans have always been specialists in relating with nonhuman others. Now *ayahuasca* shamanism offers a possibility for those young people who have the most experience with spirits to relate with nonnatives and learn more about them. Inviting non-Indians to participate in shamanic rituals offers the chance to act temporarily in a new social relationship with them. These events also provide an opportunity to bring people together and break social barriers inside the dominant society. They have the potential to create new categories, forms, and essences, and to set limits, while also reinforcing relationships between individuals.

Shamanism and myths—which have always been closely related with shamanism—have provided cultural models to deal with uncertainties across the generations. The shamanic practices of the various indigenous group helps create their self-identity. Today they are used as reference points especially related to the uncertainties provoked by urbanization, increased mobility, and political engagement within the dominant society, topics that I shall examine in the next chapters.

CHAPTER 4

Forest-Urban Communities

In the previous chapters we have examined how people in urban areas are considered to differ from those living in the forest environment and villages and the rituals practiced beyond rural-urban divides. But what do "city" and "urban" actually signify for Amazonian Indians? Urban areas have become increasingly important in terms of pursuing economic, social, political, and cultural activities that lead to new skills, experiences, forms of learning, and embodiments in more diverse social environments. The city and the reserve are seen in ambivalent ways owing to their differing vital powers, as a result of which each can manifest Otherness in divergent ways. The first section of this chapter examines Manchineri people's own sense of their translocations to urban areas and the visits to these areas as an important element in becoming an adult, insofar as they allow a new type of understanding of the self and the constitution of social difference. In the second section I address the growing forest-urban relations and how indigenous territories receive strong emotional connotations, though cities are also seen as a source of substances that enable autonomy and power. I look then at urbanization and, in more general terms, the movement toward urban areas in the region.

Transitions between Villages and Cities

For the people in the reserve, summer (the dry season from June to October) is the period for visiting other villages and municipalities. Adolescents usually travel to the urban centers for the first time in order to accompany older people receiving their pension, sell agricultural produce, and purchase essential goods, such as salt, sugar, ammunition, detergents, and clothing. Recently the growth in the consumption and use of commodities has increased the number of visits made by the Manchineri outside the reserve. Furthermore, temporary visits to urban centers are more frequent owing to health care services, negotiations with authorities, temporary paid employment on farms and in the logging industry, and the expansion in educational classes (indigenous teachers, environmental agents, health agents, etc.). The system of receiving retirement pensions and a range of benefits that need to be drawn personally every two months in the nearest municipality has resulted in the movement of whole families, since the journey is long and older people or women in particular have to be accompanied. Almost all young Manchineri people living in the reserve have visited the closest municipalities (Assis Brasil and Sena Madureira), but only a few have been to Rio Branco, usually to visit the health center.

Although visits to the nearby municipalities have increased, the people in the reserve emphasized that they go to the city only when strictly necessary. They lacked the economic resources needed to stay and live there, they said, and even traveling to Rio Branco is difficult since gasoline is so expensive. But the Manchineri young people stated that they wanted to get to know the cities, even if they could never get used to living there permanently. On one occasion, Amauri expressed his desire to enter military service and stay for a few years in the city:

> [T]oday we see the cities like this—we already have a little bit of contact with white people, you know. But our ancestors didn't know the world of the whites; they only stayed in *malocas* [community houses]. And nor did the diseases of today exist. Only our world existed. They didn't go to the city to make purchases. We knew nothing. But today it is necessary. Hence, today we need to go to the city. But this isn't because we think that the city is better than our place. I speak for myself. I think that the food and drink in the city are different, you know. And it is [the city's] way. We don't have this way of the city. Everything there is different from ours.

Boys and young men are more frequent visitors to urban areas. Usually at least one young man travels to the city to assist others. Young girls may also accompany visits to health centers and trips to purchase things in urban shops, but these tasks usually involve less negotiation. Thus mobility is gendered and has certain social age characteristics. During shorter visits young men also accompany women. For instance, a young Manchineri mother told me that her 14-year-old boy always traveled with her when she left the village to visit her relatives in other villages. If long-distance travel involves journeying by canoe, young men and boys paddle the canoes or punt the canoe standing up using a long pole (*ir varejando*). They are usually the *motoristas* (pilots) of the canoes, since they know how to use the motors. Alternatively they paddle. These are typical social roles attributed to young men (see Fernandes 1975, 71). However, girls and women may also travel *varejando*, or punting, though more for fun and over shorter distances.

The journey from the Manchineri reserve to the city is tough, because one has to sit in the canoe for several days. In summertime, the sun is scorching hot and canoes offer no shade. The river may be very low and dry, meaning that those traveling have to push or even carry the canoe. In winter, the heavy rains become the problem. In wintertime, a two-to three-day walk (50 miles/ 80 kilometers) from the river shore to Assis Brasil is particularly arduous physically. Women then simultaneously take care of their children, even carrying them at times. This trek is unnecessary during the summer as rides can be obtained from the river shore to Assis Brasil by jeep, although this depends on the local authorities, as most private drivers ask for money. Moreover, the gasoline for the outboard motors used on the canoes is a constant problem, since it is very expensive to buy the quantity required for the journey. Fuel can occasionally be received from the government or organizations, if the visits are connected to the latter. Thus, owing to their economic difficulties, the Manchineri very rarely travel to the urban centers. Nor do urban relatives have many opportunities to visit the reserve.

The Manchineri are used to walking and trekking and they enjoy visiting their relatives in the neighboring villages, as well as passing from house to house in their own villages during the evenings.[1] Adolescents especially said that they liked to wander and have the freedom to stay overnight wherever they wanted, as during their hunting or fishing trips, for example. On these occasions, they make *tapiris*, small huts of palm leaves, and look for fresh water to drink from springs. But the city is a much harsher environment for those Indian visitors coming from the reserve, since there are only a few relatives' houses where they can stay.

For anyone leaving the reserve, the daily rhythm changes and they lose the convivial proximity of people and relatedness in the village, where they are used to being offered a meal or manioc beer whenever they visit a relative's house. Generally, the young Manchineri men and women in the reserve said that they do not like visiting cities because food and water become an immediate problem. They have to be bought and "the food there is just chemicals." Furthermore, cities are unsafe and noisy, only money counts there, and there are far too many people and things.[2] In the Manchineri youngsters' descriptions of their visits to the urban areas, the experiences of urban places are marked by various differences from their own homes, as the comments of Fabia, Lazaro, Rodrigues, and Jair illustrate:

I missed my village. [Here in the village] nothing is bought. There were many people, and I found the noise of the city strange. And sometimes—here you rarely see a fight, but in the city you hear a lot.

I spent two months in Sena Madureira. I took my brother, who had been bitten by a snake [to the hospital] there. We stayed in the boat. It is very different there.

We starved a lot. If you have money, you don't starve. But we feel bad there. We go to Assis Brasil once every two months to get my mother's pension. We suffer being there. It's a big sacrifice for us to walk there and to return. And we accompany her. If we don't go, no one receives [the pension]. Myself, mother, father. We spend one day, we don't have a house to stay in.

I thought it was very busy there, houses, merchandise, people. It is just that, for me, it wasn't good, because there is no fresh smell, nor this wind. There the way people walk is different. There is a smell of waste pipes and beef. So that's what I thought of the city. I thought it was very hot there.

I'm afraid that somebody will attack me, or I'll get lost in the city, starve to death, because it's not like in our community where we have our food. Sometimes we don't eat here because we don't have enough money. We face many difficulties. We can't go out or enjoy ourselves. Because of this I don't like it here. I come here only to get information for my community.

According to many Manchineri young people, living in the city is difficult and inconvenient since they have to do lots of work there and the money earned is merely enough to buy food. In the village, though, they can make their plantations and use the cash earned from selling crops to buy clothes and other items. For instance, when I first met a young Manchineri boy from Mamoadate who was visiting Rio Branco, he seemed keen to point out the alternative wealth of his village: "[There are] the trees, the forest, the river, the sun. There is a house for me to live, meat for me to eat, game, fish, various friends—it's like when we talk about a supermarket. Everything is there inside my village. Because when we clear a plantation, it is the future for us."

On the other hand, for people coming from the reserve, the city is a space for fulfilling material needs. A girl told me that she had visited the *rua* only once in her life, when she went to Sena Madureira with her father. For her it was good there because she was able to buy many things. These she listed: clothes, shoes, lipstick, sugar, biscuits, milk powder, coffee, sardines, and jewelry. The younger girls said they are happy when something is brought from the city, such as new clothes or sandals. And once when I asked, "What is the most important place?" a girl answered, "Rio Branco, because there are biscuits and milk powder, and the city is big and beautiful!" Especially for the girls, who had not visited cities as often, they were imagined as places of many possibilities, movement, and things to see. I also noticed a young man once getting frustrated and shouting in a fit of rage, "Why don't we even have a radio?"

The Manchineri are heavily dependent on communication with and transportation to urban centers located a long distance away in order to receive crucial health care, materials, and new knowledge via training courses and personal encounters. The importance of the cities must be seen especially in relation to the well-being of the reserves. "When we are ill, we can get treatment there [in cities]," as a young boy mentioned. Some adolescents wish to have a road constructed from the reserve to Assis Brasil, since it would then be easier to travel to the municipality. According to the FUNAI documentation, this desire to improve the transportation of agricultural produce to the markets in the nearest municipalities was manifested decades ago by the Extrema community.[3] Likewise, the production of artwork and craftwork depends on transportation and market outlets.

The movement to urban areas continues because these spaces represent transformative power, knowledge, and desired capacities. The transformation associated with the non-Indians who dominate the cities has to be dealt with carefully. For the young people living in the reserve, the visits to urban places are both fascinating and fearful. The cities are overflowing with unknown people. Visiting urban areas means occupying an unfamiliar temporary space, leaving behind the social categories defined by a person's relations to others in the villages, where everybody is known by their name and personal history. Especially when negotiating with public authorities, the young Indians enter the level of the individual, marked by impersonal laws and norms. And, as discussed in relation to studying in the city, from the viewpoint of the youngsters in the reserve, visits to the urban centers involve entering new situations that have to be dealt with alone. Moreover, many people living in urban areas are attacked unprovoked. For instance, a young Manchineri man was stabbed by a stranger while he was walking in Assis Brasil in the daytime. He said that the victim could have been anybody.

Despite the anonymity of "the street," in the nearby municipality the native adolescents coming from the reserve are usually incorporated into a hierarchical social sphere by being positioned and identified according to their indigenous background. They are generalized as Indians or Manchineri. In many city contexts their marginalization and racism have obliged them to hide their differences. Even when the young Manchineri behave like non-Indians, they are not accepted as equals. In the city they are often stereotyped as street beggars, an idea compounded by media reports that generally dwelt on their poverty.[4] Social relations between white and indigenous populations in Acre, as well as other parts of Amazonia, have suffered from the idea of occupying "the last frontier" and taming its indigenous population. Even though relations between the local extractivist population and indigenous people in rural areas have usually been reasonably cordial, in urban areas Indians face more prejudice. The city is the location of the Manchineri's first encounter not only with different types of non-Indians but also with different Indians.

For the young people of the reserve, therefore, visiting the city can be seen as a kind of ritual in which new rules are applied and learned. It enables embodied transformation in various bodily ways. As has been pointed out in recent studies on the transformative relations between Indians and whites, native people are contextually becoming white through corporeal alterations that differ from the ways of speaking, dressing, eating, and working typical to life among their own kin (Vilaça [1999] 2007; Lasmar 2005; Andrello 2006; Virtanen 2010a; Kelly 2011). For Amerindians, affinity is typically produced through changing corporeal practices.

Personal experiences of the urban areas are significant in defining adulthood, and the visits gradually turn them into persons able to embody the different rules of the city. Once the person has observed the city life and learned how to walk, eat, and behave in the city, the visits—which for many indigenous peoples today are essential—become easier. Knowledge is then acted out. This is clearly apparent in one Artur's comment concerning his first visit to the city: "It [the city] gave me the shudders. I didn't know how to walk in the city. Firstly, I didn't know how to eat the food that whites eat. The other thing is that there is no way for us to buy things. And there is nowhere to take a bath. That's what I thought. I was thinking how I would return to my home. After I went to the course [of the indigenous agroforestry agents], I didn't have the shudders anymore." The training course, which had lasted several days, gave the young man the chance to observe these others more than he would have been able during the short visits more typically made to the city.

I also asked young people to draw geographical maps with the urban places they knew outside the reserve, and on some of the sketch maps produced by these adolescents in the reserve, the places visited were the only ones marked. Many of the maps sketched also illustrated that they view themselves to be living at the world's center.[5] The transitions to urban areas are similar to the wayfaring described by Ingold (2009). It is not about moving to a place and returning from there: rather, the practices, knowledge, and experience dissimilar from those of the reserve form a crucial part of the learning process throughout the entire shift toward the urban world. Sporadic exchanges of news with non-Indians on the way, a different pace of walking, greetings, and tasting new foods are all part of this general movement.

The visits to cities are also linked to local and national politics, funding from nongovernmental organizations, political struggles, and conservationist efforts including the environmental economy, all of which greatly influence the present and future of indigenous peoples (Peluso and Alexiades 2005; McSweeney and Jokisch 2007; Virtanen 2009b, 2010a). The movement toward the cities is necessary for indigenous communities, and urban experiences and relations with the state and white people are tightly interwoven with the internal and external political activities and territorial issues that constitute indigenous societies. Cities are places with different sources of power, including education, project funding, new substance, and new contacts. In order to establish development projects capable of exploiting new kinds of economic activities, even with the help of associations, the community living in the reserve needs people to become used to acting in the urban environment. Consequently young people, who visit cities more frequently and have more experiences there, often become specialists in "translating" the symbolic system of the cities into those of the reserve. Moreover, translocation, arriving in the city, and returning all tend to create feelings of belonging to one's own indigenous collective, meaning that these visits reproduce and maintain values in new ways.

The visits made by native peoples to cities are important in terms of the constitution of indigenous societies, since they play a fundamental political role: new coalitions are formed, such as those created in the recent past for the demarcation of territories and planning new projects. They also sustain native economies, allowing people to sell and purchase materials and commodities. The urbanization process driven by nonnatives has also arrived in the reserves in invisible forms, including legislation, as mentioned earlier, but also through pollution and the system of social benefits paid to citizens, for example. Its more visible forms are large-scale ranching, clandestine invasions, agriculture, logging, mining, hydroelectric energy production, and resource extraction, all of which are now swamping tracts of land bordering or within indigenous areas. The study made in 2000 showed that, even at that time, the majority of Amazonia's forested areas (74 percent) were only 31 miles (50 kilometers) away from the road system, the construction of which has allowed much easier access to many distant communities (Carvalho et al. 2002).

Although there has been interaction between rural and urban areas, as well as between indigenous groups, many of the present-day indigenous peoples live more dispersed than earlier. The rural and urban native populations should be seen as parts of complex social networks, among each other but also within their own social environments, recognizing here that the encounter with and absorption of different beliefs and social realities has never been a one-way traffic of ideas. Indigenous communities in the city and the reserves are complementary to each other. However, viewing them as the margin or the place of Otherness depends on the way one reconstructs the idea of their ability to act in the world.

For Manchineri youths living in Rio Branco, the reserve amounted to a completely different reality. This was symbolized by its food, the absence of the use of money, different forms of communication, the rhythm of daily life, and daily production. These could be either an appealing alternative to urban practices or associated with bodily suffering. For the young people from the city, visiting their reserve means encountering the home of their indigenous group and its typical ways of life, with which they identify, as well as a place where history continues unbroken. Many of the parents of these urban Manchineri youngsters had perhaps been unable or unwilling to relate with people in the village in such an open way because they had to leave the reserve involuntarily—that is, those forced to migrate in the aftermath of internal conflicts—and never returned even to visit their kin. Today the Manchineri youths in the city have more freedom to visit and can return to the reserve for good if they wish. One young man, whose father had been murdered in an internal conflict, had now moved to the reserve together with his non-Indian wife and children. However, urban indigenous adolescents rarely wanted to live in the village permanently: they said that they would miss certain conveniences found in the city, such as electricity and mobile phones. Also unavailable in the reserve is higher education, still one of their life aims.

Even those urban Manchineri youths possessing few contacts with the reality of their original villages, or the people from them, distinguish the village as a central place. But so, on the other hand, is the city. They pose certain cognitive barriers to "our way of doing things." Both are ambiguous places, the home of the Other. The difference between "us" and "them" becomes visible and is made more evident by their discourses concerning the city and village. In the indigenous territory, traditional knowledge of the past—including practices and stories—still exists, a dimension with which the young people can identify but that cannot be experienced in the same way in the city. However, the urban youngsters want to learn more about their indigenous language and history, though they still have to find a way to reembody and contextualize them in urban areas. Moreover, the natural environment plays a distinctive role in the clear distinction established between the city and the villages.

Strength in Shifting Places

The presence of Indians in urban areas has acquired a new visibility, reflecting the fact that the previous generations of urban indigenous residents, including the parents of many contemporary adolescents, chose to downplay their cultural characteristics as a means of social survival. I have identified six phases of indigenous migration typical to Acre state, and probably to other parts of the Amazon region as well. The first is the time of flight at the end of the nineteenth century when the Indians tried to escape the rubber bosses taking over their lands and determining their lives; the second, the time of captivity, when large Indian populations were subsequently transferred to rubber estates, *seringais*; the third, when indigenous territories were demarcated and people moved back to the old villages or the new settlements that had been founded.

Generally speaking, the modern urbanization of Amazonia began at the time of the rubber boom, but it was soon followed by large-scale migration from rural areas when the price of rubber fell at the end of the 1940s. The colonization started by the rubber boom was followed by agricultural reforms and more recently by industrialization. In terms of indigenous migration, the fourth and fifth phases represent the migration to urban centers. At the end of the 1970s and the 1980s, land and social issues were discussed in the cities, usually by the indigenous chiefs, who brought their closest kin to urban areas. Work for indigenous organizations, urban jobs, and internal conflicts were responsible for much of the migration to the city. This is when the first Manchineri families moved to Rio Branco.

In the 1970s, the low price of rubber also forced many indigenous families to move to the cities. The expansion of farming areas and the new occupation of the lands, as many rubber patrons switched their business to logging or raising cattle for slaughter, also maintained the movement to the cities. The state capital's outlying districts began to receive indigenous residents, though the majority of inhabitants were colonizers, as well as former rubber tappers who moved to the city due either to the lack of opportunities for marketing their produce or to being expelled by new landlords keen to invest in agriculture and cattle ranching. The large-scale migration of white colonizers occurred in the 1970s with the government's aims to colonize the Amazon region, still viewed as a marginal place (Ozorio de Almeida 1992). In general, in Amazonia, even more than elsewhere, migration policies were not designed to receive large numbers of urban residents, and the social problems of the settler population were not addressed.

The last phase started in the 1990s when many indigenous families and even small village communities started to look for better conditions, employment, and education in the cities. National and international funding increased the road and transportation systems, creating new networks of cities (Browder and Godfrey 1997). Nowadays studying is one of the main reasons for migrating to the urban areas, as was stated by my group of interviewees. When I walked in the districts of the state capital with my young native guides, they told me that even though they had worked for UNI's door-to-door population census only a couple of years ago, they now had problems finding the same houses as so many new ones had been built. These districts or *bairros* of the city are home to the majority of the state's migrants and working-class inhabitants.

One fundamental change in the Amazon region is that some indigenous communities have become settled in the cities. Elsewhere in Amazonia, whole quarters of these cities, usually the poorest suburbs, are inhabited by Indians, and there already exist so-called urban villages (*aldeias urbanas*) where the majority of residents are indigenous. There are also a number of former indigenous settlements that continue to be considered villages of Indian mestizos, though these are not officially recognized as such. It is worth noting that today 70 percent of the entire population (nonindigenous and indigenous) of Amazonia lives in cities. Nevertheless in this region, where 98 percent of native lands are located, the majority of indigenous population lives on indigenous lands (IBGE 2010). The largest urban indigenous population is found in those regions of the country with the smallest and fewest indigenous territories: northeastern and southeastern Brazil, where most of these people have lived in cities for more than a decade.

Already a significant proportion of young Indians in Acre state were born outside Indian lands. Indigenous migrants have their own communal histories of migration, and some groups have a greater tendency to be on the move than others. The Manchineri people have migrated relatively little, and often their mobility has been related to indigenous politics. The Apurinã is the largest native group in Rio Branco, and the presence of some families in urban areas dates back a few generations. The Apurinã families have been living in the urban centers of Acre and Amazonas since the 1980s mostly owing to internal conflicts, especially at the time of the demarcation of the indigenous lands. However none of the adolescents cited this as the reason for their migration—only that they had to move together with their parents or that they came because of studies. Most of the Apurinã youths currently living in Rio Branco were born in urban centers (Boca do Acre, Rio Branco itself, or Pauini) or close to farms. Migrations to cities may take place from any indigenous lands that are unable to sustain their people any longer. The native population has migrated to urban centers, since even in those cases where they do possess demarcated lands, people may lack the means of production needed to adequately feed and maintain themselves there.

Many indigenous youths also travel to urban areas with an adventurous spirit as part of their personal development or as a strategy of their people, as described in the section on schooling in Chapter 2. That was typically the case of the Cashinahua youths, who mostly came from those indigenous areas already close to urban areas or whose parents had contacts with non-Indian "friends." The need for indigenous people to embody the rules of the city in order to enhance their own autonomy in changing social situations was described to me by a 17-year-old Cashinahua boy in Rio Branco, who provided a clear explanation of why it is important for the indigenous group to have people working in the cities and how he planned to become a spokesperson for his community.

I want to spend ten years in São Paulo. To study and complete college and all that. It took me a year to get used to the city. Now the community wants me to take part in our association. But my head is still small. I shall grow more. As I am a son of a leader, I have to learn more than my father: to run after people, make contacts, and do a course to get a flight license. In the village, they need a leader who runs after people . . .

There [in the village] one learns the mysteries, stories. But I'm not only going to value and preserve, I'm also going to show. Ancient people, then their children, and now us. Now we have to undertake research and travel. And we are not going to have difficulties any more. We will receive strength, support.

A few years later, the boy traveled to Rio de Janeiro with a group of other Cashinahua people for an event presenting indigenous festivities. He had already made many contacts while in the state capital of Acre because his father was a famous indigenous leader. Eventually the Cashinahua boy stayed in the Brazilian metropolis, where he started to lead shamanic sessions that made the Cashinahua known to a bigger audience. Today he is married and has a small family in Rio de Janeiro. His story is exceptional and he is now known as a Cashinahua shaman and spokesperson even abroad. He has brought the Cashinahua and their way of thinking to the biggest cities, areas dominated by nonnatives.

For the native young people themselves, defining their presence in the city provokes some mixed feelings. Those youths who had lived in the city for a long time said that it is difficult to maintain their relationship with two very different places: their indigenous community and the city as a place of nonindigenous knowledge. Moreover, materializing indigenousness is sometimes required in order to be able to communicate with outsiders in a way that elicits respect. Similarly, Ahmed (2000) describes how Australian aboriginal women speak of learning to become aboriginal for the dominant society. Ahmed sees this as a narrative of "learning to be strange." In contrast to previous generations who were subjected to the politics of acculturation and had to dress, act, and speak like white people, the indigenous youths now have to show their indigenousness. This can be complicated when previous generations have experienced oppression and the deprecation of indigenous lifestyles, philosophy, and art.[6]

One of the Apurinã twin brothers who had lived in Rio Branco for some years explained that if they had stayed in the village, they would have learned better their indigenous language and knowledge linked to life in the reserve. But it was important for them to learn how to speak Portuguese. The other brother added that they had gone to so many offices in search of support toward their studies in the city, they could not remember all the places they had visited. The Federal Secretary of Indigenous Peoples had refused to help them, because they had already lived for some time in the city. Hence they were unentitled to demand their rights as Indians. However, the brothers had strong connections with their native community and their land. One of the brothers explained that after living in the city, though, they no longer even looked like Indians.

At first it seemed to me that those young people who had been in more contact with the dominant society were caught in a liminal zone, neither full members of the reserves nor full residents of the city (Virtanen 2010a). Later it became more apparent, though, that young Indians have learned to recognize the possibilities open to them in different social situations, which are defined by their attitudes, gestures, and issues, meaning that certain symbolic capitals are acknowledged within them. In the urban areas, a variety of social situations are produced, based on class, race, ethnicity, occupation, gender, age, and so forth, creating more struggles for power. Young indigenous people attempt to make the world comprehensible by interpreting the different social environments according to their actors, a topic discussed in Chapter 7.

On the other hand, it has been one of the characteristics and *raisons d'être* of native groups to look for resources, new ways of acting, and opportunities beyond the places where they live. Mobility in particular has been a constitutive element of their lives, at least temporarily or among some members of their communities. Even nomadism can be strategically planned (Gomes 2000, 143) and seen as part of a group's history and ecological agency (Rival 2002). However, social networks created in some places may become essential to people's everyday lives and some of the abilities learned in the reserve or in the city are inapplicable to the other context. Therefore many indigenous families and young people end up staying in the cities.

In urban areas of Highland South America, for example, indigenous populations have formed the majority of the population. By contrast, Brazilian indigenous peoples are relatively new inhabitants in modern Amazonian cities, and the dominant society still associates them with distant forest areas. However, it should not be forgotten that there were already many big settlements in the pre-Columbian period (Heckenberger et al. 2008; Pärssinen, Schaan, and Ranzi 2009) and the invisibility of Indians in urban areas only occurred, in fact, after colonization. Many contemporary cities were built on top of the previous indigenous settlements in strategical geographic locations. Gilbert ([1994] 1998, 23) also notes that the pre-Columbian heritage is largely absent in modern Latin American cities.

The municipalities of Manaus and São Gabriel da Cachoeira are among those that have recently decreed policies relating to their Indian populations. In Northwestern Amazonia, in 2003 the municipality of São Gabriel da Cachoeira approved three native languages—Nheengatu, Tukano, and Baniwa—as its official idioms along with Portuguese. Likewise, the Pankararu have become acknowledged residents of São Paulo, among its many other indigenous residents. In terms of more long-term and permanent residence in the city, FUNAI has slowly acknowledged the rise in the native population in the cities and thus recognized the fact that the entity faces new challenges. Since FUNAI's

National Conference of Indigenous Peoples, held in Brasilia in 2006, Indians in urban areas have been mentioned as a separate group needing specific assistance in matters of land, education, and health care. However, there is no special sector for urban native issues. As well as facilitating their entrance into state schools, the central issue under debate is still that of cultural education. Manaus was one of the first Amazonian cities in Brazil to attempt to offer linguistic and cultural training to those native adolescents living in the city long-term, having employed indigenous teachers residing in the city to teach indigenous students. In 2006, this initiative was implemented specifically in response to integration problems faced by native children in their school classes.

Today the reserve and city populations have generally become closer to each other owing to the number of social, political, economic, ritual, intellectual, and cultural relations between them. The populations of the city and reserve, belonging to the same native group, should be considered elements of the same social system. Borja and Castells (1997) have argued that we live in the world of *generalized urbanization* and that instead of cities, we encounter urban-regional territories that encompass the field of economic, political, cultural, and communicational relations between cities and rural areas. Indigenous people in cities usually have complex relations with their original villages, and many native populations today share knowledge and ways of acting and doing things beyond the cities and reserves, since they may be residents in both areas. This helps them differentiate themselves as the same indigenous group, insofar as they define what they are or are not. Urban centers have proved to be essential interethnic spaces in terms of strengthening indigenousness insofar as the latter is contrasted and valued in relation to new elements, especially those unconnected to urban consumerism. Indigenousness links to global urbanity and this is also where it links to international indigenous issues. Urbanity sets cultural boundaries by categorizing things in a new way and generates struggles for further power between the villages and the city. For instance, the native communities of the reserves see problems in the fact that those speaking for the community actually live in the city. In this sense, migration has been both positive and negative.

In the city, even though the urban space represents a multitude of ideologies and values, the rules of the new situations may be easier to internalize because of the role models and intermediaries potentially available. Furthermore, most urban native adolescents have already been living in the city for a long time, meaning that they are more familiar with the varying rules of social games than young people who have lived far from urban areas. For people in the villages, though, the national "development" initiatives that arrive in the form of state education, health care, environmental initiatives, and development projects can cause new experiences of oppression when no intermediaries are present or indigenous everyday lives and traditions are not properly taken into account. In fact, the clash is not between two different "worlds" but between different viewpoints on the world and the processes of learning and acting within it. In areas isolated from urban areas, the clash between two different value systems may cause more feelings of impotence due to the inability to absorb the new knowledge by perceiving it as part of one's own actions and memories, or to produce one's own ways of adapting and transforming it. Hence it is even more difficult to obtain harmony in the reserve between the world of non-Indians and individual dreams for reproduction of power. On the other hand, these contradictions are also related to the lack of state health care, education and environment policies.

Like many migrants who belong to two worlds, native adolescents living in urban area have to concern themselves with the relations between their indigenous communities and the dominant society, and with finding their place in the complex urban social structure. For native youths in the city, symbolic capital and identity may receive their strength from the reserve, a process that subsequently determines their outlook. Thus urban native youths bring new representations to the "center" from what the dominant population identifies as the margins. At the same time the "urban" has become a permanent element of the reserves. It provides an element with which life in the reserve is continually contrasted: a place to be avoided or a source of additional power. But, as is typically the case in Amazonian sociality, those who no longer live in close proximity to their original communities and territories are usually said to be "lost" (são perdidos) by the people in the reserve.[7] Simultaneously, though, Indian villages have become more visible as they have become seen from the city by urban members of their population and the nation-state. Some of the urban native residents have been important agents in creating and bringing new information to their own indigenous groups. Urban residents can make this unknown space more familiar for those living in the reserves, when people in the reserves come to learn from and in the center.[8]

In the city, tracing people's homelands therefore separates native youths into various indigenous groups, an affiliation made visible not only in their physical appearance but also in their ways of talking, eating, walking, and dressing. In many contexts in contemporary Amazonian cities, the appearance and visibility of indigenous agency with all its capacities is something new, an empowering experience for indigenous people. Beyond the family and their own indigenous group, the bonds with other known indigenous people (especially those from one's own ethnic group) also provide the basis for sociality in the city. Thus, as Lasmar (2005) noted in São Gabriel de Cachoeira, new relations of reciprocity are created through the exchange of information, such as knowing how relatives are faring in the reserve. The search for indigenous origins is an indication that native adolescents are constructing their newly embodied persons, looking to obtain self-equilibrium and develop practices that successfully negotiate between the various demands and challenges. Indigenous embodiment is actually like two sides of a coin: to Indians it represents "I am one of you" and to others "I am not like you." For example, when assuming posts in indigenous organizations or participating in cultural gatherings, young native people openly manifest themselves as part of the indigenous population and thus as people distinct from other Brazilians. It is also the individual's own attempt to communicate with the surrounding world and make it a meaningful place.

When the reserve is viewed from the urban area, the reserve becomes the invisible and external dimension of everyday life, since it is located far from the city. This establishes the contradictions between the native populations in the city and those in the reserve, but indigenous ways of doing things and relatedness can be strengthened and protected with the help of the city and the reserve working together, so that positions, actions, and objects receive different meanings in dynamic ways. In the present-day world, both the natural environment and the prominent actors in the urban areas, such as governmental officials and NGO staff, pose a kind of challenge to native groups in the reserve. The natural environments surrounding native peoples in the reserves may not sustain them in the future, a possibility that requires them to establish new positions with the state and other actors. Hence both the urban and natural environments define the symbolic limits of these communities as "the other."

What is important to note is that indigenousness relates especially to the memories of certain territories. In a sense, therefore, indigenousness is rooted in places toward which looking and speaking are directed. The territory has a fundamental meaning that unites people—not only those inhabiting indigenous lands but also those living outside them. Indian lands are the point of reference for the construction of group identity in urban areas. Even though the young urban Indians I interviewed had little or no contact with their people's reserves, whether because of internal conflicts or the fact they had migrated to the city from rural locations close to farms, they also identified with certain regions and areas where their grandparents had lived. The significance of the original territory of the native youngsters feeds into the construction of identity in the day-to-day interactions of native youths, especially in urban settings. For instance, as described earlier in this chapter, the Manchineri people in the reserve very often talked about the reserve in contrast to the city, just as those in the city contrasted the city to the "village." This fluidity of Otherness seems to explain why for both native youths in the reserve and those in the city, the original territory has an ambivalent quality. For native youths, the corporeal and spatial distinctions found in their own culture provide the primary means for categorizing behavior and, in the very same process, for creating and maintaining a traditional value system as a viable resource for adapting to the demands imposed by changing social circumstances. On one hand, the indigenous villages are the places of continuity and abundance. On the other hand, reserves are areas that lack something: there are no capacities for transformation. For both these contexts, the village or the reserve is the other—the "frontier area" where everything turns out differently. As part of the same complex, for young people in the reserve, visiting the city is a milestone in their active agency, just as visits to the reserve may be for young indigenous people from the city. They are usually the temporal spaces where cultural categories are maintained and created. Furthermore, cities are associated with knowledge and studying in the city especially prepares young people for negotiations, new posts, and responsibilities, as well as enabling them to explain their origins, history, challenges, and needs, as I discuss in the next chapter. Political negotiations usually occur in the city, and it comprises the space of indigenous politics. Translocations between the reserve and the city prepare young native people for the new economic, cultural, and political responsibilities that they now assume within their communities.

CHAPTER 5

Speaking and Acting for Many

Our analysis of the interaction between forest and urban areas—the latter linked to commodities, education, health care, negotiations, development projects, cultural presentations, and employment—has already provided a background understanding of how indigenous communities need to organize themselves differently in political and social terms. Young people's ideas show that they want to have better control of their land and resources, and to free themselves from external dominance. In achieving this aim, these communities employ creativity and their own resources. This chapter attempts to give a deeper view of the contemporary dilemmas faced by the Manchineri community and how, in a landscape riddled with difficulties but also opportunities, young people have become involved in taking on responsibilities. I examine power, the creation of alliances, and generational shifts in the roles of today's spokespeople. In the first section, I explore questions of authority and the contemporary negotiation partners of indigenous groups, and subsequently the issues of responsibility and the intermediary roles and practices that have emerged in a context where the sought-after qualities of the current spokespeople favor the younger generation and, ultimately, the movement of indigenous students in the state of Acre.

Authority and Alliances

When I first visited the Manchineri reserve to discuss my research project, a young Manchineri man would often come to talk to me during my stay. On my last day, he explained his interest in our conversations and said, "I like to speak to *payri* (whites) since that way I learn new things." At that time he remained quiet during the collective meetings, but he was becoming a gifted spokesman for the views of the Manchineri. After this young man was sent to a regional meeting to discuss the locations and characteristics of uncontacted Indians in the region, he was so well heeded that he was later asked to attend other types of meetings. In his first meeting outside the village, where he represented his people, he was able to provide a clear explanation of the Manchineri view of their close encounters with isolated nomads, the Mashco-Piro, on their lands. Another Manchineri young man thanked me greatly for coming to visit him in his house during my longer period of stay in the reserve, telling me that he had now learned how to converse. Young people often declared, "You have to know how to speak." The ability to act as a spokesman and speak Portuguese in a legitimate way with non-Indians and in changing situations is a very important mediatory skill. Learning how to talk with others means entering into a new discourse and representing things from different viewpoints, using other discourses and ways. To ensure productive relations with the state and other actors, spokespeople are expected to bring mobility and dynamics to the community by embodying the power of these others. For many Amerindians, public speaking and verbal performance are the essential marks of political power and one of the ways to embody the person's social identity (Basso 1973; Gregor 1977; Turner 1991; Hill 1993). Speech is a social practice and is often related to power in many cultures.[1]

In order to understand today's intergroup relations, we need to examine the recent history of Manchineri spokespeople and the issues on which they have negotiated. When FUNAI began to transfer the Manchineri and Jaminawa peoples to the Extrema village in 1977, it asked both groups to designate their leaders. The same happened later in new villages when more people moved to the area. Usually the village chief was a man from the family that had first arrived and "opened" the site. Most of the village leaders were still the same from this earlier period, but in some villages the leaders had changed frequently owing to their inability to run the village. FUNAI initiated the first economic projects in the reserve, such as growing coffee and rice, in order to provide a substitute for the income gained from production for bosses, but later these projects were terminated due to the contrasting views on people's remuneration for their work. In the 1990s, rice production continued, but transportation to Sena Madureira, as well as the low price and difficulty of selling rice, made the enterprise too problematic. In the mid-1980s, various indigenous groups resolved to set up cooperatives, in the area of rubber production for example, founded their own associations, and established relations with the state, international capitalism, and NGOs (Piedrafita Iglesias and Aquino 2005; cf. Fisher 2000).[2]

From the 1980s onward, Manchineri leaders started traveling to the city to participate in the meetings of indigenous peoples. As mentioned earlier, the leader of Extrema village was also a founding force in the regional indigenous movement, UNI, and started working in its Rio Branco office. He even became employed in two national indigenous organizations, Coordination of Indigenous Organizations of the Brazilian Amazonia (COIAB) and Council for the

Articulation of Indigenous Peoples and Organizations of Brazil (CAPOIB).[3] Since then, people have expected him and his family—also involved in indigenous politics—to bring projects to the village that usually result in different commodities. Everyone had heard the word *project* but few understood what it really meant. While some of the Manchineri moved to urban areas, where they were expected to negotiate for better economic production conditions, other families organized their agriculture, hunting, and fishing practices for their own use only. Recently, where the Manchineri have managed to obtain access to funds for indigenous projects, a new elite has gained control of the community's material goods, such as bank accounts.

Today many of the village leaders have participated in numerous meetings of the indigenous movement in the region. Their challenges have included negotiating in Portuguese over economic relations and demands for health care and education services (see Ramos 1988; Pacheco de Oliveira 2004; Oakdale 2004; Graham 2002). In Acre, the demands of indigenous leaders for land demarcation have also now switched to the negotiations of community spokespeople for projects for environment management, installations of telecommunications technology, equipment for processing natural resources, and other materials. The tasks and confrontations are many.

Amazonian societies have been pictured as lacking the state, coercion, authority, and power (Clastres 1974; Goldman 1963), but recently distinctive forms of Amazonian leadership have been explored. In Lowland South America, social organization and leadership are seen more as part of the production of sociality, knowledge, transformation, and kinship relations. Interaction between leaders and their peoples has been presented in asymmetrical relations to kin relations between children and their parents, as the leader's knowledge and behavior is intended to grow and nurture gendered agencies among the kin group (McCallum 1990). Leaders do not control the group (Clastres 1974), but they can regulate power among the community members and improve their potency by acting in the role of master (Fausto 2008; Costa 2010). What I wish to emphasize here is the spokesperson's importance in constructing a dialogue and acquiring resources in transformative relations with allies and partners who are turned into potential affines. Today young people are increasingly seen as spokespeople in these negotiations.

The Manchineri leader is called *whoksejeru* or *wutsrukate*, meaning "our leader." Village leaders are mostly referred with this term. Historically, the community leader ensured resources for his people and organized collective work: he sent the men to hunt, specified days for making canoes and for swidden production, and set the time for festivities and dances. The village leader's wife was usually the leader of the women, sending the women to make *caiçuma* on a certain day, for example, reflecting the fact that women have a complementary role to their husbands (see also McCallum 1990, 2001). Today these are still acts of village leaders and their wives, but people also take actions more individually. The Manchineri elders also told me that before the arrival of the rubber bosses each village in the Yaco region, besides a *whoksejeru*, had shamans (*kahontshi*) and elders who acted as counselors (*tsru yineru*) of sorts. Political power was shared among them. Moreover, social organization was based on ancestral groups, different *nerus* (*nerune*), some of whom were more powerful. The Kochitsineri, Hahamluneri, and Hijwutatuneri, for instance, started to live together among the Manchineri in the current villages, and these four groups together made one of the strongest groups. The shamans were divided into different kinds, such as the *jimatkaleru*, who was "a wise man," and the *katshinolu koshpakatshri*, "one who knows how to practice and remove sorcery."

When the traditional form of social organization was ruptured during the era of the colonization, an older man would negotiate with the rubber bosses and obtain commodities to be distributed to the group. Today *tsru yineru* still express their opinions in the meetings and are respected, but young people often say that an old person was expected not to say anything to the non-Indians at the meetings, as they do not speak Portuguese. Aside from these elder figures, only the role of village leader and the shamans have persisted as features of contemporary social organization. We can now turn to a closer examination of the current circumstances of the Manchineri in the reserve.

The Manchineri have already experienced invasions of clandestine loggers and drug traffickers coming from the Peruvian border and heading to Brazilian cities downriver. In January 2004, a Manchineri man apprehended a group of three traffickers (two Peruvians and one Brazilian) carrying 12 kilograms of coca past for cocaine. The federal police arrived and took them to Rio Branco to be charged. The drug traffickers and loggers are believed to be heavily armed, meaning the indigenous groups of the area are afraid of them. These fears reminded me of the stories about the so-called time of flight. In Extrema, the village closest to the Peruvian border, the young women were afraid that the strangers or isolated nomadic Indians, the Mashco-Piro, feeling hounded, might appear at their homes when their husbands were away hunting, leaving them alone at home with the children. A group of loggers had already arrived once in Extrema, though they were soon arrested and their GPS receivers confiscated. I asked one girl about this incident, and she replied, "We were afraid because they were the ones who had killed the Manchineri in ancient times. We already knew that, and we were afraid. We had never seen them and we were afraid."

The Mamoadate indigenous reserve is the largest in the state of Acre. None of the Manchineri has ever walked along all the borders of their reserve. The Manchineri adolescents expressed their concern over the security of their lands and the availability of adequate surveillance equipment, such as small motors that can be fitted to a canoe for use in inspecting the areas upriver with shallower waterways. For the Manchineri, the security of their lands has become an international issue as logging and oil companies operate in the frontier region, with many roads being built on the Peruvian side, the upland headwater area of their reserve. The contribution of the state and the neighboring countries in protecting and controlling access is crucial.[4] The illegal exploitation of natural resources in the indigenous reserves not only harms the fragile ecosystems; it also damages the livelihoods of the indigenous peoples who draw their different forms of sustenance from the forest. Furthermore, the forest has a spiritual meaning for these peoples.

Besides illegal logging, drug trafficking, overhunting, and overfishing on the indigenous land and in the surrounding region, contemporary threats to the Mamoadate reserve also include the impacts of the BR-317 highway (completed in 2002) and the international bridge between Brazil and Peru, opened in 2006, 50 miles (80 kilometers) from the Yaco River. Despite this fact, transportation from the city to the reserve itself remains a challenge. Sometimes it takes too long to transfer a patient to the hospital in emergency cases like snakebites. A number of telephone booths were installed in the largest villages at the end of 2007 and VHF radios are also used but they are constant problems. Communication by VHF radio with the urban health centers is made just twice a day (one hour each time) and serious accidents or other emergencies obviously do not necessarily happen at these set times. A few patients have already died because an airplane took too long to arrive. The indigenous health center, *Casa de Saúde Indígena* (CASAI), in Rio Branco, where patients usually have to stay for a long time, was also the subject of criticism. A young man told me that when you go there with one illness, you come back with two more.

The negotiation meetings and cooperation talks often take place in the reserve but are also held in cities. The contemporary Manchineri village leaders, who are older men, are not necessarily good speakers, but they think of different ways to provide things for their people. In recent years, with increased interaction with the state and many other actors, the village leaders consider who will be the right people to act in the new educational and negotiation roles to ensure that resources are acquired and properly distributed. They accept that the skills and courage of the new generation are needed. Moreover, the village leaders frequently used to host visitors in their own houses, but now they usually appoint younger people to accompany the government officials and NGO staff when they visit and to work as their interpreters. However, shamans and people performing these new roles may try to show their power by dictating who can be accepted as a collaborative partner, and by inviting people to the reserve and hosting them, the power of these outsiders can be experimented with.

Contrary to people in the new representational roles (such as association coordinators), who I shall discuss in the following section, village leaders have usually not spent lengthy periods in urban areas where they could become more familiar with the new political, environmental, and cultural programs and concepts used by nonnatives. Chaumeil (1990) and Brown (1993) have noted that leadership is no longer based on kinship or ritual expertise, because new cultural brokers have acquired authority. In the Manchineri village meetings, younger people often stood up and explained things to elders when they had knowledge from outside. The young men in particular have visited the municipalities more often. Young people may also have nonindigenous clothes and hairstyles, making them appear more visually familiar to nonindigenous visitors and in other interethnic situations. Generally speaking, young people have acquired more power in Amazonian indigenous societies. The intermediary work usually centers on cultural translation, trying to take into account the different backgrounds of their own community and the nonnatives (see Graham 2002; Virtanen 2009b).

Besides the importance of speaking in public and intermediation, there is another aspect that is typical to the relationship between a Manchineri leader and his people: respect. A Manchineri leader leaves everyone to do his or her own work and make his or her own decisions, which is also taken as respect toward them. Describing native conceptions of the good life among the Piaroa, Overing (1988) notes that the ideal is to live tranquilly, which means the person maintains a balance of responsibilities, knowledge, and emotions. These are precisely the qualities that people with leadership should possess, fulfilling their responsibilities, using knowledge to help their people, and providing resources without overlooking anyone.

The value attributed to respect is also reflected in the ideas of the young people, specifically in terms of the kinds of behavior they would like to adopt and pass on to their own children. They wish to live a life guided by the ideals of respect, harmony, responsibility, hospitality, trust, and obedience to parents. The youths said that their parents, grandparents, uncles, and aunts were the important people for them, emphasizing how much they respected them. Younger people also assert that they should obey their parents and older people. In the reserve people often remarked, "This is what my father tells me to do." Moreover, they frequently said that it is important to obey and help their parents when they tell them "not to wander around, and not to do anything that they should not do." The many different things that the community members were expected to do were listed in the answer of a 19-year-old young woman: "Not to touch the things of other people, not to abandon [our] language, always to be willing to make any kind of handicraft, welcome people who come from the outside, learn at school and all the community's activities, and respect old people."

Those young people who were already married and in preadulthood especially wished themselves to be respected and wanted other people not to gossip or circulate rumors about them. To be respected also determines how the person behaves and how he or she is received and addressed. That also creates kin relations. One Manchineri boy was doing military service in Rio Branco, and he had noticed that one of the differences with nonnatives was that the Indians have more respect for each other. Among the Manchineri, conflicts between families cause avoidance of contact, but real disputes usually arise in the festivities when drunken people start arguing and jealousies are aroused.

The village meetings still remain moments in which different spokespeople can display their oratory prowess and power relations are at stake. Negotiating skills are tested in the context of political events that create spaces for people to demonstrate their knowledge on new topics and concepts, as well as how to use new words and ways of speaking. In general, participation in the meetings is important: those attending can see who is capable of acting as a spokesperson and news is presented for discussion. People were upset if the meetings were held without their knowledge. During the communal meetings in the reserve, people can also indicate their importance simply by using a notebook and pencil. The village meetings have been typical leadership rituals where the chiefs of the settlements have shown their power through specific rhetorical techniques, forms of address, and positioning people as a group, as highlighted by researchers working in the Xingu (Franchetto 2000; Basso 1973). These verbal rites enable leaders to show their political position in relation to other community members and even to other villages. By contrast, Manchineri leaders rarely use such verbal rites, though they do coordinate which people will perform the negotiation roles with outsiders.

The indigenous groups are today broadening their networks in order to cooperate with the state, governmental organizations, NGOs, companies, people interested in native spirituality, and so forth.[5] They can be regarded as people to be turned into potential affines (Viveiros de Castro 2001; cf. Kelly 2011). The networks of Indians have enlarged and are greatly motivated by financial programs and resources directed toward indigenous peoples. In the 1980s, the political organization of Amazonian indigenous peoples was empowered by alliances with environmentalists, trade unions, NGOs, the church, and "friends of the Indians," typically journalists, lawyers, artists, university researchers, and anthropologists (Ramos 1998; Gomes 2000). Since 1985, the period of redemocratization, civic participation has changed in Brazil. Indigenous politics is composed of practices and discourses in national and international indigenous movements and associations, as well as political actions at federal, national, and international levels that oppose the dominant society and unite indigenous peoples. This politics can be called indigenism, a global and national phenomenon (Larrain 2000; Niezen 2003).[6] In the terms set out by Conklin and Graham (1995), indigenous organizations and indigenism forms a middle ground for encounters with the national population, even if the "friends of the Indians" have often maintained a romantic view of indigenous peoples.

In Brazil since the 1990s, the construction of new social identities and social actors, including indigenous movements, has been one significant consequence of postcolonialism, neoliberalism, and decentralization (Ramos 1998). International contacts and changes at the global level in relation to the world's indigenous peoples have given new strength to Brazil's indigenous peoples,[7] while also emphasizing their differences (cf. Chaumeil 1990; Warren and Jackson 2002). Indigenous peoples have become more conscious of their position and opportunities in the political arena as a result of these democratization and modernization processes, as well as the "modernization of indigeneity," a movement that had already begun among indigenous peoples themselves, though different age groups, as well as differences between indigenous peoples residing in the forest and in the urban environment, have led to distinct forms of participation in these processes. Moreover, even though the current generation of young native Amazonians may no longer be involved so heavily in pursuing territorial claims, unlike their parents, young people often act as mediators and intermediaries for their communities, as we have seen earlier. They also take representative roles and positions in interethnic politics and the indigenous movement, positioning themselves differently in relation to the state as indigenous peoples.

The biggest change is that there is now much more cooperation with the state education, culture, and environment offices; municipal governments; and NGOs, because of the financial programs these offer to indigenous peoples. The willingness of municipal leaders to work with indigenous peoples in Acre state is largely an influence of its governors. This can be seen, in my view, as a new fifth phase in the history of the Amazonian Indians: the time of partnerships (*tempo dos parceiros*). It forms a continuation of the time of rights, which followed the time of captivity, the time of flight, and the time of large community houses (Ôchoa and Araújo Teixeira [1997] 2002). Next I shall look in more detail at the new indigenous representation intermediation and spokesperson roles in more detail.

Current Positions of Responsibility and Generational Shifts

The new positions of responsibility and representation at the village and communal level have caused significant changes in the roles performed by village leaders. Contemporary challenges and contacts have led to the emergence of new social actors and social identities, such as people with new responsibilities who act as important mediators between the villages, the Manchineri and other indigenous groups, Indians and non-Indians, and reserves and urban areas. In fact, young men from the villages have gained much more symbolic capital after taking on many new kinds of pedagogic roles: the positions of indigenous teachers (*professor indígena*), health agents (*agente indígena de saúde*), and agroforestry agents (AAFi: *agente agroflorestal indígena*), as well as political posts at a broader level, such as acting as representatives within indigenous organizations or the local government. A women's representative (*representante das mulheres*) is also now nominated in every village, but besides the work of these women, there are only two female health agents in the Manchineri villages as a whole. These new positions have introduced many novel practices into the reserve, including those of the sanitation agents (*agentes de saneamento*), who take care of water supplies in the villages, environmental agents (*agentes ambientais*), responsible for environmental monitoring and legal issues, and the person responsible for the school premises.

People are appointed to these positions of responsibility in communal meetings. Both the men and women chosen for these communal representational roles usually come from prestigious families, such as those of the village chiefs, shamans, or good hunters. They have seen from very close up what it means to perform a prestigious leadership role. The children of those leaders who have been involved in indigenous politics and the native movement also tend to continue in their fathers' footsteps. They learn from their parents in urban centers, just as they would have learned different tasks in the reserve. However, the completion of training courses in urban areas, especially organized for some of these posts, is usually compulsory after the village has nominated a person for the task. In Acre in particular, the pro-Indian organizations have been pioneers in promoting education in various indigenous communities, including the training of indigenous teachers and health agents. Thus the ways in which praise and prestige are constructed have changed.

The "naming" for new positions has given a tangible "existence" to these new roles, even if the people involved do little in practice, owing to the lack of training and material resources. This is the case, for example, with the sanitation agent. Maintaining professional skills requires new resources, such as training courses and equipment. This can be seen in the problems faced by a 23-year-old village motor mechanic, Renato. When I asked him whether he had worked in the village after his course, he said that if a motor breaks, they have no spare parts in the village as they are too expensive. The same problem confronted the health agents who pointed out that they lacked the materials and equipment needed for their work. I even met some people holding a particular title who did not know what their work or responsibility was meant to be. However, the holders of these new positions do acquire symbolic capital, since they receive recognition from their group and the non-Manchineri (government officials). Naming can therefore act as "social magic" (Bourdieu [1991] 1997, 223). At the village level, other traditionally recognized social roles are good hunters and hard workers: these people are respected, though they have neither their own titles nor political importance.

Some new positions of responsibility in fact require recognition from the dominant society, such as that given to indigenous teachers by the municipal secretary of education, to indigenous health agents by the state FUNASA office, and to indigenous agroforestry agents by CPI-Acre. The role of the indigenous teacher is the most visible. The health agents also act more frequently since they see the patients in the village and contact the indigenous health center, CASAI, run by FUNASA, or alternatively give medicines to those who need them, when these are available in the village. If the patient needs to be transported to the city, health agents organize the transfer. They also accompany the FUNASA team when it visits the villages. The new social roles in Manchineri social organization offer fresh ways of understanding people, personifying them in the community and creating new hierarchies.

Consequently, the new social roles have brought new criteria for defining a person's reputation, including the competence, image of respectability, and honor linked to the moral order. On the other hand, positions of responsibility and types of leaders probably varied in earlier times, too, but some of their present-day characteristics are participation in the dialogue with non-indigenous knowledge, generational changes, and increased opportunities for young women. The gender perspective was taken into account in the projects of some NGOs and governmental organizations, and nonindigenous government officials and NGO staff work with the women. The young men were already used to working temporarily on farms, during harvests or logging, and thus had more experience of interactions with non-Indians. In fact, the new post of women's representative had to be filled in all the villages when the role was set up by the local movement of indigenous women, Group of Indigenous Women of the Union of Indigenous Nations of Acre and Southern Amazonas (GMI-UNI), in the late 1990s.

Overall, literacy skills, "indigenous knowledge" (including, for instance, the oral history of the past and shamanic skills), and the ability to speak Portuguese, along with the young person's social networks, all play a key role in their entry into this space of communication with nonnatives and natives alike. Some people may have charismatic personalities and thus become spokespeople, but success in the role after nomination to a post more often depends on a continuous process of learning how to act and how to present one's ideas in public. Good social networks can support the person in this endeavor and nonindigenous pro-Indian friends have been important figures in offering encouragement and platforms for indigenous peoples to speak. Pro-Indian friends can also teach how to benefit from technology and many other empowering tools for expressing one's views, networking, and making others into relations. Overall, acting in indigenous politics and as a spokesperson is shaped by the new possibilities for accumulating cultural, social, and economic resources. The new positions of responsibility involve an attempt to master their specialized knowledge: to produce bodies with specifically human points of view (Virtanen 2009b).

In Acre many political meetings for indigenous people are organized in such a way that only a few members of the indigenous communities, usually people known to the nonindigenous organizers, are invited to the meeting place. These encounters offer opportunities to meet new people and obtain free board and transportation for trips that would otherwise be very expensive. For the Manchineri, the change has been huge given that until the end of the 1990s they lived in fairly marked isolation. Young people are often among the participants, as they know how to communicate the views of their people. However, although the younger generation participates in these meetings, not everyone in the communities is interested in taking on a role of responsibility. In the meetings, indigenous people usually create networks with non-Indians because they are curious to learn more about the other, understand better the essences of these other beings, and acquire contextualized knowledge of certain situations, which can be empowering for themselves. They try to identify within a larger framework the points shared with the actors with whom they relate, looking to express themselves in a way that achieves understanding with these others.

In political negotiations and many other situations, the indigenous youngsters appeal to the law and speak about their rights as native people. They were aware of having special rights that were not just concepts but also of ways of relating to others. Indigenous peoples' claims for their territorial, cultural, and human rights have been one of the issues shaping South American indigenous peoples' relationship to the dominant society and to other indigenous peoples (Ramos 1998; Warren and Jackson 2002). Knowledge of legal issues forms part of new learning that has changed the identity of the village community. As 18-year-old Artur, an agroforestry agent, said,

> Cristina, I think we are improving, by knowing the law. In the past, we did not know our rights, but now many people do. Things have therefore changed a lot. It is not like before. We didn't know what we were doing then. Or what we were about to do. Now people have the knowledge needed to act. For instance, every community has a chief and agroforestry agent. And we have meetings together with the community. But before nobody did that. We shall see whether it will be better in the future.

Young people understand indigenous cultural and territorial rights in a way that is partly similar to older people. They subjectivize them and associate them with certain people and institutions, such as FUNAI, the Brazilian presidency, and pro-Indian organizations. However, older people who have not visited these institutions or participated in meetings with them have problems understanding how the laws work or what their purpose is. For older leaders, territorial and cultural rights are difficult to observe in their local contexts. An older Apurinã village leader, from the Amazonas state, complained,

> I don't know what kind of rights Indians have. The whites say that Indians have rights. In the meetings they say that Indians have to be respected by the law. But I don't see this respect, this right that Indians have. Even the government, the president, says that one has to respect Indians. But the law that the president and the whites actually design does not show respect. We even say that we have no rights because people can enter the demarcated area, they hunt, fish, cut down trees, they do whatever they want. They say that we have to photograph them, but I don't know how. I don't know what the law is about. So I don't know if Indians have rights. I know about my culture, but about the world of white people, I don't know.

In contrast, some young people have created their own speaking style, composing a hybrid language that combines fashionable concepts like diversity and rights and often contrasts the indigenous community's way of doing things with that of the dominant society, while expressing the opinions of the community during the training courses or meetings. This involved creating a new point of view and transforming the knowledge for their own use. In both the reserve and the city, we can observe young people adopting a political terminology derived from a preexisting field of actors, including public authorities, officials, politicians, and the indigenous movement. Typical discourses in this context refer to indigenous rights, environmental values, and special forms of development, and they are more and more involved with national and global issues. Tuhiwai Smith (1999) suggests that the appearance of terms such as *self-determination* and *indigenous rights* in the talks is promising, but they must also be seen as a form of wielding power. We could add: this talk must be seen as the use of power by certain community members.

Unequal power relations between elders and those of the young generation result in inequalities in both linguistic and "foreign" political skills. Those who have participated in articulating indigenous people's concerns are more able to articulate themselves, since the meetings include hours of listening of talks. Consequently, the meaning of laws and rights, for instance, becomes clearer. A young Manchineri teacher, who was at that time working in Assis Brasil, said that "our right is to know and to be acknowledged. To be acknowledged like any other citizen. White people still have lots of prejudice, and the Manchineri association helps in that. The problem is that legislation is very slow. It cannot be put into practice. That's what I learned in the indigenous movement and by traveling to other places." In Rio Branco, another Manchineri man, a son of the leader who had started to work in the UNI, active in indigenous politics, summed up his ideas about indigenous rights: "Our right is our land, but only the space we actually need. And the question of culture and how to manage it. We are consulted by ILO."

I will not enter here into a detailed discourse analysis, but the differences in forms of speech can be seen, for example, in the fondness with which some Manchineri adolescents used words of foreign origin, such as *sustainable development* or *globalization*, after they had heard and learned them from government visitors or other outsiders. They tried to use the terms and expressions that would be familiar to nonnatives (see Graham 2002). Among the Manchineri, some people tend to monopolize language associated with power.

As indigenous peoples' discussions with public authorities and other actors have increased, so they have adopted urban political structures and governmental policies. The MAPKAHA organization was established in 2003 to officially represent the Manchineri and defend their rights. The name MAPKAHA comes from the words *Manxinerune Ptohi Kajpaha Hajene*, "Organization of All the Manchineri of the Yaco River." The creation of this organization, however, altered the power relations within the Manchineri population, especially in the

Figure 5.1   Young men conversing with an embassy official in Rio Branco

terms of negotiations with non-Indians. The first executive secretary (*Secretario Executivo*) of the secretariat had been living in the city for more than twenty years, his father being the first leader to have worked for UNI. He was asked by a young Manchineri teacher to gather their people together and take care of the legal matters involved in officially registering the organization. In 2005, MAP-KAHA was the most active. The Manchineri no longer count on the assistance of FUNAI but have looked for new resources through cooperation projects with other institutions.

When I returned to Acre for the third time in 2006, I was very surprised that such a young organization had established so many new contacts[8] and project proposals aimed at preserving their cultural and natural resources. Two of the new projects were included in the IPDP (The Indigenous Peoples Demonstration Project, *Programa Demonstrativo dos Povos Indígenas*), which received funding from the Group of 7 countries.[9] The aim of the first IPDP project was cultural recuperation and unification of the ethnic group, which was something that the funders themselves expected, but in addition to the program guidelines, the Manchineri's own political organization aimed to "register and recover the Manchineri cultural tradition."[10] The project concretized an exchange with the Yine from Diamante, Peru, and a workshop was organized in Mamoadate in 2005. The results of the project (DVD and publication) are still not finished, however, owing to leadership problems in the organization. The produced material has remained in the hands of different Manchineri residing in the city and thus beyond the control of the people in the reserve. Besides the rice and beans already produced in small amounts for the local markets, the ideas for the small-scale extraction and processing of various natural resources found in the reserve, such as natural oils from the *copaiba* and *andiroba* trees, did not materialize.

When I asked the youths what qualities a village chief will need to have in the future, the emphasis was on the ability to intermediate between not only the Manchineri and non-Indians but also those working in the city and those in the village. A young man from the Extrema village said,

> I would like to have two *caciques* [chiefs]: one to represent Manchineri culture and heritage, in the community, you know, myths, ceramics. And a common chief, who would accompany MAPKAHA, to seek out partnership projects together with MAPKAHA. He would be there to look for places for people, more education for teachers, explaining how the laws work. And for us to know what goes on in the meetings, to know how to protest, to welcome people, you for instance, Cristina. To ask where you are coming from. He would ask for a meeting and all the community would go there. And he'd assumed responsibility for explaining to the community.

Young people still see it as the task of leaders to be a provider, a transmitter of knowledge, and thus a protector. The new political representation of the Manchineri has brought little dynamism to the villages. Representing Manchineri for others is also becoming so important that a specific person to master this kind of knowledge is needed. Meanwhile, village leaders need to acquire more authority and put more pressure on the state officials and decision makers.

In general, one of the most important changes regarding the indigenous population's relation with the dominant society is the arrival of capital in the area in the form of international and national funding that the indigenous peoples can obtain through their representative legal entities. Much importance is given nowadays to people who know how to negotiate financial resources with the governmental and NGOs through indigenous community projects. According to one young Manchineri man, anyone "making a project" to the community is regarded as a saint in the reserve. However, the salaries paid for some of the positions of responsibility, along with the rumors about the amount of project funding arriving for the community, have caused internal conflicts and disrupted generational relations. The fact that the village chiefs do not receive any remuneration has weakened their position. Teachers receive the highest salary, then agroforestry and health agents. Some people complain that some agroforestry agents, for instance, do not perform any work. Similar complaints are directed at those who receive salaries working in the local government. At the beginning, the MAPKAHA coordination group made its decisions at the meeting of all the villages in the reserve, but these kinds of meetings were rarely organized later. The coordinators often state the reason to be the lack of time and the transportation costs. As one example, a group of consultants for the "Indigenous Games of Brazil" had promised Extrema village a certain amount of money; however, the Manchineri in the city arranging the consultants' trip to the reserve had not informed the Manchineri there of the fact. The people in the village heard about it from the visitors. A young Manchineri man from the reserve therefore returned to the city by small airplane with the group to collect the money.

There are many other situations in which young people act as intermediaries, but here I shall focus on other examples, showing different views between the Manchineri spokespeople in the city and the reserve. The MAPKAHA representatives in the city controlled the project budgets and the bank accounts set up for the organization. The position of MAPKAHA officials in the city is more ambivalent owing to their potential links to economic resources and their distance from everyday life in the reserve (cf. McCallum 1997; Rosengren 2003; Oakdale 2004). The leadership of the organization has changed many times, and the primary motive for replacements has been project money failing to reach the reserve. Another IPDP project was designed for the territory's protection but was never fully granted as the organization's representatives and the people in the reserve could not agree on how the project should be realized. The people from the reserve were expected to carry out the physical demarcation of the reserve's borders, but they wanted material resources for this hard work.

When a young man from Extrema village started to work for MAPKAHA as its first director of finance and accountancy, he soon gave up the post saying it was too difficult for him. He had even taken part in a computing course sponsored by the IPDP but felt he was generally unprepared. Although happy with the quality of the teaching, he said that a course lasting just a few days was not enough for him to learn what was needed. Hence he wanted to spend more time in the city to broaden his knowledge of many other things. Later, when the IPDP trained the so-called indigenous project managers (*Gestores de Projetos Indígenas*), the person chosen for the course was a white woman married to a Manchineri coordinator of the MAPKAHA. The aim of the course was to teach the heads of the indigenous groups how to find financial resources and elaborate projects capable of improving the living conditions and allowing these groups to become more independent; the skills taught in the course included how to fill in forms to obtain project funding and how to deal with official bureaucracy. When I asked the Manchineri in the city why people from the reserve are not chosen, I was told that it is difficult to find people who have already completed their school education and who have learned how to live in the urban centers.

In response to these conflicts, people in Jatobá founded their own organization to control the budget money inside their village. In general, they seldom interacted with others due to the missionary presence in the village and the dominance of the Evangelical faith. At the same time, smaller Manchineri settlements with just a few houses also started to be called villages to ensure the provision of schools and sanitation facilities, for instance, to the settlements. In general, the desire for access to technological developments in the reserve was evident, including the wish to have a telephone, television, and computer in each village.

The state and local governments have become some of the villages' most important allies. Technical and infrastructural modifications that have been installed in some reserves, such as new schools, a women's house, and even sanitary facilities constructed in the biggest villages, are all the result of government projects. The youths regarded these as something new—concrete actions undertaken to improve their everyday lives and thus a kind of production that the villagers considered as evidence of the reserve's vitality. Some village residents already used showers and had access to clean water in sanitary facilities, rather than going to the river shore or a spring—although their water pumps did still have constant problems. The hope expressed by the young people in the reserve is for it to become "better organized." For them, the greatest changes faced in recent years, though, have been new encounters with various government and nongovernment agents, and the foundation of the Manchineri political organization. These are all looked upon as a positive change. Contact with the outside world was also their way of viewing the future. This desire was expressed with hope in their eyes, with isolation apparently a thing of the past. A 24-year-old man offered the following reflection: "In the future, as I see it—we shall have more knowledge of people from outside, more contacts with people who come here, like yourself now . . . Before we had no idea what FUNAI was. So knowing about all the [federal] states, this is the future, I think."

A young Manchineri man started work in the Assis Brasil local government, and two others in its municipal education office and indigenous health center. The municipal government invited Manchineri to work there with the aim of recruiting people who could speak the indigenous language and who knew the practices of the reserve. Governmental officials and NGOs are now more likely to negotiate with indigenous representatives working in local governments, with officials from indigenous organizations, and even with people in specified posts of responsibility when they want to implement activities on indigenous lands. These people find themselves in an ambivalent position due to the impossibility of fulfilling all the expectations of the people in the reserve (see Virtanen, forthcoming). The young Manchineri continue to perform different jobs in pan-indigenous organizations in Rio Branco.

The opportunities for employment in an indigenous or cultural organization or in government projects targeted at indigenous peoples that have sprung up in recent years are especially highly valued due to the political, economic, and educational power with which they are potentially associated. It is important to understand the different symbolic and economic resources of spokespeople and those holding positions of responsibility at a community level in order to perceive how prestige is constructed. At the same time various government-run indigenous projects or posts for indigenous peoples in governmental offices have become one of their main means of interacting with the dominant society. For the people already residing in the city, it is also a way to avoid the marginalization experienced by the majority of immigrants living in poor suburbs. These are often the only significant, higher-paid forms of employment that the Manchineri youths could feasibly obtain, rather than work on the farms and in logging. Therefore, indigenous people living in the city may have more power than other poor migrant populations or city dwellers in general; in some senses, they create their own social spaces. In Acre alone, there are today more than thirty indigenous organizations and associations, including cooperatives, regional associations, professional bodies (of indigenous teachers and AAFi's), indigenous women's associations, and indigenous student organizations (Piedrafita Iglesias and Aquino 2005).

Both men and women may also be employed in indigenous politics and indigenous projects that represent indigenous peoples across ethnic boundaries. The new jobs involve less need to engage in hard physical work than continuing to gain a livelihood from agriculture. They therefore alter the person's body. A Manchineri young woman, who had represented the group at the meeting of indigenous women in Rio Branco, had realized that women, too, could support themselves by taking on a paid post in an indigenous organization or by receiving the economic capital involved in some positions of responsibility. According to her, the use of the body would then be different, since these jobs would involve working with the head, easier than the physical work of the plantations. Indigenous politics traditionally involved the sphere of different types of personalized relations between indigenous and nonindigenous subjects from the forest environment, where crucial negotiations occur with forest beings. This new work, by contrast, involved other types of activities in settings different from those the Manchineri had been used to occupy (cf. Lasmar 2005; Andrello 2006, on São Gabriel da Cachoeira).

In general, women have become involved with the knowledge of nonnatives and no longer regard their sphere as just the home and the swiddens. A very young woman often came to talk to me and once asked me how she could do the type of work I was doing. She said that she would like to go and talk to people, and she had already been to city with the aim of studying there. However, in some indigenous communities women's occupation of new communal positions has been opposed. For instance, on the training course for indigenous teachers, the female teachers from other groups often said that they had suffered prejudice. The women said that the men did not like to let them work as teachers. After having a big family they usually became accepted, though, with gender no longer an issue. This can be understood in the context of Amerindian thinking concerning the potency of the female body to alter things, as discussed in Chapter 2, and the fact that only women of a certain social age, knowledge, and experience can become involved with foreign knowledge and beings. However, the women who look to take on communal roles are usually the wives or close kin of persons already in these positions. McCallum (1990, 2010) has discussed how Cashinahua women producing craftwork worked alongside their husbands who took care of the selling the products through cooperatives. Among the Manchineri, the positions of young female health agents and women's representatives have not been questioned, but in both cases the women had already entered motherhood. One of the reasons for this acceptance may also be that they are daughters of village leaders and their husbands were also in communal roles.

It can also be argued that owing to new power structures and relations with dominant society, the danger posed by women's bodies to the community is lessening, a new value having been ascribed to educated women. Education has empowered and "protected" women, especially younger women. As I discussed earlier, schooling is closely related to social age and gender roles, as unmarried young women are the ones who tend to study. In general, the more visible role of some indigenous women has changed the image of the Brazilian Indian both within indigenous communities and in the dominant society, because previously only indigenous men appeared in interethnic relations. This change must be seen in the context of Brazilian national society and to the recent value attributed to educated women with interethnic experience (Virtanen 2010b).

When young women receive salaries for certain posts (namely, as indigenous health agents and teachers), their economic wealth allows them to buy soap, detergents, salt, and other essential everyday commodities in urban areas. These are then shared among their closest kin: sisters, aunts, and grandmothers. Hence it seems that it is no longer only men who are expected to bring money home.[11]

The first women's representatives were the older women skilled in craftwork, which belongs to the women's sphere (except for the production of bows and arrows). Later when the role involved more participation in meetings in urban areas with the other indigenous peoples and non-Indian women in order to discuss the problems faced by women in their communities, younger women were appointed as representatives. The young women could speak better Portuguese and were literate. Nevertheless, part of the reason for their election was that they were usually the ones also interested in learning craftwork, such as weaving and pottery. Instead of being the most important advisors during the seclusion of the girls, older women have begun to transmit their knowledge of craftwork, given that it is becoming more valued in relations with other Indians and non-Indians. So although new positions for women as social actors sometimes bring different generations of women closer together and even empower indigenous women as a group, different social spheres value older and younger women differently.

Generally speaking, generational gaps can be identified insofar as older men and women, who are usually illiterate, have different experiences of being excluded or subordinated, including their lack of education. The young generation is more skilled in speaking outside the community about the problems or issues they consider the most important. The change must be seen in combination with the fact that young women's involvement in new tasks has transformed their positions, experiences, and power relations not only in their relations with non-Indians but also between the generations of indigenous women in terms of economic resources and the topics they bring up for public discussion. Younger women in new positions can speak about the contemporary problems affecting indigenous women, such as alcoholism in the communities or the need for new livelihoods, but they are usually blind to the fact that they are privileged members of their communities, possessing schooling and other interethnic skills, and rarely speak about the problems that the other generations in the reserves wish to air. Older women do not even have the prospect of taking on new social roles of responsibility for their community in the future.

The opinion of elders and village leaders is respected and they are heard in village meetings, but the young people have increased their power due to the new positions of responsibility roles and their knowledge of new practices and better language skills, including a more extensive vocabulary in Portuguese.[12] Many indigenous organizations and associations have tried to encourage more contributions from older people, and shamans and some elders are now called "traditional leaders." The current encouragement is also, though, an attempt to legitimize the actions of the young generation with urban experience. As well as being experts of the spirit world, elders and especially shamans are also valued for their rich knowledge of rituals, stories, chants, dances, and craftwork. Shamans and traditional leaders are more involved now in association activities brought there by the younger generation, but they seldom have the skills to control economic resources. However, since elders are respected, the final decision is usually taken when the elders and shamans agree. But their decisions depend on how things are presented to them, who presents the information, and how the message is made comprehensible. Before the political meetings, Manchineri spokespeople may be guided by the elders' or shamans' use of *ayahuasca*, as they use their visions to tell who their allies are or which people intend to harm them in the coming meeting. Shamans still play a significant role in today's interethnic relations, specifically in identifying sorcery, an aspect of the work of shamans in interethnic relations already widely described in the literature.

In fact, shamanic knowledge has increasingly become an asset for people in representative roles, and spokespeople with shamanic skills can be especially influential. This rerecognition of the shaman's role and the transformation of shamans into leading figures in interethnic relations began as early as the 1980s. This was the result of various factors, such as the recognition of shamanism as an essentially indigenous practice and their image as guardians of knowledge on the rainforest (Turner 1995; Conklin 2002). Some young Manchineri men, in the reserve and the city alike, either aspire to increase their knowledge of shamanism, nonhumans, and the past or already have a considerable experience in encountering spirits and nonhuman beings. That enables them to articulate their specifically indigenous worldview in terms understandable to Western thinking and thus enable nonnatives to understand contemporary issues from the native point of view.[13]

People dedicating themselves to a shamanic vocation usually have a long and intensive training, and during this time they prefer to be by themselves and keep silent about their aims. Anyone voluntarily aspiring to increase their shamanic knowledge must avoid sexual intercourse and certain kinds of foods, such as salty or greasy types. In addition to citing the powers of earlier shamans, the narratives on the subject typically dwell on the harshness of shamanic training and its obligations, such as the novice shaman's diet and the number of days in isolation required, though these seem to vary according to the narrator. Overall, the contemporary problem of many indigenous communities has been the lack of strong leaders—that is, people with a range of valued qualities such as literacy, shamanic knowledge, and social contacts.

New roles have brought new types of indigenous spokespeople, but there is still the expectation that they should act as providers, respecting and nursing the population. Amerindian moral principles based on humanity, personhood, and sociality limit the way in which a spokesperson's prestige is constructed. Indigenous communities complain that the incapacity of their spokespeople to interact in new situations stems either from their lack of specific nonnative skills or from the overexposure of their subjectivities to nonkin. These frequently discussed issues, such as the recent communal positions of responsibility, largely introduced by the dominant society, have increased the interaction between non-community members and the community. On the other hand, it may be difficult for people from the reserve to satisfy the community's expectations when holding a specific post, since the person may lack the skills needed to carry out his or her responsibilities well. Moreover, the new tasks usually bring with them the individual acquisition of wealth, often running contrary to the meaning of communal ties (see Virtanen forthcoming; Hill 2003). But even those who look for jobs for their own sustenance or new knowledge usually wish to assist their indigenous communities, too. The community maintains social control, since the person allocated the post will quickly be replaced if the community is dissatisfied. On the one hand, working in ethnopolitics may construct a new personhood through positions in new social networks, but, on the other, it also offers the chance for the person to become an individual within wider Brazilian society where people can act in a sphere of anonymity, possessing personal freedom, autonomy, and the right to choose. Social integration is only possible when the surrounding culture is open to the entry of new components from different cultural and indigenous groups. The key problems to solve are representativity and how the organizations share the benefits among the native population.

It is also important to mention that continuous confrontations and political struggles occur in indigenous politics, not only between Indians and the state, but also between indigenous peoples themselves. The legitimacy of Indians working in indigenous politics has frequently been questioned by community members with the allegation that they have not brought any improvements to the community or that those indigenous leaders who have been living in the city for a long time have forgotten the value systems of their indigenous communities, linked to the production of human bodies. And as we have already discussed in relation to community spokespeople, here we also have to take into account the present-day conflicts between the communities and their representatives. The issue here is successfully coping with the alteration of bodies in the community and beyond. Failure to distribute project funding successfully also reflects a lack of administrative skills. Today many indigenous officials have been accused of corruption and forgetting the interests of the groups for whom they are working, meaning that they merely end up fighting to secure economic capital for themselves. In fact, in 2004, UNI, the most important indigenous movement in Acre state, folded due to its financial debt to the local government, aggravated by internal conflicts. It was subsequently replaced by the Organization of Indigenous Peoples of Acre, Southern Amazonas, and Northwestern Rondônia (OPIN), but that, too, was shut down because of leadership problems. The most effective role in today's indigenous movement is played by the indigenous organizations and associations representing particular indigenous groups. Attempts to resolve the contradictions and conflicts in indigenous politics are made through pan-indigenous relatedness in rituals and discourses, a topic addressed in the final chapter. Here I wish to turn to the indigenous students' movement, which has continued the legacy of the indigenous movement in the Acre region.

Indigenous Students' Movement

One area in which today's indigenous people have stronger voices is indigenous youth activism. Indigenous youths have generated their own ways of taking action and questioning domination in those areas where they wish to be treated as equal actors, especially in education. Differentiated indigenous education has been guaranteed by law in Brazil since 1991 with the aim of reinforcing ethnic identity, recovering historical memory, and valuing native languages and sciences, as well as enabling access to information and knowledge valued by the national society. But in both the reserve and the city, many young people dream about better resources for study. Native youths want to reach the same level in the dominant society as their peers and graduate as lawyers, doctors, teachers, and so forth. But before this can happen, they need to be able to finish their elementary schooling. Indigenous youths, especially in urban areas, have realized that their desire for better conditions for studying can be formalized in the language of political demands. Their indigenous backgrounds have helped them make their demands, and these demands for better education have united indigenous students. Education has been the main reason indigenous adolescents have created their own organizations in Amazonia.

In the city, studying creates new social networks between young Indians from a variety of ethnic groups. In Rio Branco, some indigenous adolescents, especially Cashinahua and Apurinã youngsters, are actively involved in the indigenous students' movement, MEIACSAM (the Movement of Indigenous Students of Acre and Southern Amazonas, *Movimento dos Estudantes Indígenas do Acre e Sul do Amazonas*). There are also local indigenous student organizations in other towns in Acre, like Feijó. The student movements differ from the indigenous movement in its pursuit of equal education and its close cooperation with other peer groups, including Afro-Brazilian youths and sexual minorities. MEIACSAM was founded in 1996 and, following a lull, has been active again since the end of 2003. It aims to improve indigenous students' education and training. Its members are both young women and men. The male members have been the main spokespeople for the group, though young women have been active alongside them. The organization calls for financial support and more spaces for indigenous students in secondary schools, since they lack the financial resources to carry out their studies. For some years MEIACSAM has also been campaigning for accommodation to be built for indigenous students in Rio Branco, as well as better conditions for their relatives in the reserves.

Interacting with the dominant society via the students' movement is based on the idea of achieving equality with nonnative students. Consequently, indigenous youths are now mentioned in Brazilian government statements (e.g., those by the National Youth Office, *Secretaria Nacional de Juventude*) as minorities that need specific programs similar to those implemented for Brazil's Afro descendants. The student movements have generated a new image of native youths, overcoming a negative view prevalent in media where attention has focused on their social problems, such as their suicide and unemployment rates. Representatives from Acre have also participated in local and national youth forums. In the Second Youth Forum in Rio Branco, held in September 2004, a Cashinahua young man introduced the cultural presentation of indigenous students, who were attending the forum for the first time:

> My name is Linoa [indigenous name]. I'm from the Cashinahua people. I'm proud to be Indian wherever I am. He [pointing to a young Manchineri man] will sing to you. Every word, every song [he will sing] has a meaning for us. We have differences that only we can understand. We are students. We are organizing a movement of indigenous students, starting from here, Rio Branco. The objective of our movement and this Youth is to integrate Indian youths into nonindigenous society, since we are still somewhat marginalized. I thank you for this opportunity, and also the government for supporting us. Our people in the jungle are still suffering. But we, who are a part of them, are also contributing.

Figure 5.2 Manchineri and Cashinahua youths in the indigenous students' presentation at the 2004 Youth Forum

On the whole, young indigenous people looking for education have become excellent negotiators. They know that they have to adapt to find benefits and options for their new initiatives. The common expression is "you have to run after" (*correr atrás*) things, and the doors on which they knock are those of FUNAI, local education offices, other government departments, CIMI, political parties, and NGOs. They are like new modern warriors (*guerreiros*) looking for support for their sustenance. Owing to lack of supporters for indigenous and pro-Indian organizations in Rio Branco, MEIACSAM occasionally works together with left-wing organizations and other groups campaigning for more equality, such as the young black movement and gender movements, actively creating new social contacts and sharing similar experiences. The male leader of MEIACSAM, aged 27, explains the young Indians' arrival in the city: "[When arriving] they think one thing, but the reality is different. [They think] they will finish school and graduate soon. They arrive here but are almost abandoned. They have to run after people to give support. They have heard that they give support, but there isn't any special organ for [indigenous] students. If there was one that would take on this responsibility—If they could come here with that support already in place—and then continue [to have] the money—to do sports, courses."

Work for the indigenous students' movement tends to be urban based. New communication technologies, such as cell phones and the Internet, including e-mail and social media, are used for networking and organizing meetings. MEIACSAM's latest activities have also included selling craftwork at events such as city fairs, gaining more visibility for indigenous students in the city. The indigenous students' movements have reinforced their cultural and ethnic identity, and changed young native people's involvement in politics and other social movements. Participants in the student movement have learned about their local history as Indians. In this way they have managed to construct a single collective subject and to give meaning to their current situation. Hall (1992) has observed that blacks in the United States were formerly unable to construct self-identities from their history and culture since they were excluded from the school curricula. But today, following the reformation of the educational system, black movements are strong. In fact, the indigenous student movement has succeeded in increasing the number of scholarships for indigenous people entering universities, and today some of the young people of this study have continued their studies in the local federal university.

As in the indigenous movement, one of the main problems faced by the student organization has been the internal disputes and disagreements. Many young indigenous people blamed the organization's personnel for failing to fulfill their responsibilities and hence distrusted them. It seems that the problems encountered by the leaders of the indigenous student organization are compounded by the complicated question of the presence of native people in the city. In Acre, urban indigenous students are excluded from special education programs, since the state education office only deals with Indians in the reserves. The other government indigenous offices' main-target public is the indigenous people in the reserve. The federal secretary for indigenous peoples (today called the advisor for indigenous peoples) said that urban study would only be successful if the indigenous communities could control the studies of young people in the city and their education could be planned beforehand to match each community's needs. Anyone studying in the city should, he argued, become a professional in the areas of health care, agroforestry work, or law in order to help their communities achieve their goals. If the youths are not properly prepared for this, he argued, they will end up staying in areas where they interact with people whose influence could prove negative. The village leaders should also tell their villages what the cities and city life are like. The federal secretary of indigenous peoples also foresaw other problems:

> If a person leaves the village when young, he comes to study. And what he receives is an education about the world as it is today. That is the world of competition, the fight for survival and capitalism, which touches on everything, and his education is the prelude to obtaining a job. So he starts to be absent [from the village community], and when he returns there, he looks for a job that someone will pay

him to do. He is no longer someone from that community. Even if he is, it is difficult for him. But for him to be an instrument for the community, he has to be well prepared [about the reason for going to the city]. But if he is not prepared, he will only further complicate things for the community.

The coordinator of the UNI at that time also criticized the indigenous young people in the city for not respecting the successes of the previous generations of native leaders, who had succeeded in initiating the demarcation of indigenous lands. But as we have seen in this study, many of the young Indians in the city want to work for their communities and assume the role of specialists mentioned by the coordinator at the end of his comment, especially as teachers, lawyers, and forestry technicians. In the development programs and governmental projects, all the agronomists, biologists, and anthropologists involved are non-Indians. In the discourses of the indigenous student movement, the reserves appear more frequently and MEIACSAM's representatives say that their aim is to assist young Indians coming from the reserve to study in the city. Those who are active in the students' movement are usually from urban indigenous families whose members have already been involved in the local indigenous movement. Acting in the movement is, therefore, one of the models for taking a place in the world.

However, not all young indigenous people in the reserve plan to study in the city. In the Manchineri land, Mamoadate, I was able to talk to young people with different plans for the future, all of them important for the community. Some young people, regardless of gender, wanted simply to continue their agriculture-hunting-fishing livelihood and live peacefully on their own land. These young people also dream about some industrial goods: for example, young women wish to own dishes, a bed, and other household items. Some young people wanted to continue living in the reserve but still have more experiences of the outside world. They wanted "to have ideas," and the boys were usually willing to work outside the reserve for a while. In a third group of young people we can place a few young men who saw themselves as shamans. A fourth group of young people, a small number of adolescents, wanted to take responsibility for leading the community's development by participating in further education. They hoped "to be somebody" and "to achieve something in life." Interestingly, girls also fitted into this category of adolescents, even though leadership has not traditionally been a female role. In general, many young people thought that they had to fight for their indigenous rights and one way to do so was by becoming literate. "Studies for me are about fighting for ourselves," as a young man put it.

The young Indians' desire to extend their rights is based on their indigenousness and the history of the indigenous population's oppression. Indigeneity is the basis for the political demands made by MEIACSAM and is used as a distinguishing marker for claiming and ensuring equal opportunities. However, young people's activism differs from that of the previous generation because rather than calling for specific rights as a different (indigenous) demographic group, young activists often wish to have the same possibilities as nonnatives. They point at the power structures dominating indigenous people and their production of the image of Indians as childlike and savage—the common stereotypes of the dominant society.

Although this chapter seems to show that the proximity between community members is diminishing owing to their political participation, new positions of responsibility and new forms of leadership that involve mobility between urban and rural areas, there are current ways of producing affinity and relatedness. In Chapters 6 and 7, I shall look at how community members produce relatedness across the rural-urban divide, as well as roles with specific knowledge, their embodiments, and the political representation activities that have been created.

CHAPTER 6

Recreating Relatedness

In Amazonian social philosophies, proximity and relatedness have typically been created by common social acts that are conceived to produce similar bodies (McCallum 1996; Conklin and Morgan 1996; Vilaça 2002, 2005). This chapter looks at how relatedness is currently built between Manchineri villages, generations, urban and forest dwellers, and genders. First I look at community making through community practices and discourses and how this changes between the villages depicted in the drawings of young people in the reserve and the city. Here, I shall also shortly address the new relations of exchange. Broadening my view to other indigenous youths, the Cashinahua and Apurinã, I next examine how indigenousness is produced strategically in different encounters, while in the third section I turn to ritual practices in new environments. The ethnographic material shows how the sense of a shared past and present, as well as similar approaches in various social environments, produce similar "indigenous bodies" with a specific way of thinking—the idea of human agency with differing power and capacities.

Community Making

Producing practices of relatedness increasingly involves selecting, incorporating, and organizing certain cultural features within the social contexts in which collective representations are both possible and appropriate. Relatedness is created in daily life by small-scale sharing and exchanges between households of the closest kin within the same village. This applies to forest produce and some commodities, such as salt, detergents, and so forth, as I described in Chapter 1. What also unite indigenous communities are their memories and oral history, as well as their discourses and actions relating to ancestors and nonhuman beings (spirits). Mythologies have a special significance as boundary builders and provide the foundations for marking social differences from other beings. The myths define the relations to certain beings, and these relations are lived in everyday actions, rituals, and interactions with the natural environment. Moral values of sharing, use of certain substances, embodying similar knowledge, working together, and common practices still produce present-day kinship.

In the reserve, the increased contacts with non-Indians and other indigenous groups have created new kinds of doubts concerning which way the community is, or is becoming, similar and different from others. Attempting to focus more specifically on the ideas of young people, I examined their view of the future. In four different villages of the Manchineri reserve, I asked the children and young people at schools to draw a house in an environment they desired and some objects that would be important to them. These drawings also served to show common practices, objects, and knowledge shared by the young people in their villages. The artwork from all the villages also showed fundamental differences from those made by nonnatives. The drawings surprised me in two ways. First, differences between the villages become evident, which I took to be the result of the influence of certain people living in them, along with different forest environments of each village, particularly in relation to the distance to urban centers

Figure 6.1   Joseimar's drawing depicting his imagined home (Extrema village)

and nonnative colonies. Second, when comparing drawings from the four villages, the dissimilarities in the objects drawn around the houses, the construction materials chosen for the home, and its inner divisions, all amazed me.

The drawings by adolescents living in Extrema, the village farthest from the urban centers, clearly showed the relation to plant spirits and the importance of the different plants consumed during the life course. Students explained how different medicinal plants, such as *sanango*, were important for their lives and the process of growing up. Various kinds of natural medicines were represented, along with traditional objects such as *koshmas*, ceramics, and the traditional construction materials used for their houses.

The drawings often depicted ivory nut and *paxiúba* palms that serve as thatching material for the houses, to make a sieve, and to eat, as adolescents indicated. They also drew cotton to be used for the Manchineri clothes they would learn to make. Teaching was also emphasized: in a young boy's drawing, he shows himself reading a book.

Youths from Lago Novo, the next village downriver, drew various craftwork items, such as pottery (the village produces the most), bows, arrows, sticks used for preparing *caiçuma*, and even ritual dances. This was "what is ours." There was also a fenced area for breeding turtles in order to improve their nutritional intake. The young people also wanted a chain saw for the village in order to use the trees that had fallen down near the village for construction purposes.

Figure 6.2   Valdir's drawing depicting his imagined home (Lago Novo village)

The houses were made of wooden planks and their roofs of corrugated iron. The youths explained that these would be cleaner and keep the mosquitoes out better, and, more to the point, the village no longer had enough *paxiúba* wood for the construction of traditional Manchineri houses, which have to be rebuilt every five to seven years. In two drawings there were solar energy collectors: it was explained that these would help light the houses and facilitate cooking in the evening.

The most typical themes of the drawings in Santa Cruz were the fruit trees, as well as the bushes and animals that provide nourishment. Their drawings revealed the youths' in-depth knowledge of their natural environment; they knew how to draw and color trees, plants, and animals in detail.

In the drawings from Jatobá village, new technological equipment appeared in the place of the medical plants and Manchineri objects, including craftwork, that appeared in the Lago Novo and Extrema drawings. The houses differed the most, since according to the adolescents' explanations, some house roofs were made of bricks and plank walls. Moreover, the drawings contained televisions, radios, solar energy collectors, and even a helicopter. In their homes, the young women wanted to have an oven, since they presently have to search a long time for wood for the fire, including during the rainy season. Tending the fire also involves hard work, since the person has to blow a lot to keep the fire going at first. Gas stoves, solar energy panels, and consequently electricity and lighting were already in use in some houses—namely, those of the village teacher and the chief—providing the youths with a new pattern of living standards that they, too, wish to obtain. As I discussed previously, the young people in Jatobá wanted to have their own room in the house, a space where they could study and keep their own things. A young woman said that sometimes relatives arrive and she cannot do the things that she wants, and thus she would like a room for herself. Nor was there a boat to take agricultural produce to the urban centers and to travel.

The drawings showed the young people's thoughts about the things with which to relate and the duties and social practices to adopt and collectively value in each village. The differentiated indigenous education provided by the village schools, the proximity to urban centers, and the presence of missionaries and influential persons in the villages largely explain the differences. Undoubtedly, the drawings revealed the influence of certain people on the way the youngsters' thinking about themselves had developed: thus the images demonstrate the impact of "instructors" and other authority figures on the young people. The people who had power were shamans in Extrema, teachers from Extrema and Lago Novo who had participated for a long time in multicultural education courses, the more highly trained agroforestry agents in Lago Novo and Santa Cruz, and the converted village leader in Jatobá. Drawings from this last village also showed the strong influences of the earlier missionaries and contacts with non-Indians with whom the villagers had active trade relations. These different social networks of villages had also formed different elements that the mothers and fathers wanted to pass on to their children. When we were looking in Extrema one day at photographs I had taken at the one of the cultural meetings held on the Indian Day (*dia do índio*), where a group of Manchineri had been, a boy commented on another Manchineri person's body painting: "What a beautiful jaguar skin!" These kinds of comments showed differences of specific knowledge and values between the villages. Villages participated in different discourses as a community, especially in response to the ideas brought by the courses for indigenous teachers and agroforestry agents.

In Rio Branco, the drawings of the future made by youngsters depicted typical city houses and did not show any Manchineri objects as such, though two young men who visit the reserve regularly drew a house in the traditional style. However, young people's explanations about the future emphasized the typical values of Amazonian sociality—proximity, respect, and caring for others— but also an environmentalism that differed from the values associated with the city. For instance, immaterial things like family life and caring for others were emphasized. These appeared in their answers to the question "How should one live well?":

> By being happy and above all healthy. I don't think money can buy this. Despite the fact that it is a necessity. Money for me, money is a necessity. Happiness, health, and love. All these dominate a lot. Everyone in the world needs these.

> I would like a world of peace, without violence, and where people have lots of solidarity. To have lots of peace. And lots of solidarity for poor people, who don't have a family or any support. The other thing I would like is schools for children and lots of education in their lives.

> I don't like to think about money. It's not very important to me. But for everybody to have happiness, health, love, and harmony in their heart. This is important to me and to my family. There is no point in people having cars and money, but not having what's really necessary: love, respect and harmony.

By stating that material things are not essential to them, they expressed their moral values, which they see as different from those of non-Indians. The hopes of the young urban Manchineri for love, respect, and harmony were not the everyday reality of their neighborhoods. The problems faced by their suburbs were often unemployment, violence, drugs, alcohol, and so forth. Even though they may try to acquire material things possessed by other young Brazilians, they know that they would have great difficulty in acquiring them. In general, the young people's narratives on the need for studies, learning culture, and the importance of respect displayed their common beliefs and thoughts on the good life enjoyed by the community and its individuals and shared among themselves. They express the same ideas of being a person: a social agent related to a caring people (cf. Overing and Passes 2000; Belaunde 2001). This is also discernible in the opinion of a young Manchineri man living in Rio Branco concerning development, where he takes a stance opposed to capitalist-oriented thinking.

[*How will things be different twenty years from now?*] I think that thirty years ago all this was forest, since things change quickly. And when you cut down a tree, it's felled in ten minutes. But it takes fifty or a hundred years to grow. People say that this is progress, but it isn't. The truth is that this is not progress. I think twenty years from now there will be less forest. Things are increasing and likewise the population. If we destroy more forest, it will mean more people, more places for them, you know. I hope that people change in their hearts, since I see only wickedness. People starve and it is called power. "I'm hungry," they say. I hope that people change in their hearts. I see respect there.

In general, like the youths in the reserve, the worries of young Manchineri people in the city are not the big global issues, such as wars or natural catastrophes, that form the common fears of young people in other parts of the world, but violence in their neighborhoods and not being able to complete their school studies.

The indigenous families in the city rarely exchange or share commodities, but their visits to relatives' houses seemed to be more frequent than before, for instance, to participate in shamanic rituals. Food may be shared during the visit, but exchange applies more to various "traditional" articles, such as craftwork materials, tobacco, and *ayahuasca*. On numerous occasions these items had been transported from the reserves to the city personally or they had been obtained from there. People from the city pass new knowledge to the people in the reserve, which may be anything that the people in the reserve are willing to learn, such as martial arts taught in the city. Two young men had started to teach in the reserve and were welcomed. Previously people in the reserve had been disappointed that those living in the city did not come to teach at the indigenous schools. These exchange relations also create new relationships as the interest in producing indigenous handicrafts and organizing shamanic meetings in the city has increased. Moreover, many young people have started to visit the places where they know they can meet people from the reserve, such as the indigenous health center, training courses, political encounters, and so forth, which creates new types of relatedness between the urban and rural community members.

For youths, continuing indigenous ways of living has a purpose: as Jackson has emphasized, the dynamics of culture demonstrate the engagement of indigenous groups between "them" and "us," and thus "their struggles to preserve their self-respect, autonomy, and a life with meaning" (Jackson 1995, 18). When I started my fieldwork in the Manchineri reserve, the adolescents frequently used the word *culture*, and their opinions about what they called culture could be divided roughly into the idea of something to be recovered and something completely uninteresting. Comments by young people expressing the former set of opinions included "So far [w]e have only half of our culture. One day we will recover it all," "We are going to have to fortify our culture, handicrafts, and dances," and "If you visit us here in ten years' time, I'm sure you'll see our work here." Manchineri youth expressed their difference through negation: previously "traditional culture" had been stronger. This already showed a discourse about something conceptualized as culture.

However, the shaman of Extrema village also complained to me many times that the young people needed to become more interested in their traditions, since there would be no one to continue them after he was gone. There older people often told me that the adolescents live like white settlers on the Yaco River. The elders did not blame the period of rubber slavery and the whites' prohibition on many things, but these were often the reasons given by young people for their current situation, along with their lack of education. But as local indigenous education experts told me, education by itself cannot rescue indigenous language: it must be a part of people's everyday lives and spoken actively. Once I was interviewing two boys from the same village and only one of them had been told a story about the origin of the moon. The other boy explained that he had learned the story from a book made by indigenous teachers who had arrived at the school, though he had not been told about the story.

Once when we were talking about the cultural meeting in Cruzeiro do Sul, a young Manchineri man said that he had met the Indians who live in that region and had discovered that they knew more about their culture as a result of school education and various government measures. Later on in the reserve, the same young man told me the following:

> Today young Manchineri people are uninterested in learning traditional music or indigenous stories. Many of them don't want to recover and reinforce culture, stories, language, or those kinds of things. And because of this, I always say that when it comes to literacy, those who want to strengthen [culture] are people who know how to read and write, since when a person writes, he or she discovers that experience and tries to learn more about the culture and gives it value. So the person who tries to discover and strengthen culture and to give it value is the one who already reads and writes a little. But these people who don't read or write, and have never studied, just don't care anymore.

Speaking about culture seemed to be closely associated with community making, especially in indigenous schools and organizations (Weber 2006, 153). At the same time, it was a way to approach non-Indians, as new discourses on ethnic differences were closely related to people's desire to have more autonomy and respect in relation to the state (Wade 1997), though the discourse on culture was also closely associated with the tendency for development projects (designed by non-Indians) to essentialize and objectify indigeneity. These were often aimed at "fortifying indigenous cultures." "Culture" has become objectified in indigenous communities, and as a new instrument of self-representation and resistance, it is now used to mark their own ethnic identity and autonomy (Turner 1991, 1995). For Sahlins (1997), indigenous culturalism is a new discursive formulation of modern indigenous identities within global cultural imperialism. Indigenous peoples globally have become more conscious of their culture owing to the new means of communication and new contacts. Tuhiwai Smith (1999, 19), Maori by origin, argues that "imperialism frames the indigenous experience. It is part of our story, our version of modernity."

In relation to indigenous politics and modern mobilization, cultural differences are taken as conscious objects manipulated in the production of identities as the rise in awareness of ethnic origins came to force in the 1990s across many continents. Differentiating myths, musical rhythms, and so forth has always been a part of human societies, but the imagery expressed through them has become more powerful, since there are now many more possible lives discovered through increased interaction and communication, and the media (Appadurai 1996).

For many young people, reproducing artworks, performing rituals, using natural medicines, singing, and so forth are about forming their own part in the transitory lines of generations. The young Manchineri men said, "I would like to be as wise as my grandparents who know numerous things, like how to sing, make a sieve, make an arrow," and, "These dances, singing—I want to learn them all. The paintings, you know. Learn like my dad." In the recent past, old people were rarely asked about history, making them apparently unwilling to speak about things in which nobody seemed interested. The young people are now more aware that if they do not ask elders, their knowledge could be lost. Today the elders are actually regarded as the villages' "libraries." The young teacher from Extrema village, Lucas, explained the change in attitude toward the elders as follows:

[*Today you are looking for information from the old people. What has change?*]
[Before] I didn't really know my relatives. I was like a white man. Today we have a lot of respect [toward elders]. In the past, you could not even talk to your mother-in-law. [Or] a young person talk to an elder. Now it has changed.

[*Why?*] Since the whites have changed it [people's attitudes to elders]—I know my rights, I have read the FUNAI legislation, and this has made me respect old people more since they have more knowledge than an entire library.

During my first visit to Jatobá village in the Manchineri reserve, I asked what would happen when the old people die, who will know how to sing and tell stories. A boy told me that maybe nobody will know. But by the following year he was more positive. He had probably noticed that recently new projects in the reserve have focused on cultural preservation and hence observed that Manchineri culture is also being encouraged from the outside.

The model for organizing the community came from outside and was also criticized. For instance, during the workshop for the cultural exchange project held when five Yine people from the Diamante village in Peru visited Jatobá, I had a discussion with a young Manchineri man:

[*What are you learning here?*] How to converse in the community. I'm getting an idea of how we should talk with our people. What the difficulties are.

[*What are the difficulties?*] They wanted to organize things in the same way as white people. But now it's already being done the Indian way. Now old people have a voice to talk and young people are listening. Now everybody is learning and children and younger people are respecting older people.

[*Why did the change happen?*] Because of teachers, the coordinator of MAP-KAHA, yourself, OPIAC—those who talk about this.

[*What has changed?*] It has changed. Children and young people are respectful. Women are weaving. It is a change for the future. A young girl giving a course [on weaving] for the women. So the outcome for the community is good.

When young people say that culture must be recovered, however, in addition to those things that now count as indigenous culture—dances, chants, body paintings, clothing such as *koshmas*—they also seem to be referring to their own social organization and respect. In the most distant villages, Extrema and Lago Novo, I was often told, "We still have our culture here." This was also emphasized in terms of their dissimilarities even to other villages—for instance, their dietary restrictions, shamanism, and rituals. Moreover, knowledge in fact circulated in accordance with people's social age, gender, and roles within the group's social organization. Young people were very good at undertaking various kinds of "traditional" activities based on the application of orally transmitted information, such as building houses, hunting, or clearing a plantation, while young women processed manioc, used herbal medicine for their children and their own pregnancies, and looked for palms and other forest materials to be transformed into the objects they need, such as baskets, which are tied to their foreheads to carry vegetables and fruits. However, there are also things that are "invisible" to nonnatives and distant from their everyday lives, such as dietary rules, predicting the future, cherishing the ancestors, and so forth. It has to be remembered that for many Amazonian peoples, knowing about certain things also means a change in one's body, values, and behavior (cf. Crocker 1985, 88).

The adolescents know that old people possess the information about myths and traditional practices that can help the youths accrue more cultural capital. This includes the specialist knowledge about the particularities of Manchineri culture, history, and spirituality. Consequently, the few old people who still have a rich knowledge of myths, songs, dances, and healing have become increasingly important. Shamanic knowledge in particular is of increasing interest to nonnatives, and shamanic healing sessions can be regarded as something exotic, offering new interpretations for their life situations. Some young people who have led *ayahuasca* rituals have forged contacts with nonnative governmental and nongovernmental officials, as I discussed in Chapter 3.

Global and local are in constant dialogue, while different present-day community discourses and defining indigenousness are also sustained between the nationalized and globalized. A new awareness of indigenous culture and the preservation of cultural identity have become a political action, owing to the contemporary relations between the Brazilian nation and indigenous people. Indigenous educational politics is still trying to change the view that sees state education and indigenous knowledge, such as oral history, as parts of different systems. Ethnicity, like race, must be seen in the context of history and changing relations to the state, a process that sheds light on dynamic power relations. In Latin America, indigenousness is closely related to the experiences of domination, and in postmodern times, defining oneself as indigenous has been about claiming both specific rights and universal citizenship (Wade 1997). In addition to the everyday practices of contemporary Amazonian native peoples, their historical and political relations involve a resistance to the Cartesian framework and Western individualism, due to their communal proximity as well as the close interrelation of substances and subjectivities. The dominant society's ideas of indigenousness as something linked with place and environment can be exploited in this process.

However, indigenousness is not simply a question of political mandates and cultural expressivity, as Pacheco de Oliveira (2004) has observed: ethnicity is also about feelings, values, and an obedience to religious and political authority that is always deposited in the person's memory. Moreover, "traditions" are violations of complex inferential processes (Boyer 1997), and thus comprise histories for which young people attempt to gain a deeper understanding, even if they are produced by society's structures. The historical elements, such as continuing knowledge of the community, moral values, and livelihoods, are just as important, however (Wade 1997).

But elders still carry with them painful memories of the time when the colonizers exploited them and the state power disrespected their indigenous identities, meaning that they had to be lived invisibly. Nonnatives forbade Indians to show their cultural, political, economic, and social differences for a long period. Both in the reserve and in the city, the Manchineri adolescents said it was difficult to learn their oral history or acquire the knowledge that the older Manchineri once used to live by. It had been—and still seemed—difficult to transmit indigenous knowledge, artistic expressions, and oral history, all of which had been devalued by nonnatives for such a long time. For many young natives, these still remain to some extent no more than a learning process, or at least something difficult to grasp and maintain. For instance, one of the agroforestry agents, whose grandfather was famous for his indigenous knowledge, said that previously he had not known any medicinal plants. The young boy said that his grandfather was already too old to teach him.

Seen within this larger framework, it is somewhat ironic that now on the training courses, such as those for agroforestry agents and teachers, non-Indians and people from other indigenous groups ask the indigenous participants about traditional songs and stories, and having to admit ignorance provokes embarrassment and a feeling of inferiority. During my fieldwork, one of the youngest agroforestry agents, Artur, had just arrived from his first training course in Rio Branco. He told me that there he had been asked to present Manchineri chants or recount some of their stories, an event that made him think that now he really did have to learn them. On the training courses, the "games" of shamanic powers between the indigenous representatives are also common. According to one young teacher, through these games other groups can show him that "I didn't know anything, and that my culture was weak, as well as our cultural rules." This had made him start to practice *ayahuasca* shamanism and to seek out stories from older people. Eighteen-year-old Joseimar responded when I asked him what his biggest dream was, "To study more about the whites and our culture. If I can learn, I have to teach my relatives. If I am a shaman, I have to teach other relatives, so our knowledge is remembered and other people can be helped. So shamanism does not end. We shall have more reinforcements one day."

Another example concerns musicality, which may involve an arduous search for the knowledge involved. A boy in Lago Novo village told me that it took a long time for him to learn just two chants used in *ayahuasca* rituals. While working in the health center in Rio Branco, he had heard the Manchineri *ayahuasca* chants there for the first time, because the shaman from the other Manchineri village had also been visiting for treatment. Another boy described his thoughts to me:

He was really happy since he thought that one day he would take *cipó* [the vine used to prepare *ayahuasca*], if there was someone to take *ayahuasca* with him. He would take it with someone willing to take *cipó*. He hopes to learn [*ayahuasca*] chants one day—the "spirituality" that other peoples also know. Because just recently when he took part on the course [of environmental agents], there were people looking for him [to ask about *ayahuasca*], but he didn't know. So he was happy when he saw a relative taking it [*ayahuasca*].

The circulation of discourses, even about the lack of a certain type of knowledge and experiences, is what makes the communities possible, not the existence of groups per se. This discursive circulation links the reserves and the forest world to the urban, where a new kind of indigenous discourse appears as part of the new encounters of the cities in general. Native oral history can be viewed as a "metaculture" that, as Urban (2001) suggests, moves through the world and is replicated in different types of social relations. However, we also have to note that nonindigenous classifications of "indigenous" dominant culture and its ways of seeing Indians transforms indigenous representations and the relationships and attitudes of native peoples to the past and present. The changes toward "us as a community," self-governance, and sovereignty are reflected in indigenous political and cultural meetings, and in encounters with nongovernmental associations and state organizations, as well as training courses in which the Manchineri had participated.

As the amount of information to process today is vast, the transmission of oral history and knowledge has changed. Currently, transmission occurs both from old people to young and from young people to old, and from the city to rural areas and rural areas to the city. This is an important turnaround. Many young indigenous people also anticipate the need for new tools and organizational structures for oral history to be transmitted. Youngsters in the villages very often asked me how they could record chants, body paintings, or myths. In the Manchineri reserve, for instance, young people wanted to obtain a simple voice recorder to record the chants of the oldest woman in the village, who still remembered a great variety of them. "She will be dead soon and we want to learn the songs." In fact, some people did possess cameras or voice recorders, but there were rarely enough batteries to use them or, indeed, other small electronic items such as radios. One of the problems faced by many indigenous groups is that they lack the necessary economic capital to invest in the new commodities, tools, and equipment that could help them produce and document their cultural manifestations.

Due to new interethnic contacts, young people have become increasingly aware of their cultural differences, sometimes meaning that they consciously look for more knowledge about their history and differences. At a national level, the Ministry of Culture has also been running a new initiative over the last few years, the Indigenous Culture Prize (*Prêmio Culturas Indígenas*). Applicants have discovered what things and practices are seen to have a value, and young Manchineri teachers have also tried to apply for funding for their individual projects as these kinds of opportunities have appeared. For instance, they have drafted proposals for registering traditional designs, chants, and medicinal plants.

For most native communities, though, studying Portuguese and nonindigenous culture was still the most effective means of defending themselves, since they could communicate with people from outside the reserve and thereby transmit their own culture. This implies the need for indigenous traditions to be materialized for nonnatives, yet for the young natives this is not an easy task, even if they wish to do so. Today ethnicity can offer an important model for the future and a sense of one's responsibilities.[1] Overall, it seems that, in terms of ethnicity, Amazonian indigenous peoples are more inclined to redefine their position in society than to construct the kind of resistance identity generated when a devalued group builds a new survival strategy. This may also explain why there are so few violent riots involving indigenous groups in the cities they inhabit, compared, for instance, to some other neighborhoods of the larger Brazilian cities where marginalized poorer citizens live. In both urban and rural settings, indigenous people can produce meanings that are held by certain sociocultural processes highlighting the boundaries that set them apart as distinct ethnosocial groups. Some objects and elements, such as craftwork, indigenous bags, dresses, jewelry, natural medicines, chants, and practices, offer a link to ancestors, the present indigenous community, and cultural values. Certain practices and objects can carry special meanings and emotions of belonging. They both unite native groups, among the Amazonian youths living in both the reserve and the city, and establish ethnic differences. The relations to specific things and people become symbols that mark identity, producing a sense of group cohesion and togetherness. This can also be employed strategically.

Strategical Indigenousness

One of the ways of recreating relatedness is strategical. In some social situations, young people may admit to being an Indian when "Indianness" is a potential asset. Especially in urban areas, indigenousness can be spatially wielded. However, contemporary social spaces designated as "indigenous," or "indigenous, too," where young natives interact only unite people temporarily and may exclude them from others, creating imagined boundaries between them. In Rio Branco, for instance, I often observed that when native adolescents left the cultural meetings or the shops to sell their craftwork—which features their own symbolism—they avoided using objects that could readily identify them as

Indians or removed them. For example, when a Cashinahua boy left the shop where he had been selling indigenous handicrafts, he took off his traditional woven headdress. Indigenous youths rarely wanted to be personalized as Indians in public social spaces owing to the discrimination still present.

Moreover, I realized that since Brazilians can have a number of surnames, the indigenous name is frequently left out in situations where this may elicit more positive treatment, as mentioned. Young people very often cite their indigenous group as their only surname. This naming locates a young Indian within the social world as someone belonging to a distinctive social group. For indigenous youngsters, this represents the continuation and reproduction of their communal ties. Nonnatives may also use the indigenous group as a surname for Indians. Moreover, the native youths in the city rarely said that they were from the city, saying instead that they were from a certain place, indicating their indigenous origin, or stating that they come from such-and-such an indigenous family. They used their indigenous surnames according to context. In some situations, ethnicity allows them to show that they belong to their indigenous communities living in the villages, despite the fact that the indigenous territory is located a long distance away. Ethnic minorities may attempt to integrate into the dominant culture in one area but refrain from doing so when it is of no value for them to do so (Modood 2004).

Speech act theory has already noted that the speaker always speaks to someone, meaning that a speech act cannot be separated from its context. But in order to understand contemporary spatial reorganizations of indigenousness, we must take into account relations of power, culture, and space, as Gupta and Ferguson ([1997] 2001) propose. The notable element in the practices of young people is their new voice, the content of their present practices and speeches. This spatial and temporal identification can be seen in changing comments by youths, for instance, concerning their presence in urban areas. A 22-year-old Cashinahua woman living in an urban area told me, "In Tarauacá, in my home, I use white things. But because I live in the city, I have to accompany the rhythm of white people. If I lived in the village, of course I could live in the traditional way." The girl was involved in selling the craftwork of Cashinahua women in urban markets and in the city very proudly presented herself by her indigenous surname. However, as the comment of a young Cashinahua woman shows, it can be very different to be an Indian in the reserve and in the urban area, though they form part of the same identity. Although the idea of Indians changing clothes and using different shoes and so forth is not novel, we have to interpret it as bringing indigenousness to spaces without the essentialization of indigeneity expected by the dominant power structures.

Indigenousness may be valued and used as a source of prestige, helping the young person receive some form of positive treatment. Many Amazonian indigenous adolescents have realized that having access to specific knowledge—such as knowledge about medicine, stories, or singing and knowledge of one's own cultural beliefs and customs—produces special resources: skills and values transmitted within the ethnic environment that may benefit a young person. They can display valuable cultural expertise, even beyond their own indigenous community and other indigenous groups. Some changes at the federal and state level have legitimated indigenous knowledge as cultural capital that may be an advantage, for instance, when selecting people for a communal representative role. Knowledge of the environment, indigenous art, oral history, handmade objects, and natural medicines have turned this resource into a source of power, since information can also pave the way for new social interactions. This kind of resource, which some authors have also called ethnic capital (see, for instance, Borjas 1992; Modood 2004), also increases social capital, since it promotes new social networks, including those in which interaction occurs between the indigenous peoples and those sectors of the non-Indian population that value native cultures and knowledge. Shamanic knowledge, for instance, can be converted into new social networks during the training courses, visits to the reserves, or encounters with indigenous officials, as it allows personal relations with foreigners and can turn them into more known subjectivities. Moreover, cultural and social capital may be transformed into forms of economic capital, including, for example, gifts, project funding, or the salaries paid for some new posts such as indigenous teachers and agroforestry agents.[2] The new valorization of "Indianness" can offer a mark of distinction that even helps open up spaces within the school and job markets. Interestingly, the attitudes of some interviewees actually changed during the course of my fieldwork. Especially in the city, ethnic preservation gained a new importance for young people as they saw that someone was interested in them precisely because of their status as native adolescents.

However, such spatial alterations do not necessarily mean a change in identities. According to a 23-year-old Cashinahua man, even though he had stayed in Rio Branco for many years, indigenousness is produced in his speaking, eating, singing, and the rituals that accompany him: "I've been here since 2002. I speak the same language, I sing. I haven't changed in any way! I'm still an Indian. I have the material to paint, my shamanic things, and food. The question is all about presenting it [to others], isn't it?" Overall, the presence of indigenous people in the cities or the contacts between the reserves and urban areas do not necessarily mean a decrease in indigenous identity and culture. The majority of those now living in the city have never had the opportunity to live on Indian lands, but that does not make their identities any less indigenous.

On the other hand, indigenousness may be used as a tool to create personal codes and cognitive models at times of uncertainty—such as when moving to urban areas and when the urban space of anonymity is "too much"—insofar as being indigenous is about belonging and even authenticity. Indigeneity, a special way of doing and being, provides feelings of proximity, relatedness and care, and maintains social values across generations. Hence indigenousness produces social capital at least, even where it is not recognized as cultural capital. For a young native person, indigenousness offers a social and cultural space amid a dominant society that sometimes appears to represent confusion. It is important to note its usefulness for indigenous youngsters. It stimulates a desire to create something and a sense that they should and can control the period of change. Young Indians strive to add order to their individual worlds by identifying some social situations as areas of continuity. Ways of doing things and relating to others offer not only a feeling of continuity but also something totally fresh and new, when it has not been an object of conscious objectification. On the other hand, indigenousness functions differently in relations with the native community; it operates within relations with "Others." Native young people make various uses of specific symbolic resources, which are produced and recognized by others and constantly redefined in changing situations, producing different bodies. We can regard the social spaces as temporary communities, since they have their own symbolic systems. Shared symbols and meanings construct their own social and cultural boundaries.[3] The encounter with various cultural traditions has afforded an experience of different forms of symbolic resources that other young Brazilians lack.

Usually when among their own native group and other indigenous peoples, in the context of the indigenous movement, or among people interested in indigenous cultures and spirituality (such as shamanism), indigenous youths benefit from presenting indigenous bodies that share something acknowledged as indigenousness as a basis for social relationships. Embodied indigeneity reflects a common history underlying the unity of different indigenous groups, constituting what they share as native peoples in general. There appears to be a special orientation to other nonhuman subjects and the past, since embodied indigenousness shows particular relations to the environment, something from the past actualized in the present, and emphasizes the exchange between actors. In the Acre region, indigenous people have succeeded in making themselves visible, expressly arguing and demonstrating their cultural differences from the surrounding population, telling their own histories, and allying themselves with other indigenous peoples in the region and beyond. In some sense, they can also embody their Indianness in more visible ways than before. New urban indigenous cultures are being produced and native residents in the cities openly display their own ethnic characteristics, as I show regarding indigenized youth cultures in the next chapter.

Aside from at home, indigenous youngsters can show their identity as indigenous young people more openly within a network of people who value and respect their indigenous knowledge. In Acre these are people who can be said to have the same values as those who participated in the alliance of the *Povos da Floresta* (People of the Forest), including environmentalists, NGO workers, governmental officers, academics, and those interested in indigenous traditions such as shamanism. In Acre some indigenous youths have been invited to parties in the private homes of these people, an opportunity that many other nonindigenous youths never have. The non-Indian friends were usually from southern states or had traveled to foreign countries, introducing the youngsters to new global influences. For young people, the relations with new actors alter their relations with members of their own indigenous group, though they also challenge the way in which they define their presence in the city and among their nonindigenous friends.

However, some native youths are ashamed of their indigenous roots and differences, and neglect them. Even where they have memories of their original places, it may often become strategical to ignore them in order to avoid prejudice. On the other hand, for some people, being ignorant of the cultural differences of their own indigenous group, or being unable to speak the indigenous language, may cause a loss of self-esteem in the eyes of their own community, other native peoples, or nonnatives. The dominant society seldom if ever recognizes the fact that not all native populations have had the opportunity to be socialized within their own indigenous cultures. The result may be called "ethno-stress" (Lindgren 2000, on the Sámi), when the person cannot live up to what society expects him or her to be, a phenomenon observed among many other indigenous peoples. Learning "to be indigenous" can be complicated owing to the discontinuity of certain practices during the years when the negative pressure from the surrounding society was at its worst. For whatever reason, there are various deep-rooted prototypes and stereotypes related to being an Indian,[4] and the ability to speak an indigenous language is still one of them. The endangerment and disappearance of the original native language is very common among villages and reserves located near urban centers and for Indians actually living in these urban areas. Portuguese is used in interethnic relations, and a shift toward its use in place of indigenous languages is very common.

However, the city can also become a place for native people to reflect on their origin and future in a new way and produce new personal goals. In Rio Branco, a Cashinahua girl who seemed to have a large number of non-Indian friends told me how she had been introduced to her indigenous origins. She explained how she had learned the Cashinahua language, songs, and body paintings from her parents and grandparents visiting her urban home. Her

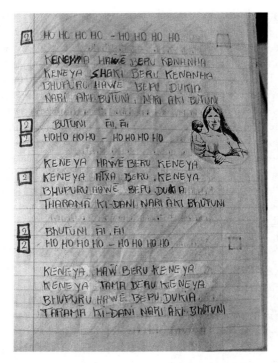

Figure 6.3 Notebook of a Cashinahua girl living in Rio Branco, containing Cashinahua songs

father always brought a recorded tape of Cashinahua chants for her when he visited the village, and she wrote down the words in her notebook.

For some young people learning the oral history, chants and ritual practices of their own indigenous group can be considered a form of acquiring knowledge that is not necessarily passed on through everyday actions, especially if there are no older relatives to accompany the youth in the learning process. By contrast, in the reserve, young people lack qualified teachers at their state-funded schools.

Those young native migrants in cities with the least knowledge of their past and cultural traditions usually had the biggest problems in terms of marginalization. This applied to both Apurinã and Cashinahua boys and girls living in the city, who all said that their parents had never told them what life was like before in the village or the traditions of their people. Some of them spend time with the most marginalized people of their neighborhoods, were even involved in criminal activities, used drugs, or had early pregnancies. For their parents, it was very sad and difficult. These young people had been unable to produce strong links with any place[5] and consequently suffered from identity problems and finding their place in the world. In Acre, one of the indigenous leaders told me that the best thing for the youths is to have an objective when staying in the city and generally to focus on the kind of knowledge important to the community. On the other hand, heavy consumption of alcohol can be linked, for instance, with learning nonindigenous ways of being (cf. Calavia Sáez 2004), and the men from the reserve, old and young alike, indeed have the habit of getting drunk in cities. But it has already turned into a real social problem among many indigenous young people. Generally speaking, certain practices and types of knowledge that only young Indians can master widen the gap between generations in indigenous communities. Ritual encounters can introduce new sounds, designs, beings, and smells across urban and rural, as well as generational, backgrounds.

New Ritual Encounters

In addition to shared practices and value-laden discourses, rituals and their networks and objects create relatedness in new ways, as well as producing indigenousness in contextual everyday relations. In every society, certain territorial and temporal spaces exist where a person enters into a zone of disorder and anonymity. These are gateways to different communicational and codified systems. The ritualistic behavior denotes important cultural values and thus displays the things that divide cultural potentialities: those things to be valued and pursued, those to be avoided, and those to be remembered or forgotten (Cormier 2003; Anttonen 2000). Through rituals indigenous adolescents can acquire the knowledge of how to be real humans. Ritualistic practices connect generations to each other and connect the past to the present and to new ways of doing and being (see Hill 1993; Cormier 2003; Calavia Sáez 2004; Lagrou 2007). It is important to note that in ritualistic spaces feelings of placelessness, corporeality, and noncorporeality are experienced, enabling a type of relatedness beyond generational, ethnic, rural-urban, and gender differences. As has become apparent, and as the new social organization and political actions reveal even more clearly, "community" and kin are increasingly understood in a broader sense, including the Manchineri residing in the other villages, in urban areas, and occasionally even Indians from other groups.

Political and cultural gatherings can also be regarded as new modern ritual spaces, because these events are marked by a particular kind of symbolism and involve a shift to different symbols and habits through the setting of specific times and spaces. When participating in them, young indigenous people openly show themselves to be part of the indigenous population and thus a population distinct from other Brazilians. Certain things are worn here with pride, and people become symbols that mark identity, producing a sense of group cohesion and togetherness. These events enable embodiments that carry memories of the past and reproduce its values. Manchineri youths living in the city and the reserve can take part in large-scale ritual dances in political and cultural meetings.

One Manchineri boy told me that the Manchineri started to practice their traditional dances in 2001, when a group from their people took part for the first time in a cultural meeting of indigenous peoples held in Rio Branco. He said that before then, he had never even heard about the Manchineri dances, *yikaklu*. Manchineri from the furthest village, Extrema, usually participated in these indigenous cultural meetings in the urban centers, since these were attended by people who knew the most elaborate body painting designs, who sang the best, and who knew how to make *yikaklu*.

However, symbolic manifestations do not have to be exclusively those of one group. Nor do cultural elements have to be ancient or ancestral, since they have always been adapted to the current time and space. New manifestations do not mean the people involved are no longer indigenous and do not lessen their authenticity (cf. Pacheco de Oliveira 2004). The power clashes between Indians and nonnatives today are about recognition. The indigenous representations chosen are usually those that indigenous people know are easily interpreted by "the Other" as exotic: the highly colorful feathers and body paintings that the nonindigenous others want to see. This is also what attracted the eco-political movements to take the Amazonian Indians as leading media figures as early as the 1980s (Conklin and Graham 1995). Non-Apurinã Indians in Rio Branco sometimes used the Apurinã word *xingané*—or an Indian from a non-Panoan-speaking group the Pano word *mariri*—to refer to their peoples' traditional dances. They were criticized for not being real Indians. Besides the concepts, those Indians who borrow cultural objects for cultural presentations from their "ethnic neighbors" usually say that they no longer possess the material culture of their indigenous group. However, there is a desire to persuade people to accept that indigenous peoples have specific rights and that they should be respected as they are or have been. This is a result of the history of domination and conflicts.

Ritual practices enable the creation of a space of communication and interaction for the present-day indigenous community, connecting it to the past, present, and future. In many rituals, the focus is on the ancestors and the sociocosmos of the jungle, and the ritualistic objects convey not only memories but also images of the different ways of seeing the world and interacting with its entities. The use of certain objects and visual imagery like body paintings, musical instruments, headdresses, and pipes marks out the rituals. The rituals reflect the consolidation of social categories since they amount to techniques for dealing with cultural boundaries that in other contexts may be difficult to discern.

Ritual practices strengthen the social values and identity of the group. They also allow a bond to be created with their own indigenous land and community, which for those in the city, in their everyday life, is effectively a nonexistent community whose lifestyle is very different. Rituals also differ from the everyday context of the community in the reserve, which usually considers the people living in the city to be non-Indians. The rituals can be bearers of old values against new insecurities, as they make it possible to access shared knowledge and memories of the indigenous communities.

For some indigenous youths in the city in particular, it seemed to be more important to represent something generically indigenous rather than their own indigenous origins. I realized just how much indigenous cultures influenced each other when Indians asked other people from indigenous groups at cultural and political events to paint them and exchange different cultural objects, such as craftwork, jewelry, snuff, and so forth. These can also be conceived as new forms of relatedness with potential affines. The nature of the object involved is secondary; what matters is the desire and the mode of representation, such as body painting. This is precisely what Urban (1996, 189) says about rituals: "Ceremonies create an image of community by shrinking the spatial distances between families, but they also transform the spatial relationships." While indigenousness has united various indigenous groups, it has also caused the hybridization of indigenous cultures. Yet it is not only about hybridization but also about self-representation as such. The social space of indigenous politics is also, in effect, a space of cultural learning.

In specific manifestations, nativeness can be represented in a variety of ways, including body painting and the use of decorative and symbolic objects. The intercultural political and cultural events maintain the symbolic order of society since they are moments that can act as models of collective values. When indigenous representations are used, it is to show the difference maintained by a certain social group, reflecting the struggle of indigenous populations to establish their position in society as indigenous peoples. Indigenous identities are thus also shown in new ways. For instance, a young Manchineri environmental agent used a Cashinahua indigenous cotton bag that he had received on his training course, wearing it proudly as a sign of his indigenousness. As has been argued in terms of the ethnic identity of indigenous groups, indigeneity is about self-definition and the distinction imposed by mainstream society. And as Bourdieu ([1991] 1997, 221) argued in relation to ethnic identity and power struggles, "struggles over ethnic or regional identity—in other words, over the properties (stigma or emblems) linked with the origin and its associated durable marks, such as accent, are a particular case of the different struggles over classifications, struggles over the monopoly of power to make people see and believe, to get them to know and recognize, to impose the legitimate definition of the divisions of the social worlds and, thereby, to make and unmake groups." Thus people's bodies are produced in this social space in relation to their own community and other indigenous groups but also in relation to the dominant society's power.

The media has played a fundamental role in creating indigenous politics and cultural manifestations as a space of interaction between Indians and non-Indians. In Acre, the local newspapers created a new image of the Indians and supplied important information in support of the Indian movement.[6] But today it is not only the media that enables "imaginations in collective forms," to use the term introduced by Appadurai (1996), but also essentially different articulations, discourses, and modern rituals such as cultural and political encounters that connect indigenous youths with politics and the nation-state from a young age. During the political negotiations, indigenous spokespeople may articulate their cultural and political demands and express their existence with special needs as specific groups or as indigenous peoples as a whole. Besides their role as political manifestations, the political and cultural events have a considerable spiritual significance.

The present-day rituals can also be understood as recreating a human perspective that infiltrates and partially dissolves different contemporary divides between generations, genders, and rural and urban dwellers. These ritual actions transform the youths into independent thinkers and provide important psychological support for their development and identity formation: the construction of personal and group identity. Many rituals, such as *ayahuasca* rituals, cultural and political meetings, and traditional dances, should also be seen as purifying and healing actions, since they often make the young people feel that "now it is all right," "we are all here," "this is like it was before" (or as they would act on the reserve), "this is my community," and "now we can be at peace." Especially as a healing act, shamanism represents the indigenous knowledge and oral history that protect their identity and dignity.[7] Furthermore, people performing shamanic practices usually feel the need to reproduce the knowledge in the present in new ways in order to continue strong and firm.

The ritual practices are transmissions between the urban and rural residents, and different times, generations, and places. They permeate the cultural flows from the center to the periphery (from the urban area to the reserve, or the opposite, depending on the point of view) and vice versa (Hannerz 1997) where things can transform into other things. In this sense, the rituals still perform the same function—namely, that of crossing cultural categories. Ritual practices are the most important ways of learning about the myths, histories, beings, and viewpoints of each native group. They also increase the social inclusion of the native population and help build a sense of community through, for example, community discourses in village meetings, indigenous cultural and political events, and shamanic rituals. There is even a certain seriousness required, as in the *ayahuasca* rituals, and older people are more respected. Consequently, communal rituals also contribute to producing kinship relations.

For instance, a young Manchineri man living in the city, who had been interested in shamanism and was experienced in *ayahuasca* shamanism, moved to his original village and took a position in the community as a teacher. Through shamanism he maintained his relationship with his community, and this also helped him reproduce his kinship relations. He had also previously been involved in the student movement and the Manchineri association. Cultural knowledge he had acquired in the city, where he had finished the upper secondary school, his social networks, and shamanic knowledge were all important resources for him. However, he also had to work on farms to earn money for the things he needed for his small family in the reserve. The teachers' salaries are paid irregularly. He was invited to the village school where classes were given at advanced level. The village leader wanted to replace the teacher as he was a son-in-law of the veteran Manchineri teacher who had started to work in the city. According to the leader, this experienced teacher should not have abandoned teaching the village class and should not have accepted a new governmental job in the closest urban center.

The indigenous women are also needed in many communal roles. Some young women have in fact become experts in ritual practices, such as in shamanic techniques. In Acre, two young Yawanawa women have turned into shamans through vigorous shaman training. These Yawanawa sisters completed a long period of shamanic training in 2006, including one year of isolation in the jungle. In the media, they were presented as the first shaman women. One of them said that she had observed that shamanic knowledge was weakening in her community and she therefore wanted to do something about it. The sisters were even invited to the senate and were granted the *Mulher-Cidadã Bertha Lutson* award on International Women's Day. Their wish to learn shamanistic skills was initially opposed by the community members, but since their father was an important leader and they would not desist, the oldest shaman eventually relented and passed his knowledge on to them. He took the sisters to the forest where they had to observe a special diet and experience the effects of sacred hallucinogenic plants. Today, one of these sisters has participated in the course for indigenous project managers in the neighboring state and has started studies at the local federal university. The shamanic knowledge has allowed them both to reproduce their indigenous practices in new ways, such as creating new designs for clothes and body paintings and new chants, even though they do not work as shamans. Some people in their community still think that the sisters should not be allowed to interact with the nonhuman world. This fact shows how gender norms in the relations with the nonhuman (spirit) world have changed little, though in interethnic relations the danger posed by the female body and its difference seem no longer to be so significant. On the other hand, the increased interest and participation of young women in shamanic practices is one of the outcomes of the change in the contemporary challenges involved in reproducing the community and its knowledge.

Moreover, in order to be a legitimate and acknowledged social actor, whether man or woman, and continue the work as representatives of the indigenous community, close relations with the community members have to be continuously produced. Rituals reproduce reciprocity, trust, and group identity, all of which are central concepts in Amazonian sociocosmologies. Consequently, the participation of spokespeople in these rituals, especially if they live for long periods away from the community, is extremely important. Involvement in the ritual practices, along with many other current practices discussed in this chapter, bring together people with different ways of experiencing their belonging to an indigenous community. In the next chapter, I end the book by examining the diverse ways of being Indian and the new image of Amazonian indigenous populations.

CHAPTER 7

The Diversity of Being an Indian

After exploring Manchineri sociocosmology, the passages to adulthood, shamanism, mobility between urban and rural areas, young people as spokespersons, and the current views of relationality in the previous chapters, it has become clear that a highly diverse range of human and nonhuman actors are viewed as a source of transformative power. Young people have an active role themselves in constituting their relations to these actors and thus in constructing hteir agency. Likewise for Amazonian indigenous peoples the natural environment has been related to various types of animal, plant, and tree beings and other spirits. In particular the differences represented by non-Indians in Amazonian sociocosmology deserve more attention, because today indigenous groups increasingly act with different humans. This chapter begins with an analysis of young native people's relations to the humans of their age group: I shall discuss youth culture and the sense in which this has been indigenized. Then I shall describe the new image of Indians to which the young generation has been contributing greatly, since young people wish to be indigenous anywhere and in their own way. This helps us better understand what counts as "identity" and "agency" for young Indians and how young Amazonian indigenous people negotiate and deal with the new social, cultural, and political situations in the global world.

Indigenized Youth Cultures

National and global youth cultures offer the possibility of new conducts and manners and the crossing of cultural and social boundaries. Young people's tastes in clothing, items, and music are representations of global youth cultures that can also be considered to be deterritorialized (Ortiz 1998; Tomlinson 2004). Among Amazonian youths, the "participation" in youth cultures appears to be especially related to the educational sphere, including school, studying, and being a student, all related to accessing the power of the dominant society and its youngsters. In the reserve, different clothing and language are also used at the indigenous schools. The neat young people's "city clothes," purchased in the nearby municipalities, could be the clothing of any adolescent from the region. Youth cultures are expressed in jeans and shoes and many other objects and personal items. Moreover, schools are one of the contexts for government policies, despite the fact that the villages try to construct educational programs adapted to their own social realities. Leisure time may also be marked by the use of certain attitudes and leisure activities in which youth cultures become visible.

For indigenous adolescents in urban areas, television, leisure activities, various ideologies, media sources, outfits, the use of language, and music all carry different ideas and values that can help them feel more independent, enabling them to construct their own opinions. Moreover, in urban areas, certain places are sites for the young people to hang out, such as town squares, along with the venues for activities organized specifically for youngsters, such as concerts. However, young Indians usually prefer to remain in the company of their relatives or other indigenous people. When I met with youngsters in their free time hanging out in the city center, they were often with their kin—sisters, brothers, or cousins.

Figure 7.1 Manchineri siblings in Rio Branco

In the city, youth cultures are social contexts formed by relatively anonymous actors in collective groups that meet in public squares where communication is possible, desirable, or even obligatory.[1] When the indigenous adolescents from the reserve visit urban areas and walk in the city during their visits, they try to achieve this bonding, albeit just temporarily. In this space, young indigenous people may feel relatively strong ties with other adolescents—Indian and non-Indians alike. However, youths coming from the reserves rarely speak Portuguese well, so membership in the dominant society can be expressed in other ways: by certain objects, personal items, and clothing or by going to *forrós* (popular dances) in the city.

As we have seen, when young Indians visit the urban centers, it is easier for them temporally to embody youth cultures other than their own. For some young Indian adolescents, being personified as Indians—for instance, being thought as unknowledgeable of urban life—may also represent an experience of feeling subject to strict personal rules and possessing distinctive characteristics. Thus they sometimes prefer to enter into the social system of anonymity and "hide" their "Indianness." In the city, this can be strategical, but it can also be unintentional and more familiar to personal life histories of a young person, as is typical to Apurinã youngsters, whose families have very often moved to Rio Branco as the result of internal conflicts in their villages and seldom have contact with their homelands. Moreover, usually neither of their parents is white. Many of the indigenous adolescents who have resided in the city for a long time do not seem to have any marked experience of displacement. When a young person wants to avoid being identified by his or her indigenous background, ethnocentrism may lose its meaning in the context of national and global youth cultures (cf. Tomlinson 2004), since various positions that are normally marked, along with the internal rules of domination, may be temporarily abolished. Indigenous youths may adapt to behavioral codes that help bypass not only the social spheres of indigenousness but also the older age groups of Brazilian society. Girls, boys, young women, and young men mobilize youth cultures.

Youth cultures relate young Indians to the members of the dominant society and to knowing its manners and codes in their own ways. Besides the clothing already mentioned, these connotations—found in both the urban and reserve contexts of Amazonia—are linked to regional and national music cultures, such as *forró* and *sertanejo*, and to technologies. In the city indigenous young people also listen to other genres typical to their age group, including pop and rock music. For instance, some urban young people at the time of my fieldwork were fans of Charlie Brown Jr., a Brazilian pop rock group associated with skateboarding culture. Young people want to experience different new things, and this is equally true for indigenous adolescents.

Indigenous youths in the city also frequently use the Internet to converse with their nonindigenous and indigenous friends. In the beginning of my fieldwork girls also started increasingly to visit cyber cafés with their friends. Today many young indigenous people of my study use email and social media, which is a powerful tool to express opinions, to organize meetings, and to access the latest information. In social media they have almost an equivalent number of indigenous and nonindigenous contacts.[2] Some of the indigenous youths living in Rio Branco use Facebook, for instance, almost daily to talk about their family life, indigenous politics, problems related to studying, spiritual things, and love life. Indigenous languages are also increasingly used on the Internet.

Youth cultures are not homogeneous, nor do they refer only to counter-cultures or subcultures but to something that can enable a break from typical ways of relating, talking, eating, clothing oneself, and celebrating in indigenous communities. Youth cultures have different meanings for different indigenous young people in different situations, and adapting to national or global youth cultures depends on the will to act in certain social environments. Through youth cultures, indigenous youths are creating something of their own and distinguishing themselves from their own indigenous community, previous generations, the dominant culture, or all these simultaneously. The intergenerational arguments that the youths in the city mentioned in my research were often over issues related to their ways of dressing and hairstyles or over housework. Some mothers did not want their girls to have short hair, for example. In the city, therefore, these issues can be seen within the intersections of generations, ethnicity, and gender, as some of the issues were related to aspects of youth cultures that nonindigenous parents would have opposed, too. In the reserve, the generational conflicts are more often about the young generation's capacity to take the lead in the community's relations with non-Indians. However, in the reserve, the word that appeared the most in the answers given by the Manchineri adolescents when talking about cultivating a good life was "respect," to older generations especially, along with other closely associated themes, such as harmony, responsibility, hospitality, trust, and obeying parents. In the city, respect for parents as such was not emphasized, but Manchineri youngsters thought that family life, proximity, and caring for others were important.

Language also separates young people from their elders, since even in the city some elders speak only the indigenous language. Some youths in the city cannot speak the indigenous language at all, widening the gap between young people and the community's elders. Furthermore, they would sometimes laugh at words or their indigenous names that their grandparents told them about. Many elders also worry that nonindigenous practices are replacing the community's own ways of doing things. Producing and participating in global youth cultures may increase when traditional ways of doing things are no longer reproduced in the community and young people's social environment, but in this case youth cultures are no longer just an attempt to master the embodied knowledge and power of the dominant society.

Indigenous youths have also brought new elements to Amazonian youth cultures that, so far, have lacked indigenous contributions. Young nonindigenous people may be a reference group, even though indigenous youths carry their own ethnic differences and thus introduce new indigenous representations. New artistic expressions are created, for example, mixing youth styles with indigenous objects such as necklaces, bracelets, and cotton bags traditional to their indigenous groups. A few "interethnically skilled" young people have also made contacts with nonindigenous DJs, mixing rhythms from their indigenous groups with electronic sounds. This kind of networking is also about constructing new types of sociality and new indigenous identities.

Most of the youngsters do distinguish themselves from nonindigenous youths, even if they adopt youth cultures in their clothing styles and other ways. Indigenous youth cultures in the Amazon region are on the way to becoming subcultures to "mainstream" youth cultures or parallel cultures. In Southern Brazil, a group of Guarani youths in the state of Mato Grosso do Sul called Brô MCs received widespread media attention in January 2012 for rapping in Guarani about the circumstances and reality experienced in their indigenous territory. Elsewhere, for instance, rock and rap music has recently been produced in the Sámi language in Scandinavia and, similarly, in the Maori language in New Zealand. Some of the first indigenous rappers were probably Maori adolescents in the 1980s, who boosted their self-esteem through break-dance, hip-hop and rap music. According to Mitchell (2001), they indigenized rap and hip-hop by singing in the Maori language about their beliefs, as well as about the political and social problems the Maori face. However, the Maori youths initially said that they used black American street culture symbols instead of Maori symbols to compensate for their lack of indigenous knowledge. Moreover, if they had worn Maori symbols, others would have thought that they had no respect for their own culture. Later the Maori language was used without English translations and new hybrid musical expressions were created. In general, the symbols of black American cultures are fairly uncommon among Amazonian indigenous youths, despite the frequency with which they are found among youths globally.

In the Amazon region, many indigenous youths give visibility and feeling to their indigenous identity in new ways. As elsewhere in the world, in Latin America there seems to be a close relationship between migrant youths and the creation of marginal cultural phenomena. Some young migrants, for instance, have been linked to subcultures in urban areas, such as rap music (on Mexico, see Ariza 2005). For indigenous young people living in the city, adaptation to a new dwelling place that is different from their home may be a life-changing experience, and integration depends on a series of familiar, personal, and contextual factors.

It should be borne in mind that a sense of disunity with the dominant society usually results in stronger feelings of ethnicity among indigenous groups, and young indigenous people still face racism. Looking at Amazonian youngsters shows that there is not just one view of the world, as has often been presumed in discussions of a so-called indigenist identity for Latin America, for example (see Larrain 2000). Although this may be closer to the aims of some extreme indigenous political movements, which see a complete return to indigenous values as the only solution, young people demand more autonomy and respect as members of indigenous populations, even if they also decide to pursue non-Indian or urban lifestyles. Overall, for indigenous young people, youth cultures offer bridges to act with people across class, race, gender, and ethnic divides. Young people's construction of bodies is a continuous activity, and youth cultures provide them with one more layer that can be applied. Youth cultures offer an environment for new conduct and manners and the crossing of cultural and social borders.

Continuing to Be Mobile

Throughout this study we have seen that in various social environments, indigenous adolescents integrate, exclude themselves, and play a part in new encounters with their own indigenous groups, other indigenous groups, age groups, and the various subgroups of the dominant society, creating new ways of relating. Their process of sociality is therefore multidimensional. Recently, many Amazonian indigenous young people have made their own films, websites, records, educational materials, and radio programs to show off their new image and views to the world. New knowledge and forms of cooperation, for instance with nonindigenous artists, filmmakers and musicians, have allowed transformations and the possibility to continue to be mobile.

Some indigenous Amazonian peoples have managed to benefit from new technologies to reproduce their "rituals" and cultural practices, celebrating the splendor of living oral histories and enhancing the community's relatedness in an effective way.[3] In Acre, Internet connections via satellite have helped the Ashaninka and Yawanawa populations develop in the way they want, better protect their lands, and strengthen their cultures through new contacts. The Yawanawa have also worked together with clothing and fabric designers, reproducing their body paintings in new forms. Youngsters often intermediate with partners who later become friends, but community members may also consume new products and are proud of their dynamic traditions. The groups are internationally known and respected for their image of sustainable living, which has helped them acquire more contracts with business enterprises, artists, organizations, and many other private actors. Possessing some degree of economic capital can therefore help boost the sense of dynamic indigenousness.

Contrary to the aims of integrationist politics decades earlier, many Indians continue to identify themselves as Indians. During that time there had been a silent resistance to acculturation. New forms of communication and new connections have allowed them to discover differences between their indigenous cultures and the fact that some indigenous groups still "practice their culture" or the contrary. They have also noticed that their own cultural change cannot be explained exclusively by the impact of rubber production and colonization in the region, but has also depended on other social, political, and economic factors. Overall, many of today's indigenous young people are more actors than members of excluded communities, and they have already ensured the continuity of indigenousness in a fresh way.

In indigenous cultural and political events where indigenousness was embodied in body paintings, headdresses, and cotton bags, for instance, indigenous young people also wanted to mix traditional body painting designs with totally new ones, such as hearts or even the flags of football teams, when they were painted by others or were painting themselves. Although using the traditional means of representation—decorating one's body through painting that relates to nonhuman agencies important to the community and its value systems—they also lived their indigenousness through those things that played a part in their everyday lives, such as football teams and other iconography used by their indigenous and nonindigenous peer groups alike. In such ways indigenousness can be contrasted to non-Indians but also to the indigenous groups. Being in a particular indigenous group exists within a continual process of transformation and organization of diversity in which knowledge is embodied according to different environments. This can be pictured more as a movement, since being is a series of temporary transformations rather than a state. As one young Manchineri man said, "our culture will change. Before it was different and now it is different."

As challenges vary, the available physical and symbolic materials are used dynamically to construct what needs to be created. Once when some young girls were talking about body paintings in the reserve, one of them went inside the house for a moment: she came out again soon after, holding her baby covered in traditional designs made with a red felt-tipped pen. In the past, such designs would only have been applied using paint made from genipap fruit. Ancestors and other beings of the forest activated in the paintings, for instance, can be related in various forms and ways to different people.

Young people especially seem to modify and integrate new elements into traditional forms. Some traditional practices receive new shapes, without which they are considered too old-fashioned and lacking in movement. When I arrived once at Jatobá village, for instance, I was wearing a traditional necklace made of seeds and using a handmade cotton bag, both made in the villages I had visited previously. A girl told me that these items were extremely ugly. I already knew that they preferred pieces of jewelry made of plastic gems that they bought and threaded into a necklace for themselves.

For indigenous youths, the notion of well-being is still based on proximity and establishing interactive subjectivity (cf. Overing and Passes 2000). However, collectiveness can be represented in diverse forms, creating memberships in new ways and participating in different social groups. The similarities can be produced to unite people from one's own indigenous community, people living in the city and the reserve, or people beyond ethnic frontiers. These actors can also be identified by expertise, age, gender, place of living, and history. Consequently, so-called real people are constituted in relation to various types of humans and in different encounters with indigenous and nonindigenous agents. Since my study was carried out in many different social contexts, I came to realize that all these strategies contribute to their agency and interaction with beings, nonhuman and human, in the contemporary world.

In general, young people adopt different roles in changing social situations, a practice akin to code shifting. School, communal meetings, political negotiations, and rituals in which young Indians participate all outline social spaces where different languages and gestures are used and the different qualities of actors are valued. The changing social environments have their own ways and styles of dress, language, bodily practices, values, and obedience to rules that indicate the positions young indigenous people create and adopt when confronting today's power structures. The urban school environment, for instance, usually enables the embodiment of Brazilian or global youth cultures, and at the same time exacerbates the invisibility of indigenous backgrounds. Some other encounters support other types of embodiments, but they can be interrelated and may overlap and affect each other, reflecting difference making among the youths.

Indigenous youths in different socially constructed environments may deal with many different embodiments, each of them potentially empowering in its own way. Mobility and multinaturalism, various perspectives in the world, have been noted as characteristic of Amazonian peoples in general, alterability being their typical state of being, so to speak (see, for example, Viveiros de Castro 1996, 2002; Stolze Lima [1996] 1999; Vilaça 2005). The way in which beings see the world is the same, but they see and understand things differently. In order to approach others, to see the world in the same ways as the others do, one has to change bodily. Alterability allows the acquisition of strength, transformation, and continuity by relating to others and being influenced by their agency. Scholars have noted how Amazonian Indians are open to the Other, and enemies and predators are fundamental in the reproduction and the production of distinctions (Lévi-Strauss 1966; Viveiros de Castro 1992; Fausto 1999; Fausto and Heckenberger 2007). The Other is thus an essential element of "us."

However, corporeal transformations have principally been examined in terms of the relations between humans and animals (Viveiros de Castro 1996; Stolze Lima [1996] 1999), with enemies (Viveiros de Castro 1992; Fausto 1999), or between Indians and non-Indians (Vilaça [1999] 2007; Gow [2003] 2007; Lasmar 2005; Kelly 2011). But the alteration of bodies constitutes a variety of categories of difference, such as being young or educated, knowing indigenous traditions, living in the forest environment, or working close to the state power. Corporeality is considered to alter depending on the knowledge embodied, the age group, other indigenous groups, or with youths in general regardless of their ethnicity, class, or gender. Young people produce bodies based in everyday actions and lifestyles, depending on what the person eats, what kind of work they perform, what clothes they use, and the social interactions in which they engage (Vilaça [1999] 2007; Lasmar 2005), but the approaches are not about becoming more white or indigenous, or more similar to people of the city or the community. The study has shown that these groups, especially other humans (indigenous groups and non-Indians), are much more diverse and heterogeneous. Hence they are related differently depending on the mutual understanding reached, which may be based on a similar world view (shamanism), urban cultures (youth cultures), political opinions (indigenous rights or the environmentalist movement), and so forth.

Approaching an increasing variety of indigenous and nonindigenous actors in different corporeal ways enables indigenous people to benefit from distinct social contexts and temporarily create relatedness with different groups. In other words, these altering embodiments guide young people in different social situations vis-à-vis their possibilities in social structures, and this sense they comprise different kinds of *habitus* that generate and organize practices and representations.[4] However they are not necessarily learned at home or during childhood, and thus they are not similar to the *habitus* originally understood by Bourdieu ([1980] 1990). Even though embodiments may be unconscious or conscious actions and reflective positions (Gibbs 2006), they are produced by socially structured conditions. An examination of the different social situations helps us understand what kind of bodies young people produce according to the subjects, power relations, possibilities, and environment at hand. The body is produced in relation to the social structures and power relations involving Indians and non-Indians, Indians and other indigenous groups, genders, generations, and community members. Thus indigenous youths alter their bodies to obtain the power and knowledge possessed by different groups in multilayered and intersecting ways, such as being an urban-educated, young indigenous person or a young indigenous person with shamanic skills, experienced in interethnic relations. The understanding of the world is embodied and gained through acting in the world.

Social mobility has contributed to the appearance of new images of Indians both within the indigenous community and among the dominant society. Indigenous youths therefore contribute to the new image of indigenous people. Even though the Indian population often experiences disrespect, especially in the cities, they still want to remain as they are, possessing their own cultural differences, while simultaneously being recognized as full Brazilian citizens. They do not wish to become whites: rather, they want more autonomy and respect as different peoples and individuals. Moreover, the "indigenous" bodies produced in human networks with non-Indians and other Indians alike differ from those of older generations or those associated with indigenous people in general (see Virtanen 2010a). For the dominant society, for instance, the sight of indigenous people painted in traditional designs while holding mobile phones, using the latest models of laptop computers, or walking in cities is still changing stereotypes of Indians.

Figure 7.2 Cashinahua girl, Raimunda, at the Indigenous Cultures Encounter held in Cruzeiro do Sul in 2004

However, indigenous youths are often expected by the dominant power structures to engage as Indians only in "indigenous" encounters, such as their own territories, rituals, and indigenous politics. Amazonian indigenous people are seldom regarded as professionals other than in "indigenous" sectors of the dominant society. Today's Amazonian youths are living at a time when Indians have slowly come to be considered persons beyond their own kin groups, yet there is still only one classification admitted by society: the traditional one. Young indigenous people have ruptured the idea of the Indian who has "tenacity and synchronization with nature" (DaMatta 1995, 273), and they resist the tendency for Indians to be seen as people purified of all urban and "modern" elements. Indigenousness may refer to primordial claims of blood, language, soil, territory, and cultural values, and to a certain extent cultures, but it does not exclude other elements from it. Heterogeneity, complexity, and diversification are all ways in which contemporary "traditional" cultures continue to survive (see Hall 1992). Indeed, this has always been the case.

In contrast, the Brazilian nation-state and media usually still prefer to present the indigenous population with beautiful body paintings in a natural setting whenever they appear on television or in official state publications. Consequently only in this way have indigenous peoples been considered "real" Indians and seen as a homogenous group. Overall, Indians have been taken for granted as part of the Brazilian identity, insofar as in Latin American "the cosmic race" has traditionally consisted of Indian, black, and white elements (Freyre [1963] 1966; Ribeiro 2000). In Latin America, the racial heritage and the proclamation of racial democracy have formed the cornerstone of the establishment of the nation-states, yet this is frequently criticized as a myth owing to the persistent prejudice shown against Afro-descendent and indigenous populations, who are still unable to exercise full citizenship (Ramos 2003; Costa Vargas 2004).

The stereotypes persist of Indians as primitive, irresponsible, wild, lazy, treacherous, and vagrant (Aquino 1977; Ramos 1998; cf. Appadurai 1988; Rosaldo 1989). Occasionally it is still assumed that the only place for Indians lies in the reservations and jungle. Urban areas are still reserved for the "high cultures" responsible for governance and politics. I remember how once when I was visiting an upper-class Brazilian family in Rio Branco, their two-year-old daughter was drinking from a jug (instead of the glass) and the mother reproached her, saying, "Don't behave like an Indian!" I was disappointed as she knew about my work with the indigenous population and did not even recognize her own reaction and use of words.

On the other hand, as a legacy of the romanticism prevalent during the period of state building, and especially more recently following the end of the region's military regimes, many Latin American state leaders have promoted the existence of indigenous groups as symbols of the nation's strength. They have also consequently been seen as a tourist attraction in many places in Latin America. In Acre, from the early 1990s onward, a change has taken place in attitudes toward its first inhabitants—that is, indigenous groups, traditional extractivist communities, and river dwellers. Today, they are seen as the roots of Acrean identity. Local politics have played a key role in increasing interethnic contacts and acknowledging the traditional ways of life of the river dwellers and indigenous peoples living in Acre. The state government has also initiated indigenous education and sociocultural development projects. "Traditional communities" have become discussed more frequently in public statements calling for the preservation of indigenous knowledge, although their proposals are rarely fulfilled. These initiatives can be seen as attempts by the state government to recognize the tragic history of local communities and acknowledge them as special groups. The recent recognition of the history of the *Povos da Floresta* (rubber tappers, indigenous peoples, and riverside and rural communities) has formed part of this attempt to improve the cohesion of the state's population, advocating that when these become more active agents, they will be able to help build present-day Acre and ensure its future development.

To some extent this can be seen as an attempt to integrate these populations into the capitalist system—to help them become producers and consumers. As Hill (2003, 173) notes, "Official state recognition of indigenous cultural practices can be a mixed blessing. State appropriations of indigeneity have often become part of broader neonationalist or global agendas as failing liberal states desperately seek new ways of authenticating national identities." This means that indigenous peoples have also become more equal members of society when they have entered consumer culture and through it the process of globalization. Thus, according to García Canclini ([1999] 2000, 82), "the construction of democratic interculturality and opening of the Other" is related more than ever to market forces. At the same time, though, by displaying a multicultural face, Acre's acknowledgment of the indigenous population can be seen as part of a search for regional identity, counteracting the fact that the country's largest metropolises usually define Brazilian identity.

Indigenous people have used their image as "traditional" peoples as symbolic capital in new political situations and in making their demands (De la Cadena 2000; Ramos 2003; Bacigalupo 2004). Embodied indigenousness includes the idea of power, a factor we have to take into account. The emergence of this newly embodied indigeneity is especially linked to a *strange fetishism* (Ahmed 2000), since in order to achieve recognition, the indigenous youths have to move closer to becoming a stranger, contrary to the colonial period when Indians had to assimilate the whites. Whereas indigenous peoples once had to downplay their differences, they are now expected to display them vividly in order to be regarded as full human beings. Discourses on the dominant society's multiculturalism emphasize the encounter between the other and the self, but it is often taken for granted that there were or still are historically determined differences. This increases the strangeness. Hence, for indigenous adolescents to change their social place "from distant to close," they are still expected to appear something like the *noble savage*, the classic image of Indians.

For example, when one of my non-Indian Acrean friends heard that I was working with the Indians, she asked if I knew "the powerful Ashaninkas" (*Ashaninka poderosa*). The Ashaninka had become renowned in the media as one of the most traditional and sustainable communities in the state. The image of indigenous people has been changing particularly in response to growing awareness of their cultural knowledge and ecological conservationism. They have switched to being regarded as promoters of modernity, for instance by being recognized as the best conservers of nature (Carneiro da Cunha and Almeida Barbosa 2000, 2002; Ramos 2003; Nepstad et al. 2006). Today there are also various national and international nonindigenous NGOs supporting the Indian population. Thus, contrary to earlier ideas, indigenous peoples' voices have in some respects strengthened since national and global changes have actually helped bolster their cultural and ethnic identity.[5]

In Brazilian society, as in many others, indigenousness is still taken as an essential quality that has to be shown in the person's way of speaking and embodied in every relationship with others. Otherwise it cannot act as symbolic capital. In addition to encounters at an everyday level, many adolescents in my study also said that they are not taken as Indians at offices dealing with indigenous peoples if they live in the city and do not speak their own language. The difficulties center on the need to represent something you do not know, or something your people have never been, and being located between two cultures. As an Apurinã boy who came to the city to study once told me, "We who have studied today, we Indians—I don't mean just those from our own indigenous group—were prohibited from speaking in their language, weren't they? And today we are almost asked for money if we can't speak our mother tongue. But they don't think it was them who did that to us. And today we have this knowledge, and we are studying." Indigenous youths also aspire to interact with others without any need to be strange, exotic, the Other. This involves a move beyond nostalgia and cultural romanticism, the terms in which the eco-political movement, for instance, still saw Amazonian Indians in the 1980s and 1990s (Conklin and Graham 1995). Instead, young Indians already give a very realistic picture of their communities, whether they live in the reserves or the cities.

The new definitions of indigenousness found among young native urban Amazonians is reminiscent of the Argentinean Mapuche punks resisting the univocal image of Mapuche Indians created by the indigenous political movement itself, ignoring the diversity found among the Mapuche people (Briones

2007). When their indigenous background answers certain questions for adolescents themselves, they share this with others, but in their own ways. This is a new challenge for the contemporary young generation, a battle over classification and the introduction of a new vision of indigenousness: it does not have to be shown, so much as thought and felt. Young indigenous people seem to say that they have a right to adopt any lifestyle and cultural value. They can be indigenous anywhere, even if this is not shown in their physical bodies, speech, and behavior.

The challenges that young indigenous people experience today in terms of economic development processes and urbanization have prompted them to elaborate their own strategies, such as valuing education, organizing their groups politically, and reworking their rituals. Indian youths create their own marginal cultures, not only blurring cultural and social borders, but also renewing and recreating them. Young natives may embody their subject positions on a day-to-day basis in different social spaces, such as networks of shamanic practices, indigenous students, the forest-urban indigenous community, and (indigenized) youth cultures. They produce, recreate, and adopt rules prevalent in each structured framework, which involves employing different embodiments. Moreover, even gender issues are included in this new era of change, as a more active role for women is gradually being taken for granted among indigenous young people, whether in the reserves or the urban areas. Indigenous youngsters' production of specific bodies can be understood in the context of the local histories of indigenous peoples and today's power relations, rather than urban people joining urban movements as a resistance to individualization and social atomization (cf. Castells [1997] 2004).

Residents of the forest environments have to be prepared for new challenges and demands. The fact that many indigenous peoples are dealing more and more with governmental and nongovernmental officials and other agents means that skills and positions differ from the past. Previously living was directly dependent on the natural environment, including a wide variety of nonhuman beings, but today other powers affect indigenous peoples from the outside, such as the nation-state—especially in the form of health care, education, and territorial legislation—and people outside the reserves, such as NGOs. However, these other actors form a very heterogeneous group with their own intentions and histories. The power of the Other with which the Indians have to deal is more complex than it used to be, at least in terms of the relations between Indians and non-Indians. People attempt to achieve nonharmful relationships and close bonds with these powers in order to interact differently with the new actors, seeking to maintain balance and tranquility—in other words, to control various unknown social environments. The actions linked to these powers are a recreation of the world and were usually only seen previously in the traditional ritual cycles. Just as the forest environment was never a separate entity for Amazonian peoples (Viveiros de Castro 1996; Rival 2002), neither are these new unknown elements for contemporary indigenous communities. Current transitions to adulthood, the dynamics of shamanism, mobility, urbanization, and embodiments in different social encounters can all be understood in this context. Previously, the Manchineri puberty rituals involved a variety of physical ordeals designed to reinforce the person's spirit and physical strength. Today, for instance, showing a puberty body painting to classmates is more of a psychological ordeal, since the young person is making his or her difference visible and openly manifesting values that are typically questioned in Brazilian society. This is a way of showing indigenous identity, which is reconstructed in any place. Moreover, the puberty ritual, studying, certain types of matrimony, shamanism, and experiences with others in new environments are all different means for forming ways of belonging to certain indigenous peoples with specific traditions and knowledge. They have an essential meaning for the young person's identity construction. The experience of coming into adulthood is gendered, because it involves becoming women and men in generational lines mapped according to gender roles, though these are in some senses criticized and reevaluated.

Various indigenous adolescents in the reserve and the city are actively contributing to what is today defined as indigenousness, taking a dynamic approach to culture. Indigenous youths—who have various bodies and circulate between various social situations, ranging from the school where they dress in jeans, to ritual encounters in which a very different logic and epistemic system are deployed—have been especially viewed as people who fail to match the traditional image of indigenous peoples. They break with the image of Indians as people who are different only in terms of their ethnicity. By taking part in shamanic practices and the indigenous movement especially, they have also challenged the ideas informing many gendered practices.

From this perspective, we can see the activities of indigenous youths in indigenous politics, urban cultures and their leadership of shamanic healing sessions as a generational question. Young Indians constitute their agencies in multiple ways in relation to the power relations constructed through interaction with wider Brazilian society, the indigenous community and other Indians. Since adolescents are more familiar with this logic of multiple new social situations than older generations, they have tended to assume active roles in their indigenous communities. Meanwhile, they have received a new form of power by being viewed as Indians with certain rights. Indigenous adolescents have become noteworthy social agents and assumed various responsibilities, since they have recognized the new possibilities for producing their own symbolic social and cultural capital from various sources, including indigenous knowledge and history, their knowledge of new concepts, and the national education system. These can also be converted into economic capital.

Apprehending the dominant society's view of indigenousness is an important factor in reshaping young people's experiences, but it is not passively adopted. Rather, it has encouraged new encounters between the Indian populations of the cities and reserves, and between Indians and the various sectors of the dominant society in a new power relationship. It is important for these young people to feel that others are listening to them and that their actions are valued. While state policies have recognized the indigenous population living in urban areas, the policies have often started to look for their relatives in Indian lands and those working for their indigenous population in the cities. Young Indians still differentiate themselves from other migrants and make their own claims to cultural and political autonomy. In urban areas especially, the poor migrants coming from Brazil's hinterlands do not have such a powerful resource.

However, social mobility can also occur in response to a lack of opportunities. Many indigenous young people still suffer from serious marginalization, and adapting to set situations is painful. Those young people who have been able neither to become familiarized with their indigenous background nor to integrate into national Brazilian culture are on shakier ground. In my study, young people with social problems, such as unemployment, abandoning school, failure to study, or even criminal activities, were typically in such situations. They had not managed to construct their own version of the kind of humanity required in the context of modern urban Brazilian society.

Overall, frustration and a loss of self-esteem occurs when the person does not know in his or her socialized body how to act and talk with new people, or, therefore, how to be guided by the rules of the game of the social field in question. This occurs, for instance, when indigenous adolescents have to negotiate with new actors in constantly changing situations. Then the new perspective cannot be established, maximized, or lived through. It means that certain qualities and abilities cannot be activated in the human body. The conflict arises not because of the encounter with new things and situations but because the young person has no control over the situation or because access to the required new information is denied. If a certain perspective cannot be taken, one cannot protect oneself—just as Ahmed (2000) writes in his description of the skins of people's bodies as borders that feel and mark differences. In this case, an adolescent is unsure how to react and behave in certain situations and thus lacks any scripts for the other person's behavior. Ignorance about what is going on, such as the kinds of decisions made in the city, affects people in the reserves. In turn, this ignorance causes fear and uncertainty. This is very common in the Amazon region where distances are huge and new forms of telecommunication have yet to be introduced to all remote areas. Information from the reserve or city cannot always be obtained when wanted. In the indigenous communities young people are expected to have more knowledge of nonindigenous ways of doing things and thus to become better accustomed to acting in new social situations. Many young Amazonian Indians wish to be less dependent on the state but cannot achieve this.

In a way, the situation of Amazonian indigenous youths is similar to the struggles of the indigenous movement as a whole, which still mainly fights for ethnic recognition in Brazilian society. But the fight of the young generation is different. Moreover, even if indigenousness serves as a basis for identity formation, indigenous identities can vary just as much as other types of identity. Young indigenous people are changing the stereotypes of Indians. For the dominant society, "Indianness" does not have to be consciously shown, but it must be perceptible in relationships. Due to their position constructed in the dominant society as indigenous people, but also due to the empowering process of Amazonian native communities, indigenous ways of doing and thinking have become more visible: they have been "rediscovered" and contested.

Recent global changes have caused new subject positions and social identities to emerge (see, for example, Hall 1992). Contemporary indigenous identities are among them. The main reason for this is the sociopolitical change in indigenous issues at national and international levels, but it is also a factor at local levels. In addition to state policies as a whole, debate over multiculturalism has increased in Brazilian society owing to changes in power relations and the process of democratization. In a way, indigenous populations have taken their place in some sectors of Ibero-American social systems (DaMatta 1995) where they can also apply their expertise and where their authority is becoming visible to others. But this multiculturalism is a different view from Amerindian multinaturalism, in which different things represent similar culture for human and nonhuman beings alike (see Viveiros de Castro 1996) and mobility between the different ways of seeing the world is essential.

It has also been argued that the constant alteration of bodies in indigenous Amazonian sociocosmologies implies a change in people's identities, especially the change between Indian and non-Indian (Vilaça [1999] 2007; Gow [2003] 2007; Lasmar 2005). However, when it comes to identity issues, the diversity of relations between non-Indians and Indians also has to be noted. The body is continually altering as young indigenous people in Amazonia engage in different social environments with different non-Indians and their groups with their many different lifestyles. By employing various embodiments, indigenous youngsters claim the right to adopt any lifestyle or cultural value. Sometimes indigenous youths dress and act more like Brazil's youth population as a whole, while at other times they prefer to maintain their distinctiveness from the dominant society. In the identity construction of indigenous youths, social distinctiveness is intimately related to the interplay of day-to-day practices, interactions, values, and knowledge of the places from which young people originate within various social groups.

Acting and relating are multidimensional since in some situations, depending on people's age, gender, and indigenous background, the place of residence can create group unity and serve as a basis for identity, or it can be "left out." The different bodies and perspectives produced by indigenous Amazonian peoples comprise ongoing negotiations of different lifestyles and forms of embodiments, which are in effect claims of identity (Bhabha 1994). Transforming the body by approaching certain types of being involves producing images for others. Power structures are embodied in the intersections of different elements meaningful to indigenous youth. This is all part of the contemporary diversity of being an Indian. Indeed identity is not fixed in the body (Shilling 1997). Identity is also formed in movement and paths of becomings: a process in which only some aspects are embodied or even visible to others.

In this book we have seen that indigenous adolescents operate with various social encounters: indigenousness is translocational and has to be considered in complex relations between a diversity of human and nonhuman actors. In this way native youths live what Westerners might term a postmodern subjectivity and lifestyle. For the youngsters, though, this is nothing new, since they grow up accustomed to transformations among a plurality of perspectives, a wide range of different points of view. They are familiar with the rapid changes between the visible and invisible, as well as between different concepts of time—both linear and cyclical. This is in sharp contrast to many nonindigenous young people, for whom seeing things from unusual perspectives may demand more time to become acquainted with them and whose social mobility may be more limited. Many poststructuralists have argued that cultures are fundamentally multiple and shifting and that the use of different representations is an important strategy when coming into contact with new social groups (García Canclini 1995; Gupta and Ferguson ([1997] 2001). Moreover, it has been typical for Westerners to see "nature" and "culture" as separate entities (Latour 1993). Knowledge has also been classified in this bipolar manner and identified with bounded places. Western cultures have overlooked the integration of knowledge produced by our movement, paths, and relations (Ingold 2009). By contrast, the actions and thinking of indigenous youths always contain elements from different social environments, nonhuman, and human agents, and various cultural influences, and in this sense the changes in relation to the past are less substantial.

The big change is young people's own agency and subjectivity in their transition to adulthood. This also constructs their current age-based identities as young people. The attitudes of young people change, assume new forms, and remain forever contextual. The forest environments of indigenous communities also change and are equally variable. It should be noted that indigenous traditions will almost certainly be lost, changed, or reproduced according to their capacity, as well as how valuable they are to people and whether they help recreate and reproduce relatedness. The key question for the future is what kind of elements will be absorbed into these complex cultural dynamics and the constitution of the lived worlds of indigenous adolescents, and how they will cope with new technologies without losing the sensitivity to forest environments that many of them still nurture.

Notes

Introduction

1. "Urban indigenous population" refers to indigenous population living in cities and does not refer to population that would be essentially different due to their urban presence.
2. On the Apuriná, see the work of Juliana Schiel (for instance, 2004) and Sidney Facundes (for instance, 2000). On the Cashinahua, see the recent studies of Ken Kensinger, Cecilia McCallum, and Els Lagrou, for example.
3. Population numbers of the three indigenous groups are from FUNASA (2010).
4. On the Yine in the Urubamba and Madre de Dios Rivers, see the studies of Peter Gow and Minna Opas.
5. Law 6001 of the Statute of the Indian, proclaimed on December 19, 1973, set out the new relationship between indigenous populations and the Brazilian state. Indian lands would be officially demarcated when they were shown to have historical bases. The Indians were released from tutelage as part of the broader aim of integrating them into Brazilian society. Following the provisions of the 1988 Constitution, Indians now had now the right to education and health care, civil and political rights, employment, their own forms of social organization, customs, language, beliefs and traditions, and land rights.
6. Deforestation has increased during the presidency of Dilma Rousseff, even though many efforts to reduce the process have been made at local and national levels.

Chapter 1

1. The mapped area is approximately 261 miles (420 kilometers) × 180 miles (290 kilometers).
2. *Maklojni* means "young woman"; *maklujni* means "young man."
3. See Rivière (1984); McCallum (2001).
4. The local government constructed the so-called women's houses at the beginning of the 2000s, but they were seldom used as the local government had failed to take into account that the women undertake some productive activities, such as weaving, at home where they can take care of the children and prepare food at the same time.
5. The missionaries left Jatobá in 1991, but only because there was already a trained Manchineri priest who could continue running the village church.

6. The kin terminology used is very similar to that described for the Piro of the Urubamba (Gow 1997), the difference being that father's sisters and mother's sisters are called by different terms.

7. An American missionary group translated hymn books and some of the gospels into Manchineri and produced a first reader book in the native language.

8. For instance, I visited a small house shared by a Cashinahua family of approximately ten people. It had only two walls but was the only place they could afford to live, thanks to a generous friend who had lent it to them. The adolescent girls of the family did not work or study.

9. See Chapter 4 for migration phases to cities.

10. Similarly, see Wulff (1995) on young people in different cultural contexts.

11. See DaMatta ([1979] 1991) on the social levels of "individual" and "person."

12. In very similar fashion, Gow (1991) states that the Piro (Yine) opposed themselves to their ignorant ancestors, who were enslaved by the rubber bosses since they did not know how to speak, write, count, or do similar things. Those native peoples who still lacked schools were called "uncivilized forest people."

13. See Amazonian historicities and histories in Whitehead (2003).

14. See the version of the myth narrated by the Piro in Gow (2001).

15. Flood myths are found across all the world's continents (Dundes 1988). In my view, these Amazonian narratives are normally related to the rainy season, when the rivers begin to flood and the new cycle of production starts, as well as to climatic change.

16. A similar myth is narrated by indigenous groups in the Amazon, both Arawak and Pano speakers.

17. See Cormier (2003), for example.

18. Where no name is given, the individual interviewed prefers to remain anonymous.

19. See Chapter 3.

20. See Gow (2001); Gebhart-Sayer (1985); Lagrou (2007); Virtanen (2011a).

21. A detailed discussion can be found in Chapter 3.

22. This is also called removing *panema*, the local word for bad luck, a term used, for instance, if a hunter fails to find any game or misses a target (Carneiro da Cunha and Almeida Barbosa 2002, 16).

23. See Virtanen (2011b) for a detailed discussion.

24. See Regan (1983).

25. Bracketed italics denote my interpolations.

26. Cf. Regan (1983); Gow (1991).

27. The government arranged for participants from the Yaco River area to travel to the *Encontro de Culturas Indígenas*. The meeting has also been held in Rio Branco.

28. See Gow (1991); McCallum (1997).

29. The girl refers here to the death of Pataxó man in Brasília in 1997. He was burnt alive at a bus stop by a group of young people.

30. Three hyphens have been used to indicate a pause in the interviewee's speech.

31. See Chapter 4 for a discussion of the ways in which today's young urban Indians define and interpret their new cultural and social situations.

Chapter 2

1. "*Nalixinitka . . .*" in Manchineri.
2. See Van Gennep ([1909] 1960); V. Turner (1969).
3. Gow (2001) sees the ritual as a part of constructing the mythic relations with anaconda and jaguar described in the origin myth and thus with history.
4. See, for instance, Rosengren (1987).
5. See, for instance, Eliade ([1959] 2004); Douglas ([1966] 1989); Héritier (1996).
6. See Gow (1991); Héritier (1996); Conklin (2001). Eliade ([1959] 2004) also suggested that the young woman is kept in isolation during her puberty ritual, unable to see the sunlight and kept separate in the darkest corner of the house, because there is a mystic relation of dependency between the girl and moon.
7. I was asked how people "graduate" in my place and what kind of food we eat. The question could be translated as a desire to know what protects the body during its change in my country.
8. Later on, new indigenous education policies were formulated, and multicultural and bilingual education was guaranteed by Presidential Decree No. 26 on February 4, 1991; Interministerial Decree No. 559 of April 16, 1991; the Law of Directions and Bases of National Education No. 9394; Constitution, Decree of the Ministry of Education No. 6 of 1992 (decreed on December 20, 1996); Resolution CEB/CNE No. 03/99; CEB/CNE Resolution No. 14/99; and CP/CNE Resolution No. 10/2002. Indigenous education was initially the responsibility of FUNAI, but is now under the control of a special sector of the Ministry of Education.
9. For Bourdieu ([1980]1990), logic of practice refers to implicit bodily practices and body knowledge designed by power relations and domination in different social fields.
10. See Rival (2002).
11. School festivals are also common elsewhere: see, for example, Rival (2002, 170–71) on Huaorani schools.
12. See Bourdieu ([1979] 1984) on the symbolic efficacy of cultural capital.
13. Cardoso de Oliveira (1968) mentions a common expression among young Terena, *aprender o regulamento* (learning the rules), which refers to learning the rules of good behavior in the urban space.
14. Gomes (2000), for instance, mentions that the Indians first had to learn to wear shoes in towns.
15. See also Gow (1991).

Chapter 3

1. The founder of the Santo Daime church, Raimundo Irineu Serra, had taken *ayahuasca* with Indians in Acre. After experiences in which the *Rainha da Floresta* spirit appeared to him, Irineu Serra founded a spiritual cult in the 1930s in which *Banisteriopsis caapi* was consumed. The ritual is reminiscent of a Catholic liturgy.
2. See also Seeger (1987) on a similar meaning attributed to music in Suyá rituals.
3. This setting is very different, for instance, from the Tukano way of consuming *ayahuasca*, as described by Reichel-Dolmatoff (1975), where the men dance and bodily movements form part of the collective trance.

4. See Hill (1993) on the exercise of ritual power.
5. See also Lagrou (2001).
6. See Stokes (1994) on ethnicity and music.
7. See too, for example, Gow (1991); Lagrou (2001, 2007). According to Lagrou, *ayahuasca* results in seeing *yuxin*, spiritual agents that lack solid bodies but produce images that confuse and scare humans.
8. See Douglas ([1966] 1989), on taboo and totemism. See also Lévi-Strauss (1966).
9. Similar experiences are also shared within the ritual community during the peyote hunt of Central American Indians (Cohen 1985).
10. See Massey (1998), depicting her journey through Mexico's Yucután region, where she filmed the Maya women preparing bread in their ancient way in the late afternoon, and an example of spatially constructed space of young people: the Maya youngsters playing computer games loudly in the next house.
11. It should be remembered that Viveiros de Castro (1996) also uses the concept of *habitus* when formulating his version of perspectivist theory.
12. See Chapter 2.
13. See Smith (1996); Carneiro da Cunha and Almeida Barbosa (2002).
14. See Rose and Langdon (2010).
15. See Luna (1986).
16. Gow (1991) and Seeger (1987) have argued that shamanic knowledge comes only from the spirits. Nevertheless, Gow (1994) later observed that in the Urubamba region, cities are regarded as one of the origins of shamanic knowledge.

Chapter 4

1. Chandless (1866, 102) reported, "The Manetenerys are essentially a water-side tribe, always on the move up or down river."
2. For me, the experience of returning from the village to the city was neither easy nor simple. I was surprised by the amount of things, the variety of food and furniture, and the automation of our lives by different gadgets and devices. In the city, I felt unable to breathe inside the house.
3. See Chapter 5.
4. See McCallum (1997, 119–20).
5. See Virtanen (n.d.) for a detailed discussion.
6. I return to this issue in Chapters 6 and 7.
7. See Chapter 1; McCallum (1996); Lagrou (2001).
8. See Hall (1992); Sahlins (1997).

Chapter 5

1. See Basso (1973); Gregor (1977); Shertzer and Urban (1986); Bourdieu ([1991] 1997).
2. The cooperatives have also been important entities in terms of political representation.
3. These two other national Indian organizations, COIAB and CAPOIB, were set up in 1989 and 1992. Their work has included organizing meetings of Indian

leaders, launching campaigns to inform the public about the problems affecting Indians, and circulating documents. At a transnational level, COICA was created in 1992.

4. Forest certification, fees and fines for illegal logging, local governance, and control of land use have already shown some positive results, such as a reduction in the rate of deforestation.

5. Some native peoples like the Yawanawa have managed to make deals with companies, selling annatto dye to the cosmetics industry, for instance.

6. The roots of indigenism in Latin America also lie in the final colonial period and the formation of the nation-states.

7. In the 1970s indigenous peoples were recognized in the Economic and Social Council of the UN. In 1989, the International Labour Organization decreed Convention 169 on indigenous peoples. In the 1990s, indigenous peoples launched a campaign for a permanent forum at the UN, which was officially founded in 2002.

8. Such as Amazonlink and *Origem Jogos e Objetos*. The latter is a Brazilian company that develops board games, such as Indigenous Games of Brazil, having examined the traditional games and toys of various Brazilian indigenous peoples.

9. The IPDP is one of the subprograms of the so-called Pilot Program to Conserve the Brazilian Rain Forest (*Programa Piloto para a Proteção das Florestas Tropicais do Brasil*) coordinated by the Brazilian Ministry of the Environment and one of its offices: the Amazonia Coordination Office.

10. The Embassy of Finland also funded the project.

11. According to Gow (1991), men satisfy their women with money and game.

12. See Bourdieu ([1979] 1984, [1980] 1990) on symbolic capital.

13. Davi Yanomami, for instance, who has worked as mediator between the whites and his own people from a young age, has managed to combine native concepts and discourses with nonnative ones, interpreting them both in new ways (see Kopenawa and Albert 2010; cf. Graham 2002).

Chapter 6

1. Following Bourdieu ([1994] 1998), this investment in the future comprises the interest in what we can call the field's *illusio*, or social libido.

2. Previously health agents also received a salary from the government. However, despite being cut, the health agents have continued their work as before.

3. See Cohen (1985) on the symbolic construction of community.

4. See the discussion in the next chapter.

5. Belonging to different cultures may create cultures of hybridity (fusion between cultures) as has been the case for many peoples in diaspora. It can lead to creative new forms of representations, but it may also offend traditionalist members of the community (see Hall 1992).

6. An example is the *Papo do Índio* column, launched in 1986 and still published today in the Acrean daily newspaper, *Jornal Página 20*.

7. See also Taussig (1987) on violence and shamanism.

Chapter 7

1. See DaMatta ([1979] 1991).
2. By 2012, one Manchineri young woman living in Rio Branco had over 2,000 "friends" on Facebook, one of the highest numbers among my own Facebook contacts. Today she is a university student and has participated in various indigenous meetings.
3. See Turner (1991) on Kayapo social and ethnic images in their filmmaking.
4. In his use of *habitus*, Bourdieu ([1980] 1990) explains that social actors do not act according to a self-conscious reflection on their own actions, or a logical control, but according to a reason or motive: they have or do not have an interest in acting in a certain way. Bourdieu follows in the footsteps of Marcel Mauss, his objective being to find an alternative to Sartre's subjectivism and the objectivism of Lévi-Strauss.
5. Cf. Turner (1991); Warren and Jackson (2002); and Pacheco de Oliveira (2004) on the new cultural and indigenous consciousness.

References

Ahmed, Sara. 2000. *Strange Encounters: Embodied Others in Post-Coloniality*. London: Routledge.

Andrello, Geraldo. 2006. *Cidade do índio*. São Paulo: Edunesp/ISA/NuTI.

Anttonen, Veikko. 2000. "Sacred." In *Guide to the Study of Religion*, edited by Willi Braun and Russell T. McCutcheon, 271–82. New York: Cassell.

Appadurai, Arjun. 1988. "Putting Hierarchy in Its Place." *Cultural Anthropology* 3 (1): 36–49.

———. 1996. *Modernity at Large: Cultural Dimensions of Globalization*. Minneapolis: University of Minnesota Press.

Aquino, Terri Valle de. 1977. "Kaxinawá: De Seringueiro 'Caboclo' a Peão Acreano." MA thesis, Universidade de Brasilia.

Århem, Kaj. 1993. "Ecosofia makuna." In *La selva humanizada: Ecología alternativa en el trópico húmedo colombiano*, edited by Francois Correa, 109–26. Bogotá: Instituto Colombiano de Antropología/Fondo FEN/Fondo Editorial CEREC.

Ariza, Marina. 2005. "Juventud, migración y curso da vida: Sentidos e vivencias de la migración entre los jóvenes urbanos mexicanos." In *Jóvenes e niños: Un enfoque demográfico*, edited by Maria Mier Terán and Cecilia Rabell, 39–61. Mexico City: FLACSO.

Bacigalupo, Ana Mariella. 2004. "Shamans' Pragmatic Gendered Negotiations with Mapuche Resistance Movements and Chilean Political Authorities." *Identities: Global Studies in Culture and Power* 11 (4): 1–41.

Basso, Ellen. 1973. *The Kalapalo Indians of Central Brazil*. New York: Holt, Rinehart and Winston.

Belaunde, Luisa Elvira. 2001. *Viviendo bien, género y fertilidad entre los airo-pai de la Amazonia peruana*. Lima: CAAP.

———. 2005. *El Recuerdo de Luna*. Lima: Fonde editorial de la facultad de ciencias sociales.

Belisário, Franca. 2007. *Estratégia Xavante*. Brazil. Film, 86 min.

Bhabha, Homi K. 1994. *The Location of Culture*. London: Routledge.

Borja, Jordi, and Manuel Castells. 1997. *Local & Global: Management of Cities in the Information Age*. In collaboration with Mireia Belil and Chris Benner. London: Earthscan.

Borjas, George J. 1992. "Ethnic Capital and Intergenerational Mobility." *Quarterly Journal of Economics* 428 (1): 123–50.

Bourdieu, Pierre. (1979) 1984. *Distinction: A Social Critique of the Judgment of Taste.* Translated by Richard Nice. London: Routledge and Kegan Nice.

———. (1980) 1990. *The Logic of Practice.* Translated by Richard Nice. Cambridge: Polity Press.

———. (1991) 1997. *Language and Symbolic Power.* Translated by Gino Raymond and Matthew Adamson. Cambridge: Polity Press.

———. (1994) 1998. *Practical Reason: On the Theory of Action.* Cambridge: Polity Press.

Boyer, Pascal. 1997. "Recurrence without Transmission: The Intuitive Background of Religious Ontologies." In *Present Is Past: Some Uses of Tradition in Native Societies,* edited by Marie Mauzé. Lanham, MD: University Press of America.

Briones, Claudia. 2007. "'Our Struggle Has Just Begun': Experiences of Belonging and Mapuche Formations of Self." In *Indigenous Experience Today,* edited by Marisol de la Cadena and Orin Starn, 99–121. Oxford: Berg.

Browder, John D., and Brian J. Godfrey. 1997. *Rainforest Cities: Urbanization, Development, and Globalization in the Brazilian Amazon.* New York: Columbia University Press.

Brown, Michael F. 1993. "Facing the State, Facing the World: Amazonia's Native Leaders and the New Politics of Identity." *L'Homme* 126–28: 307–26.

Calavia Sáez, Oscar. 2004. "In Search of Ritual: Traditional, Outer World and Bad Manners in the Amazon." *Journal of the Royal Anthropological Institute* 10 (1): 157–73.

Cardoso de Oliveira, Roberto. 1968. *Urbanização e tribalismo: A integração dos índios Terêna numa sociedade de classes.* Rio de Janeiro: Zahar.

———. 1972. *O índio e o mundo dos brancos: Uma interpretação sociológica da situação dos Tukuna.* São Paulo: Livraria Pioneira.

Carneiro da Cunha, Manuela, and Mauro Almeida Barbosa. 2000. "Indigenous People, Traditional People, and Conservation in the Amazon." *Dædalus: Journal of the American Academy of Arts and Sciences* 2 (129): 315–38.

———, eds. 2002. *Enciclopédia da floresta. O Alto Juruá: Práticas e conhecimentos das populações.* São Paulo: Companhia das Letras.

Carvalho, Georgia, Daniel Nepstad, David McGrath, Maria Carmen Vera Diaz, and Marico Santilli. 2002. "Brazil's Amazon Development Policy: Democratic Transition and Enduring Policy Patterns." In *Currents of Change: Globalization, Democratization and Institutional Reform in Latin America,* edited by Jaime Behar, Ulf Jonsson, and Mats Lundahl, 303–17. Stockholm: Institute of Latin American Studies, Stockholm University.

Castells, Manuel. (1997) 2004. *The Power of Identity.* Oxford: Blackwell.

Castelo Branco, J. M. Brandão. 1947. "Caminhos do Acre." *Revista do Instituto Histórico e Geográfico Brasileiro* 196: 74–255.

———. 1950. "O gentio acreano." *Revista do Instituto Histórico e Geográfico Brasileiro* 207: 13–83.

Chandless, William. 1866. "Ascent of the River Purus." *Journal of the Royal Geographical Society* 35: 86–118.

Chaumeil, Jean-Pierre. 1990. "'Les nouveaux chefs . . .': Pratiques politiques et organisations indigènes en Amazonia péruvienne." *Problèmes d'Amérique Latine* 96 (2): 93–113.

Clastres, Pierre. 1974. *La Société contre l'État*. Paris: Les Éditions de Minuit.

Cohen, Anthony P. 1985. *The Symbolic Construction of Community*. London: Tavistock.

Cohn, Clarice. 2005. *Antropologia da criança*. Rio de Janeiro: Zahar.

Collet Gouvêa, Celia Letícia. 2006. "Ritos de civilização e cultura: A escola bakairi." PhD diss., Universidade Federal do Rio de Janeiro.

Conklin, Beth A. 2001. "Women's Blood, Warriors' Blood." In *Gender in Amazonia and Melanesia: An Exploration of the Comparative Method*, edited by Thomas A. Gregor and Donald Tuzin, 141–47. London: University of California Press.

———. 2002. "Shamans versus Pirates in the Amazonian Treasure Chest." *American Anthropologist* 104 (4): 1050–61.

Conklin, Beth A., and Laura R. Graham. 1995. "The Shifting Middle Ground: Amazonian Indians and Eco-Politics." *American Anthropologist* 97 (4): 695–710.

Conklin, Beth A., and Lynn M. Morgan. 1996. "Babies, Bodies, and the Production of Personhood in North America and a Native Amazonian Society." *Ethnos* 24 (4): 657–94.

Connell, John, and Chris Gibson. 2003. *Sound Tracks: Popular Music, Identity, Place*. London: Routledge.

Cormier, Loretta. 2003. "Decolonizing History: Ritual Transformation of the Past among the Guajá of Eastern Amazonia." In *Histories and Historicities in Amazonia*, edited by Neil L. Whitehead, 123–40. Lincoln: University of Nebraska Press.

Costa, Luiz. 2010. "The Kanamari Body-Owner: Predation and Feeding in Western Amazonia." *Journal de la Société des Américanistes* 96 (1): 169–92.

Costa Vargas, João. 2004. "Hyperconsciousness of Race and Its Negation: The Dialectic of White Supremacy in Brazil." *Identities: Global Studies in Power and Culture* 11 (4): 443–70.

Crocker, Jon Cristopher. 1985. *Vital Souls: Bororo Cosmology, Natural Symbolism and Shamanism*. Tucson: University of Arizona Press.

Dalmolin, Gilberto Francisco. 2004. *O papel da escola entre os povos indígenas: De instrumento de exclusão a recurso para emancipação sociocultural*. Rio Branco: EDUFAC.

DaMatta, Roberto. (1979) 1991. *Carnivals, Rogues and Heroes: An Interpretation of the Brazilian Dilemma*. Notre Dame: University of Notre Dame Press.

———. 1995. "For an Anthropology of the Brazilian Tradition; or 'A Virtuade está no meio.'" In *The Brazilian Puzzle—Culture on the Borderlands of the Western World*, edited by David J. Hess and Roberto da Matta, 270–92. New York: Columbia University Press.

———. 2000. "Individualidade e liminaridade: Considerações sobre os ritos de passagem e a modernidade." *Mana: Estudos de Antropologia Social* 1 (6): 7–29.

De la Cadena, Marisol. 2000. *Indigenous Mestizos: The Politics of Race and Culture in Cuzco, Peru, 1919–1991*. Durham, NC: Duke University Press.

Descola, Philippe. 2005. *Par-delà nature et culture*. Paris: Gallimard.

Douglas, Mary. (1966) 1989. *Purity and Danger: An Analysis of the Concepts of Pollution and Taboo*. London: Ark Paperbacks.

Dundes, Alan, ed. 1988. *The Flood Myth*. Berkeley: University of California Press.

Eliade, Mircea. (1959) 2004. *Ritos de iniciação e sociedades secretas*. Translated by Isabel Debot. Original title: *Initiation, rites, sociétés secrètes*. Lisbon: Ésquilo.

Esteinou, Rosario. 2005. "La juventude y los jóvenes como construcción social." In *Jóvenes e Niños: Un enfoque demográfico*, edited by Maria Mier Terān and Cecilia Rabell, 25–37. Mexico City: FLACSO.

Fabian, Stephen Michael. 1992. *Space-Time of the Bororo of Brazil*. Gainesville: University Press of Florida.

Facundes, Sidney da Silva. 2000. "The Language of the Apurinã People of Brazil (Maipure/Arawak)." PhD diss., University of New York at Buffalo.

Fausto, Carlos. 1999. "Of Enemies and Pets: Warfare and Shamanism in Amazonia." *American Ethnologist* 26 (4): 933–56.

———. 2008. "Too Many Owners: Mastery and Ownership in Amazonia." *Mana: Estudos de Antropologia Social* 14: 329–66.

Fausto, Carlos, and Michael Heckenberger. 2007. "Introduction: Indigenous History and the History of the 'Indians.'" In *Time and Memory in Indigenous Amazonia: Anthropological Perspectives*, edited by Carlos Fausto and Michael Heckenberger, 1–46. Gainesville: University Press of Florida.

Fernandes, Florestan. (1948) 1988. *A organização social dos Tupinambá*. Brasília: Editora Universidade de Brasília.

———. 1975. *Investigação etnológica no Brasil e outros ensaios*. Petrópolis: Editora Vozes.

Ferri, Patricia. 1990. *Achados ou perdidos? A imigração indígena em Boa Vista*. Goiás: MLAL.

Fisher, William. 2000. *Rain Forest Exchanges: Industry and Community on an Amazonian Frontier*. Washington, DC: Smithsonian Institution Press.

Foucault, Michel. 1980. *Power Knowledge*. Brighton: Harvester.

Franchetto, Bruna. 2000. "Rencontres rituelles dans le Haut-Xingu: La parole du chef." In *Les rituels du dialogue—Promenades ethnolinguistiques en terres amérindiennes*, edited by Aurore Monod Becquelin and Philippe Erikson, 481–510. Nanterre: Société d'ethnologie.

Freyre, Gilberto. (1963) 1966. *The Mansions and the Shanties. The Making of Modern Brazil*. Translated by H. de Onís. New York: Alfred A. Knopf.

FUNAI (*Fundação Nacional do Índio*). 2006. *Documento final da conferência nacional dos povos indígenas. Propostas aprovadas: Plenárias temáticas*. Unpublished report. Brasília.

FUNASA (*Fundação Nacional de Saúde*). 2010. "Demografia dos povos indígenas." Accessed March 30, 2012. http://sis.funasa.gov.br/transparencia_publica/siasiweb/Layout/quantitativo_de_pessoas_2010.asp.

García Canclini, Nestor. 1995. *Hybrid Cultures: Strategies for Entering and Leaving Modernity*. Minneapolis: University of Minnesota Press.

———. (1999) 2000. *La globalizacíon imaginada*. Buenos Aires: Paidós.

Gebhart-Sayer, Angelika. 1985. "The Geometric Designs of the Shipibo-Conibo in Ritual Context." *Journal of Latin American Lore* 11 (2): 143–75.

Gibbs, Raymond W. 2006. *Embodiment and Cognitive Science.* New York: Cambridge University Press.

Giddens, Anthony. 1984. *Constitution of Society: Outline of the Theory of Structuration.* Cambridge: Polity Press.

Gilbert, Alan. (1994) 1998. *The Latin American City.* London: Latin American Bureau.

Goldman, Irving.1963. *The Cubeo: Indians of the Northwest Amazon.* Urbana: University of Illinois Press.

Gomes, Mércio P. 2000. *The Indians and Brazil.* Translated by John W. Moon. Gainesville: University Press of Florida.

Gow, Peter. 1991. *Of Mixed Blood: Kinship and History in Peruvian Amazonia.* Oxford: Clarendon Press.

———. 1994. "River People: Shamanism and History in Western Amazonia." In *Shamanism, History and the State,* edited by Nicholas Thomas and Caroline Humphrey, 90–112. Ann Arbor: University of Michigan Press.

———. 1997. "O parentesco como consciência humana: O caso dos piro." *Mana: Estudos de Antropologia Social* 3 (2): 39–65.

———. 2001. *An Amazonian Myth and Its History.* Oxford: Oxford University Press.

———. (2003) 2007. "'Ex-Cocama': Transforming Identities in Peruvian Amazonia." In *Time and Memory in Indigenous Amazonia: Anthropological Perspectives,* edited by Carlos Fausto and Michael Heckenberger, 194–215. Gainesville: University Press of Florida.

Graham, Laura R. 2002. "How Should an Indian Speak? Amazonian Indians and the Politics of Language in the Global Sphere." In *Indigenous Movements, Self-Representation, and the State in Latin America,* edited by Kay B. Warren and Jean E. Jackson, 181–226. Austin: University of Texas Press.

Gregor, Thomas. 1977. *Mehinaku.* Chicago: University of Chicago Press.

Gupta, Akhil, and James Ferguson. (1997) 2001. "Culture, Power, Place: Ethnography at the End of an Era." In *Culture, Power, Place: Explorations in Critical Anthropology,* edited by Akhil Gupta and James Ferguson, 1–29. Durham, NC: Duke University Press.

Hall, Stuart. 1992. "The Question of Cultural Identity." In *Modernity and Its Futures,* edited by Stuart Hall, David Held and Tony McGrew, 273–325. Cambridge: Polity Press.

Hannerz, Ulf. 1997. "Fluxos, fronteiras, híbridos: Palavras-chave da antropologia transnacional." *Mana: Estudos de Antropologia Social* 3 (1): 7–39.

Heckenberger, Michael, J., Christian Russell, Carlos Fausto, Joshua R. Toney, Morgan J. Schmidt, Edithe Pereira, Bruna Franchetto, and Afukaka Kuikuru. 2008. "Pre-Columbian Urbanism, Anthropogenic Landscapes, and the Future of the Amazon." *Science* 321: 1214–17.

Hemming, John 1991. *Amazon Frontier. The Defeat of the Brazilian Indians.* London: MacMillan.

Héritier, Françoise. 1996. *Masculin/Féminin: La pensée de la différence.* Paris: Odile Jacob.

Hill, Jonathan. 1993. *Keepers of the Sacred Chants: The Poetics of Ritual Power in an Amazonian Society.* Tucson: University of Arizona Press.

208 • References

————. 2003. "Shamanizing the State in Venezuela." *Journal of Latin American Lore* 21 (2): 163–77.

Hugh-Jones, Stephen. 1979. *The Palm and the Pleiades: Initiation and Cosmology in Northwest Amazonia.* Cambridge: Cambridge University Press.

IBGE (The Brazilian Institute of Statistics and Geography). 2005. *Tendências demográficas—Uma análise dos indígenas com base nos resultados da amostra dos censos demográficos 1991 e 2000.* Rio de Janeiro: IBGE.

————. 2010. *Censo 2010.* Accessed March 1, 2012. http://www.ibge.gov.br/home/estatistica/populacao/censo2010/tabelas_pdf/total_populacao_acre.pdf.

Ingold, Tim. 2009. "Against Space: Place, Movement, Knowledge." In *Boundless Worlds: An Anthropological Approach to Movement,* edited by Peter Wynn Kirby, 29–44. New York: Berghahn Books.

Jackson, Jean E. 1995. "Culture, Genuine and Spurious: The Politics of Indianness in the Vaupés, Colombia." *American Ethnologist* 22 (1): 7–27.

Kelly, José Antonio. 2011. *State Healthcare and Yanomami Transformations: A Symmetrical Ethnography.* Tucson: University of Arizona Press.

Kensinger, Kenneth M. 1973. "*Banisteriopsis*: Usage among the Peruvian Cashinahua." In *Hallucinogens and Shamanism,* edited by Michael J. Harner, 9–14. London: Oxford University Press.

————, ed. 1984. *Marriage Practices in Lowland South America.* Urbana: University of Illinois Press.

Knott, Kim. 2005. "Spatial Theory and Method for the Study of Religion." *Temenos* 41 (2): 153–84.

Kopenawa, Davi, and Bruce Albert. 2010. *La chute du ciel: Paroles d'un chaman yanomami.* Paris: Plon.

Labre, A. R. P. 1872. *Rio Purús, notícia.* Maranhão: M. F. V. Pires.

Lagrou, Els. 2001. "Identidade e alteridade a partir da perspectiva kaxinawa." In *Fazendo antropologia no Brasil,* edited by Neide Esterci, Peter Fry, and Mirian Goldenberg, 93–128. Rio de Janeiro: DP&A Editora.

————. 2007. *A Fluidez da Forma: Arte, alteridade e agência em uma sociedade amazônica.* Rio de Janeiro: Topbooks.

Larrain, Jorge. 2000. *Identity and Modernity in Latin America.* Oxford: Blackwell.

Lasmar, Cristiane. 2005. *De Volta ao Lago de Leite: gênero e transformação no alto rio Negro.* São Paulo: Edunesp/ISA/NuTI.

Latour, Bruno. 1993. *We Have Never Been Modern.* New York: Harvester Wheatsheaf.

Lauer, Matthew. 2006. "State-led Democratic Politics and Emerging Forms of Indigenous Leadership among the Ye'kwana of the Upper Orinoco." *Journal of Latin American Anthropology* 11 (1): 51–86.

Lévi-Strauss, Claude. 1966. *The Savage Mind.* Chicago: University of Chicago Press.

Lindgren, Anna-Riitta. 2000. *Helsingin saamelaiset ja omakieli.* Helsinki: Finnish Literature Society.

Londoño Sulkin, Carlos D. 2005. "Inhuman Beings: Morality and Perspectivism among Muinane People (Colombian Amazon)." *Ethnos* 70 (1): 7–30.

Lopes da Silva, Aracy, Angela Nunes, and Ana Vera Lopes da Silva Macedo, eds. 2002. *Crianças Indígenas: Ensaios Antropológicos*. São Paulo: FAPESP.

Luna, Luis Eduardo. 1986. *Vegetalismo: Shamanism among the Mestizo Population of the Peruvian Amazon*. Stockholm: Almqvist and Wiksell.

Massey, Doreen. 1998. "The Spatial Construction of Youth Cultures." In *Cool Places: Geographies of Youth Cultures*, edited by Tracey Skelton and Gill Valentine, 121–29. London: Routledge.

Massey, Doreen, and Pat Jess. 1995. "Places and Cultures in an Uneven World." In *A Place in the World? Places, Cultures and Globalization*, edited by Doreen Massey and Pat Jess, 45–77. Oxford: Open University Press.

Matteson, Esther. 1965. *The Piro (Arawakan) Language*. Berkeley: University of California Press.

McCallum, Cecilia. 1990. "Language, Kinship and Politics in Amazonia." *Man* 25:412–33.

———. 1996. "The Body That Knows: From Cashinahua Epistemology to a Medical Anthropology of Lowland South America." *Medical Anthropology Quarterly* 10: 347–72.

———. 1997. "Comendo com Txai, comendo como Txai: A sexualização de relações étnicas na Amazônia contemporânea." *Revista de Antropologia* 1 (40): 110–47.

———. 2001. *Gender and Sociability in Amazonia: How Real People Are Made*. Oxford: Berg.

———. 2010. "Escrito no corpo: Gênero, educação e socialidade na Amazônia numa perspectiva Kaxinawá." *Revista da FAEEBA* 19 (33): 87–104.

McSweeney, Keandra, and Brad Jokisch. 2007. "Beyond Rainforests: Urbanisation and Emigration among Lowland Indigenous Societies in Latin America." *Bulletin of Latin American Research* 26 (2): 159–80.

Métraux, Alfred. 1948. "Tribes of the Juruá-Purus Basins." In *The Tropical Forest Tribes*. Vol. 3 of *Handbook of South American Indians*, edited by Julian H. Steward, 657–86. Washington, DC: Smithsonian Institution of American Ethnology.

Mier Terán, Maria and Cecilia Rabell. 2005. *Jóvenes e Niños: Un enfoque demográfico*. Mexico City: FLACSO.

Mitchell, Tony. 2001. "Kia Kaha! (Be Strong!) Maori and Pacific Islander Hip-Hop in Aotearoa-New Zealand." In *Global Noise: Rap and Hip-Hop outside the USA*, edited by Tony Mitchell, 280–305. Middletown, CT: Wesleyan University Press.

Modood, Tariq. 2004. "Capitals, Ethnic Identity and Educational Qualifications." *Cultural Trends* 13 (2): 87–105.

Monte, Nietta Lindenberg. 1996. *Escolas da floresta: Entre o passado oral e o presente letrado*. Rio de Janeiro: Multiletra.

Nepstad, D., S. Schwartzman, B. Bamberger, M. Santilli, D. Ray, P. Schlesinger, P. Lefebvre, A. Alencar, E. Prinz, G. Fiske, and A. Rolla. 2006. "Inhibition of Amazon Deforestation and Fire by Parks and Indigenous Lands." *Conservation Biology* 20 (1): 65–73.

Niezen, Ronald. 2003. *The Origins of Indigenism: Human Rights and the Politics of Identity*. Berkeley: University of California Press.

Nunes, Angela. 1999. *A Sociedade das crianças A'uwe-Xavante: Por uma antropologia da criança*. Lisbon: Instituto de Inovação Educacional.

Oakdale, Suzanne. 2004. "The Culture-Conscious Brazilian Indian: Representing and Reworking Indianness in Kayabi Political Discourse." *American Ethnologist* 31 (1): 60–75.

Ôchoa, Luiza Pinedo, and Gleyson Araújo Teixeira, eds. (1997) 2002. *Índios no Acre: História e Organização*. Rio Branco: MEC, CPI, OPIAC.

Opas, Minna. 2008. "Different but the Same: Negotiation of Personhood and Christianities in Western Amazonia." PhD diss., University of Turku.

Ortiz, Renato. 1998. *Outro territorio. Ensayos osbre el mundo contemporáneo*. Bogota: Convenio Andres Bello.

Overing, Joanna. 1988. "Personal Autonomy and the Domestication of the Self in Piaroa Society." In *Acquiring Culture: Cross Cultural Studies in Child Development*, edited by Gustav Jahoda and I. M. Lewis, 169–92. New York: Routledge.

———. 1992. "Wandering in the Market and the Forest: An Amazonian Theory of Production and Exchange." In *Contesting Markets: Analyses of Ideology, Discourse and Practice*, edited by Roy Dilley, 180–200. Edinburgh: Edinburgh University Press.

———. 2003. "In Praise of the Everyday: Trust and the Art of Social Living in an Amazonian Community." *Ethnos* 68 (3): 293–316.

Overing, Joanna, and Alan Passes, eds. 2000. *The Anthropology of Love and Anger: The Aesthetics of Conviviality in Native Amazonia*. London: Routledge.

Ozorio de Almeida, Anna Luisa. 1992. *The Coloniazation of the Amazon*. Austin: University of Texas Press.

Pacheco de Oliveira, João. 2004. "Uma etnologia dos 'índios misturados'? Situação colonial, territorialização e fluxos culturais." In *A viagem de volta: Etnicidade, política e reelaboração cultural no Nordeste indígena*, edited by João Pacheco de Oliveira, 13–42. Rio de Janeiro: Contra Capa.

Paden, William E. 1988. *Religious Worlds: The Comparative Study of Religion*. Boston: Beacon Press.

Pärssinen, Martti, Denise Schaan, and Alceu Ranzi. 2009. "Pre-Columbian Geometric Earthworks in the Upper Purus: A Complex Society in Western Amazonia." *Antiquity* 83 (321): 1084–95.

Peluso, Daniela M., and Miguel N Alexiades. 2005. "Indigenous Urbanization and Amazonia's Post-Traditional Environmental Economy." *Traditional Settlements and Dwelling Review* 16 (11): 7–16.

Piedrafita Iglesias, Marcelo. 2010. *Os Kaxinawá de Felizardo: Correrias, trabalho e civilização no Alto Juruá*. Brasília: Editora Paralelo 15.

Piedrafita Iglesias, Marcelo, and Terri Valle de Aquino. 2005. *Povos e terras indígenas no Estado do Acre*. Programa Estadual de Zoneamento Ecológico-Econômico do Estado do Acre—Fase II. Rio Branco: Secretaria de Meio Ambiente e Recursos Naturais do Governo do Estado do Acre.

Portes, Alejandro. 1998. "Social Capital: Its Origins and Applications in Modern Sociology." *Annual Review of Sociology* 24: 1–24.

Ramos, Alcida Rita. 1988. "Indian Voices: Contact Experienced and Expressed." In *Rethinking History and Myth: Indigenous South American Perspectives on the Past*, edited by Jonathan D. Hill, 214–34. Urbana: University of Illinois Press.

———. 1998. *Indigenism: Ethnic Politics in Brazil*. London: University of Wisconsin Press.

———. 2003. "The Special (or Specious?) Status of Brazilian Indians." *Citizenship Studies* 7 (4): 401–20.

Regan, Jaime. 1983. *Hacia la tierra sin mal: Estudio de la religion del pueblo en la Amazonia*. Iquitos: CETA.

Reichel-Dolmatoff, Gerardo. 1975. *The Shaman and the Jaguar: A Study of Narcotic Drugs among the Indians of Colombia*. Philadelphia: Temple University Press.

Revkin, Andrew. 1991. *Amazônia em perigo: O assassino de Chico Mendes*. Translated by Ana Barradas. Lisbon: Círculo de Leitores.

Ribeiro, Darcy. 2000. *The Brazilian People: The Formation and Meaning of Brazil*. Translated by Gregory Rabassa. Gainesville: University Press of Florida.

Rival, Laura M. 2002. *Trekking through History: The Huaorani of Amazonian Ecuador*. New York: Columbia University Press.

Rivière, Peter. 1984. *Individual and Society in Guiana: A Comparative Study of Amerindian Social Organization*. Cambridge: Cambridge University Press.

Rosaldo, Renato. 1989. *Culture and Truth: The Remaking of Social Analysis*. Boston: Beacon Press.

Rose, Isabel Santana de, and Esther Jean Langdon. 2010. "Diálogos (neo)xamânicos: Encontros entre os Guarani e a ayahuasca." *Tellus* 10 (18): 83–113.

Rosengren, Dan. 1987. *In the Eyes of Beholder: Leadership and the Construction of Social Power and the Dominance among the Mantsigenka of the Peruvian Amazon*. Gothenburg: Göteborgs etnografiska museum.

———. 2003. "The Collective Self and the Ethnopolitical Movement: 'Rhizomes' and 'Taproots' in the Amazon." *Identities: Global Studies in Culture and Power* 10 (3): 221–40.

———. 2006. "Matsigenka Corporeality, a Nonbiological Reality: On Notions of Consciousness and the Constitution of Identity." *Tipití: Journal of the Society for the Anthropology of Lowland South America* 4 (1): 81–102.

Ruiz, Maya Lorena Pérez, ed. 2008. *Jóvenes indígenas y globalización en América Latina*. Editora INAH.

Sahlins, Marshall. 1997. "O 'pessimismo sentimental' e a experiência etnográfica: Por que a cultura não é um 'objeto' em via de extinção (parte II)." *Mana: Estudos de Antropologia Social* 3 (2): 103–50.

Schaden, Egon. 1969. *Aculturação indígena: Ensaio sôbre fatôres e tendências da mudança cultural de tribos índias em contacto com o mundo dos brancos*. São Paulo: Pioneira.

Schiel, Juliana. 2004. "*Tronco Velho. Histórias Apurinã*." PhD diss., Universidade Estadual de Campinas.

Seeger, Anthony. 1987. *Why Suyá Sing: A Musical Anthropology of an Amazonian People*. Cambridge: Cambridge University Press.

Seeger, A., R. DaMatta, and E. B. Viveiros de Castro. 1987. "A construção da pessoa nas sociedades indígenas brasileiras." In *Sociedades indígenas e indigenismo no Brasil*, edited by João Pacheco de Oliveiro, 11–29. Rio de Janeiro: UFAC.

Shertzer, Joel, and Greg Urban. 1986. *Native South American Discourse*. Berlin: Mouton de Gruyter.

Shilling, Chris. 1997. "The Body and Difference." In *Identity and Difference*, edited by Kathryn Woodward, 63–107. London: Sage.

Silva, Aracy Lopes da, and Mariana Kawall Leal Ferreira, eds. 2001. *Antropologia, história e educação: A questão indígena e a escola*. São Paulo: FAPESP.

Smith, Nigel J. H. 1996. *The Enchanted Amazon Forest: Stories from a Vanishing World*. Gainesville: University Press of Florida.

Stokes, Martin. 1994. "Introduction: Ethnicity, Identity and Music." In *Ethnicity, Identity and Music: The Musical Construction of Place*, edited by Martin Stokes, 1–27. Oxford: Berg.

Stolze Lima, Tânia. (1996) 1999. "The Two and Its Many: Reflections on Perspectivism in a Tupi Cosmology." *Ethnos* 64 (1): 107–13.

Taussig, Michael. 1987. *Shamanism, Colonialism, and the Wild Man: A Study in Terror and Healing*. Chicago: University of Chicago Press.

Taylor, Anne-Christine. 1996. "The Soul's Body and Its States: An Amazonian Perspective on the Nature of Being Human." *Journal of the Royal Anthropological Institute* 2 (2): 201–15.

Toffler, Alvin. 1990. *Powershift: Knowledge, Wealth, and Violence at the Edge of the 21st Century*. New York: Bantam.

Tomlinson, John. 2004. "Global Culture, Deterritorialisation and the Cosmopolitanism of Youth Culture." In *Resituating Culture*, edited by Gavan Titley, 21–30. Strasbourg: European Council.

Tuhiwai Smith, Linda. 1999. *Decolonizing Methodologies: Research and Indigenous Peoples*. London: Zed Books.

Turner, Terence S. 1991. "Representing, Resisting, Rethinking: Historical Formations of Kayapo Culture and Anthropological Consciousness." In *Colonial Situations: Essays on the Contextualization of Ethnographic Knowledge*, edited by George W. Stocking Jr., 285–313. Madison, WI: University of Wisconsin Press.

———. 1995. "Social Body and Embodied Subject: Bodiliness, Subjectivity, and Sociality among the Kayapo." *Cultural Anthropology* 10 (2): 143–70.

Turner, Victor. 1969. *Ritual Process: Structure and Anti-Structure*. London: Routledge and Kegan.

Urban, Greg. 1996. *Metaphysical Community: The Interplay of the Senses and the Intellect*. Austin: University of Texas Press.

———. 2001. *Metaculture: How Culture Moves through the World*. Minneapolis: University of Minneapolis Press.

Valentine, Gil, Tracey Skelton, and Deborah Chambers. 1998. "Cool Places: An Introduction to Youth and Youth Cultures." In *Cool Places: Geographies of Youth Cultures*, edited by Tracey Skelton and Gill Valentine, 1–26. London: Routledge.

Van Gennep, Arnold. (1909) 1960. *Rites of Passage*. Chicago: University of Chicago Press.

Vilaça, Aparecida. (1999) 2007. "Cultural Change as Body Metamorphosis." In *Time and Memory in Indigenous Amazonia: Anthropological Perspectives*, edited by Carlos Fausto and Michael Heckenberger, 169–93. Gainesville: University Press of Florida.

———. 2002. "Making Kin out of Others in Amazonia." *Journal of the Royal Anthropological Institute* 8 (2): 347–65.

———. 2005. "Chronically Unstable Bodies: Reflections on Amazonian Corporealities." *Journal of the Royal Anthropological Institute* 11 (3): 445–64.

Virtanen, Pirjo Kristiina. 2009a. "Shamanism and Indigenous Youthhood in the Brazilian Amazonia." *Amazônica: Revista de Antropologia* 1 (1): 152–77.

———. 2009b. "New Interethnic Relations and Native Perceptions of Human-to-Human Relations in Brazilian Amazonia." *Journal of Latin American and Caribbean Anthropology* 14 (2): 332–54.

———. 2010a. "Amazonian Native Youths and Notions of Indigeneity in Urban Areas." *Identities: Global Studies in Culture and Power* 17 (2/3): 154–75.

———. 2010b. "New Social Roles of Indigenous Women in Brazilian Amazonia: Gender, Education, and Age in Intersections." In *Islas de la locura: Normatividad y marginalización en América Latina*, edited by Minna Opas, Pirjo Kristiina Virtanen, and Sarri Vuorisalo-Tiitinen, 88–107. Madrid: Instituto Iberoamericano de Finlandia.

———. 2011a. "Constancy in Continuity: Native Oral History, Iconography and the Earthworks of the Upper Purus." In *Ethnicity in Ancient Amazonia: Reconstructing Past Identities from Archaeology, Linguistics, and Ethnohistory*, edited by Alf Hornborg and Jonathan D. Hill, 279–98. Boulder: University Press of Colorado.

———. 2011b. "Guarding, Feeding and Transforming: Palm Trees in the Amazonian Past and Present." In *The Archaeological Encounter: Ethnographic Perspectives*, edited by Paolo Fortis and Istvan Praet, 125–73. Saint Andrews: University of St Andrews Centre for Amerindian, Latin American and Caribbean Studies.

———. Forthcoming. "Indigenous Spokespeople in Urban Amazonia: Partial Elites Facing Multiple Spaces." *Journal of Latin American and Caribbean Anthropology*.

———. n.d. "Movement, Centrality, and Embodied Encounters—Amazonian Indigenous Conceptualisations of Place."

Viveiros de Castro, Eduardo. 1987. "A Fabricação do corpo na sociedade Alto Xinguana." In *Sociedades indígenas e indigenismo no Brasil*, edited by João Pacheco Oliveira Filho, 31–41. Rio de Janeiro: Marco Zero.

———. 1992. *From the Enemy's Point of View: Humanity and Divinity in an Amazonian Society*. Chicago: University of Chicago Press.

———. 1996. "Os Prononomes cosmológicos e o perspectivismo Ameríndio." *Mana: Estudos de Antropologia Social* 2 (2): 115–44.

———. 2001. "GUT Feelings about Amazonia: Potential Affinity." In *Beyond the Visible and the Material: The Amerinidianization of Society in the Work of Peter Rivière*, edited by Laura Rival and Neil Whitehead, 19–44. Oxford: Oxford University Press.

———. 2002. "O nativo relativo." *Mana: Estudos de Antropologia Social* 8 (1): 113–40.

Velho, Gilberto and Luiz Fernando Duarte, eds. 2010. *Juventude contemporânea: Culturas, gostos e carreiras.* Rio de Janeiro: 7 letras.

Wade, Peter. 1997. *Race and Ethnicity in Latin America.* London: Pluto Press.

Warren, Kay B., and Jean E. Jackson, eds. 2002. *Indigenous Movements, Self-Representation and the State in Latin America.* Austin: University of Texas Press.

Weber, Ingrid. 2006. *Um copo de cultura: Os Huni Kuin (Kaxinawá) do rio Humaitá e a escola.* Rio Branco: Edufac.

Weinstein, Barbara. 1983. *The Amazon Rubber Boom 1850–1920.* Stanford: Stanford University Press.

Whitehead, Neil L. 2003. Introduction to *Histories and Historicities in Amazonia,* edited by Neil L. Whitehead, vii–xx. Lincoln: University of Nebraska Press.

Wulff, Helena. 1995. "Introducing Youth Culture in Its Own Right: The State of the Art and Possibilities." In *Youth Cultures: A Cross-Cultural Perspective,* edited by Vered Amit-Talai and Helena Wulff, 1–18. London: Routledge.

Index

CPSIA information can be obtained at www.ICGtesting.com
Printed in the USA
LVOW10*1815171213

365740LV00012B/544/P

9 781137 265340